Conversations with Ann Beattie

Literary Conversations Series

Peggy Whitman Prenshaw
General Editor

Photo courtesy of Richard Watherwax

Conversations with
Ann Beattie

Edited by
Dawn Trouard

University Press of Mississippi
Jackson

www.upress.state.ms.us

The University Press of Mississippi is a member of the Association of American University Presses.

First edition 2007

∞

Library of Congress Cataloging-in-Publication Data

Conversations with Ann Beattie / edited by Dawn Trouard. — 1st ed.
   p. cm. — (Literary conversations series)
   Includes index.
   ISBN-13: 978-1-57806-922-4 (cloth : alk. paper)
   ISBN-10: 1-57806-922-X (cloth : alk. paper)
   ISBN-13: 978-1-57806-923-1 (pbk. : alk. paper)
   ISBN-10: 1-57806-923-8 (pbk. : alk. paper) 1. Beattie, Ann—Interviews.
2. Authors, American—20th century—Interviews. I. Trouard, Dawn, 1954–
II. Series.

   PS3552.E177Z63 2007
   813'.54—dc22   2006015022
   [B]

British Library Cataloging-in-Publication Data available

Books by Ann Beattie

Distortions. New York: Doubleday, 1976.

Chilly Scenes of Winter. Garden City, New York: Doubleday, 1976.

Secrets and Surprises: Short Stories. New York: Random, 1978.

Falling in Place. New York: Random, 1980.

Jacklighting. Worcester: Metacom Press, 1981.

The Burning House: Short Stories. New York: Random, 1982.

Love Always. New York: Random, 1985.

Spectacles. New York: Workman Publishing, 1985.

Where You'll Find Me and Other Stories. New York: Linden Press, 1986.

With Alex Katz. *Alex Katz.* New York: Abrams, 1987.

Picturing Will. New York: Random, 1989.

What Was Mine: Stories. New York: Random, 1991.

With Bob Adelman. *Americana.* New York: Simon and Schuster, 1992.

Another You. New York: Knopf, 1995.

My Life, Starring Dara Falcon. New York: Knopf, 1997.

Park City: New and Selected Stories. New York: Knopf, 1998.

Perfect Recall: New Stories. New York: Scribner, 2001.

The Doctor's House. New York: Scribner, 2002.

Follies: New Stories. New York: Scribner, 2005.

Lincon Perry's Charlottesville. Charlottesville: University Press of Virginia, 2005.

Contents

Introduction

In the nearly three decades since she first erupted on the literary front, Ann Beattie has proved herself prolific. On top of the reviews and essays, she has published eight collections of short stories and seven novels, written introductions and commentaries for a variety of art and photography books, and earned the honors and awards befitting such talent. With Beattie another project is always in the offing. When her book *Chilly Scenes of Winter* was made into a movie (*Head over Heels*), she even made a cameo appearance in it as a waitress. She radiates a willingness to give it a try and, is, from all evidence, free of envy and only mildly afflicted by artistic angst. The author photo chosen for her 2005 collection, *Follies: New Stories*, tells the tale. Half hidden by a ball cap, she smiles, snuggled with Sandy, the beloved, fourteen-year-old summer loaner dog. The moment was captured by Lincoln Perry, artist, husband, and lover—of atlases and Ann. The pure relaxed bliss emanating from the photo, however, turns out to be ever so slightly complicated by the dissonant concept of "loaner dog." When I asked for confirmation on the dog's name, Beattie responded sadly: "I've got to be honest here. We only get him for a month or so in the summers." It turns out that Sandy, alas, belongs to dear friends and so leads a double life.

I first met Ann Beattie at a Summit County Democratic "dog and suds" in 1983. She was visiting a friend in Akron and a snapshot taken that day records her standing beside a six foot six fellow. They are smiling in front of some patriotically festooned beer kegs in a picnic area. Living in New York then, she looks a bit quizzical, displaced, but game. It was early in her career arc. Over the years, Beattie's own discerning commentary on captured images becomes, I think, one of the best ways to understand her as a writer. Or rather, it is her work on photography that provides some vital clues on how to read her. In her introduction to the photographic collection, *Flesh and Blood: Photographers' Images of Their Own Families*, she reveals secrets about her technique.

I sidestep solving mysteries by presenting alternative mysteries. . . . When characters talk, I want you to be able to envision their world; when they are placed in that
world, I want you to be able to guess, before they speak, what they'll say. Then I
hold my breath and hope things go out of control— . . . what was clearly in focus
blurs. . . . Maybe it's all an elaborate, and even perverse, way of putting myself at
ease, this insistence that the picture I'm looking at, which I try to transcribe in
words, has a life of its own. (7)

In her introduction to photographer John Loengard's collection, *As I See
It*, Beattie again clarifies how to read an image. She likens Loengard's photographic method to the work of a novelist, "a perceiver of inner realities
[where] things can work only if the photographer intuits something true
about the subject, so the moment . . . isn't an outtake, but an interpretation . . .
he finds a way to put himself in a symbiotic relationship with the subject,
and then not miss the tenor of what is revealed" (7).

In this collection, there is a telling black and white photograph of Beattie
and Perry. It was shot in 1990 amidst the cluttered shelves of their friend
Michael's Charlottesville bookstore. The couple's bodies are dramatically
inclined as Perry bends Beattie into a deep dance dip. Initially, in Beattie's
account of the photograph's backstory, Loengard intended to pose them on a
sofa at home but decided it was too awkward, artificial. When pressed to
reveal what they might ordinarily do on an afternoon without a photographer around, the couple disclosed a preferred activity—what Beattie termed
"Bothering Michael" at his shop (10). At the bookstore, she and Perry danced
and, as Perry tipped her into the dip, they kissed. They could fall, but they
don't.[1] Loengard has preserved a moment of grace.

Just outside the photograph's frozen moment—before and after—is a
felt vitality. The photograph does not reveal if there were customers nearby,
or if anyone bought a book that day. We cannot know from the photograph
even what Owner Michael thought about the hubbub or even if Mission:
"Bother Michael" proved a success. But there is, as Beattie claims for
Loengard's art (and by extension her own), a clear life beyond the frame.
Loengard's photographs embody what Beattie has described as "a split-
second decision to capture the moment when the subject has done something truly revelatory . . . [when] the limitations of the orchestrated moment
will have been overcome. That, it seems, is the exhilarating moment for all
artists" (Beattie, *At Twelve* 11).

Beattie delights in such moments of artistic exhilaration, moments often obdurately, and not coincidentally, full of mystery. And in her willingness to honor mystery, Beattie reveals strong affinities with one of her favorite authors, Eudora Welty, a writer who has also exploited the intersections of photography and narrative.[2] This connection was serendipitously borne out in October 1998 when Beattie joined a group of artists and scholars for "A Tribute to Eudora Welty" hosted by the 92nd Street Y. As her tribute text, Beattie chose Welty's story, "Old Mr. Marblehall," and it too provides another reminder on how best to read Beattie's own fiction. "Old Mr. Marblehall" is a fanciful story, a kind of ironic parable of artistic intensifications. It is about a Natchez man who leads a double existence in order to outrageously and literally store up life. Welty's comically perverse take, however, has Mr. Marblehall redoubling an utterly prosaic existence: two households, each with its own dreadful wife and tedious child. Yet, in Welty's imagining, Mr. Marblehall revels in his completely unextraordinary secret life. (It is as if Welty inverted Nathaniel Hawthorne's "Wakefield" and unleashed its latent inclinations to the comic.) In a classic Welty tableau, the story's narrator provocatively describes Mr. Marblehall (a/k/a Mr. Bird) as he bends over the garden he has planted apparently smelling the zinnias. The zinnias, however, are, botanically, without scent: "Just what Mr. Marblehall is bending over the zinnias for is a mystery, any way you look at it. But there he is, quite visible, alive and old, leading his double life" (94).

Rife with similarly inconsequential collisions and duplexing, Beattie's own fiction compels closer scrutiny. Though nothing much may appear to be happening, *anyway you look at it,* the fine-tuned reader of Beattie's fiction is well advised to stop and bend over Beattie's zinnias closely. For instance, "Find and Replace," a story from *Follies,* embodies Beattie's approach to the notion of double lives which require a double take. In it, Ann, a writer home for a delayed commemoration of her father's recent memorial service, discovers that her widowed mother, far from bereft, has accepted an e-mailed marriage proposal. The suitor, a very nearby neighbor, has even spoken at the memorial service. Provided with a series of discordant images of this unrecognizable mother, Ann balks. The story oscillates between Ann's resistant exchanges with her mother and a series of encounters with a variety of intrusive males (rental car clerk, manager, and cop). She yo-yos between the car rental agency and her mother's driveway. "Find and Replace" unfolds like a film sequence, or perhaps a *Seinfeld* segment, as Ann confronts both memory and the transitoriness of all things.

The story works reflexively. When Ann's mother encourages her to send Drake, the fiancé "a teeny note," Ann cannot imagine what she could write. Her mother reminds her: "Well, you think up dialogue for characters, don't you? What would you imagine yourself saying?" (120). Later, when the rental car clerk is curious about her work, she confides that drawing from real life isn't a problem: "People don't recognize themselves" (124). Precariously comic and painful, the story finds its operating trope in the computer jargon of the title, "find and replace." As always, Beattie complicates: the techno-mechanistic origin of the phrase takes on a pained humanity as it confirms our capacity to accommodate loss.

While she is master of the portentous ordinary, she is not afraid of the outlandish. With more than a hundred stories, plus the novels, Beattie's fictive output has never flagged. Comparisons to writers like Chekhov and Turgenev suggest some of her literary power while critical readings that liken her technique to Hemingway's or to Henry James's indicate how various Beattie's writing actually is. As she has put it: "To come to conclusions about the writer is irrelevant to the writer's work. We can only hope that our work transcends us" (Beattie, "Essentials" 18).

Though critics have angled to reduce her daunting range to a period (sixties angst) or a type (*New Yorker*), Beattie has resolutely refused to be contained by reviewers' or critics' needs to limit her. As a result, she has experimented with point of view (*The Doctor's House*), form (*Love Always*), and time (*Picturing Will*). A story like "It's Just Another Day in Big Bear City, California" relies on the quotidian, but it is a quotidian that requires portaging—not just from its title town, but from Mars to Vietnam. By contrast, "Spiritus," seemingly static, emerges from the oscillating thoughts of a man on the brink of forty merely preparing for his day—shaving, boiling an egg for his wife's breakfast. From his inchoate relationship with a woman named Susan to his grandmother's opinions on Depression glass, he ruminates; his thoughts drift and waft, ultimately lending the story a shimmering coherence and a distinct vitality.

Though Beattie's work has garnered some substantive scholarly attention with a Twayne volume by Christina Murphy and Jaye Berman Montresor's edition, *The Critical Response to Ann Beattie*, it has too often been confined by catch phrases—minimalist, sixties chronicle, nihilism, and family trauma. When readings of her fiction recognize her range, they too often default to a thematic reading of generational malaise, short circuiting analyses of its rampant irony, preternatural fictive reinvention, and dark verbal whimsy. Her best critics detect what is being left out of the story; they hear the message in the ambient music that pervades her fiction, and they recognize the deft freeze frames that so often amplify the moment. They are willing to contend with the complex and allusive redoubled narratives.

Critic Carolyn Porter, for instance, has praised Beattie's ability to render "a comic epiphany . . . but, with a punch" (85). Blanche Gelfant locates Beattie's achievement in the way her stories "fill the silence that remains when the song is over, the way they say nothing when there is nothing to say" (22). Perhaps even more critical to an understanding of Beattie is an appreciation for what Gelfant identifies as her "magic—all the wonderful, indelible aspect of Ann Beattie's secrets and surprises. She has the secret of exact infallible perfectly timed dialogue" (29). There is, however, still so much more to be done on Beattie. For all the close attention paid to her dwarves, her Vietnam vets, her lost children, her later works, especially *My Life, Starring Dara Falcon* (1997) and *The Doctor's House* (2002), call for reconsideration. Further, her growing body of nonfiction, especially her art commentary, must be fully addressed. It is my hope that these interviews will recall readers to the full possibility and prodigious pleasure in reading or rereading Beattie.

In this prelude to the "conversations," I must confess that the process of selecting interviews for this collection sharpened my appreciation for the suicide note in *Jude the Obscure*: "DONE BECAUSE WE ARE TOO MENNY." Of the thirteen interviews finally chosen, I regret not having room for twenty others. Since interviews often coincide with the publication of a new work, I tried, when possible, to choose ones that covered the career and gave context. Though I did not always succeed, I tried to avoid ones where too many of the most frequently asked questions occurred. It is, however, a hazard of such collections (and the practice of interviewers) to succumb to an apparently irresistible need to cover familiar territory. Beattie has been interviewed since the mid-1970s and is somewhat hostage to her early legend: a *New Yorker* short story darling by twenty-seven; and Doubleday, in 1976, fanned her celebrity by publishing both her first short story collection *and* her first novel simultaneously. She was not even thirty and so it is the stuff of literary fantasy. No wonder there is a palpable need to hear her tell and retell certain tales from that gangbuster start.

Finally, of course, I feel compelled to mention the author embodied. Beattie is striking, almost glamorous, especially in the early author photos. In interviews she is direct, confident, accessible, and patiently bemused. Beattie once commented that it "had never worked to [her] disadvantage" to have "long blond hair" (Seshachari) and her interviewers, true to form, cannot resist morselizing her. The interviews are riddled with comments on that blonde hair, her cheekbones, her nail polish, her shoes, her attire, how she sits—whether her legs are crossed or not—how she looks in the spaces she occupies. More often than not, like the stations of the cross, she is asked variations on the following: Education? [all but dissertation and two courses shy of a Ph.D.]; Schedules? [sleeps late; writes late into the night—or used to]; Influences? [some and none]; First publication? ["A Rose for Judy Garland's Casket," appeared in the *Western Humanities Review*]; Reactions to criticism? [avoids reading reviews]. She is also asked about her moods (depressed? [no]) and the relationship of her art to her personal life (autobiographical? [no—and the characters aren't case studies either]). Her vaunted productivity? [rapid, but not regulated—months may pass with no summons to her writing desk]. Children? [no, never on the want list].

I favored broader interviews over those, however interesting, where the interviewer tended to deploy a set of questions designed to test and get approval for a particular pet reading of Beattie's latest collection or novel. I tried and mostly resisted including interviews that were very short or that had been collected elsewhere. However no introduction to Beattie would be complete without Larry McCaffery and Sinda Gregory's 1980 interview. In it, we learn some of her early views on other writers, her own reputation, and the all important source of her favorite typing paper. I was partial to interviews where Beattie's delight showed through as it did in her interview with Joyce Maynard. Her proclivity to be wry though kind, earnest and bemused, are irrepressible here and in many of the other interviews as well. And if Fred Sokol hadn't gotten her to talk about television writing, we'd not know that she finally quit watching *Saturday Night Live* since the "Mr. Bill Show" was on too rarely. I also tried to include interviews, like Patrick Samway's, where it is clear how very smart and articulate she is on matters literary, a consistent but unremarked quality in all of her interviews.

Ultimately, another round-up will need to gather together the interviews where readers learn she followed the tabloids on the Royals (Montresor 253), has encountered literary shake downs for endorsements (Romano), sometimes gets character names from *What Shall We Name the Baby* (Sitesh), and left New York, not to write a novel, but because she finally "couldn't stand talking about real estate" (Rothstein). In rereading my choices for this collection, I note with some amusement that in the first three interviews (and elsewhere), she mentions, with some exuberance, the falsies she wore in her *Head over Heels* appearance. Like other editors in the Literary Conversations series, I have arranged the selections chronologically, made minor silent corrections, and reproduced them, except where noted, as originally published. In the tradition of the series, I offer apologies for the inevitable repetitions.

For the record, to hear Beattie's best handling of the fatiguing moniker of "spokesperson," readers must listen to Kay Bonneti's wonderful 1987 audio interview where Beattie recounts the time her best friend's car got a flat and her friend said, "well, as spokesperson for your generation what should we do?" For readers whose appetites are whetted by the sampling in this collection, I especially encourage them to listen to the other audio interviews, particularly those by Don Swaim and Michael Silverblatt, both available online. These give what print cannot—at least a small sense of Beattie's voice, her poise, her whimsy, and her sheer professionalism. Swaim's relentless efforts to convince her she should really want to work on a computer instead of a typewriter make for the kind of curious moment Beattie so often preserves in her stories.

At the risk of cheating the collective Beattie fantasy a bit, I want to share Ben Yagoda's account of Beattie's launch to fame from *About Town: The New Yorker and the World it Made.* It offers a clarification worth retelling for those readers just getting to know her—especially since it illustrates persistence, the quality she credits for some of her success, but which is too often lost in the mythic origins of Beattie lore. Yagoda's account confirms that her submissions arrived at the *New Yorker* without agent, the nearly mythic over the transom success story. However, over a twenty-two-month period, editor Roger Angell rejected the first thirteen of those submissions, but always with advice and encouragement. Finally, according to Yagoda, she produced what Angell said he wanted from her—a "modest" story: "one that relies on no devices and is content merely to bring us to its discoveries." Yagoda preserves Angell's acceptance letter for what was "A Platonic Friendship": "Oh, joy . . . there is nothing that gives me more pleasure . . . than at last sending an enthusiastic yes to a writer who has persisted through as many rejections and rebuffs as you have. It's a fine story, I think—original, strong, and true" (Yagoda).

Though collections of interviews like these are intended to speak to serious readers as well as those who will now discover the author, I think they can also serve a mischievous function—especially for the community of readers who understand the world Beattie is writing about and the lens through which she views it. And so I will close by offering a few corrections and suggestions. It is "BEE TEE." It is not *also* BAY TEE, as infoplease.com ("all the knowledge you need") has decided. She shares a September 8 birthdate with Confucius and Aimee Mann. She is not the Ann Beattie with the border collie on North Lapeer Canine Academy's website. And she is most definitely not to be confused with Melody Beattie, author of *Talk, Trust, and Feel* (though I suspect Beattie would be delighted by the irony of a self-help book like this finding its way onto her publication list courtesy of this Amazon.com search glitch). Finally, while no one should write to the Jessica who has posted on gnooks.com and who is soliciting help on her paper on Beattie's story, "Snow," I think "el hombre" (same story, same site) should be deluged with replies on his cry for help: "cant figure out exactly what the two lovers and the chimpmunk [sic] would represent."

Jon Stewart, Beattie is waiting for the call to start the alt.Oprah book club with you.

There is always much to be grateful when a project like this comes to an end. Kathryn Seidel and the former happy kingdom of University of Central Florida's College of Arts and Sciences supported me on this with travel and time. An itinerant troop of students were variously attached to the project over the last few years: Renee Gosnell, Carrie Groebner, Melanie Romney, Patrick Quinlan, Jennifer Goodin, and Sarah Sayahi. They skulked and tracked with good humor and perseverance. Linda Hargreaves, again, applied her relentless eye to editing. Pat Coderre transcribed interviews with heroic fortitude. Clint Bowers and Rudy McDaniel gave technical, moral, and fluid support. Lisa Logan, Lynn Hepner, and Jorge Raimerez provided various rescues at critical points. Bookie Patrick, Georgia Peeples, Mark Kamrath, Dan E. Moldea, Susan V. Donaldson, Rebecca Mark, Joan Morris, Jon Glover, Keith Folse, Jose Fernandez, Jim and Nikolai Gilkeson have all provided comfort and distraction as necessary. And finally I need to thank Emily Searcy for nagging me and Jesse Marquette for not. Lakey and KD kept the pages warm when I was missing.

Needless to say the University Press of Mississippi knows how to midwife these collections. Hunter Cole provided the essential start-up giggle; Walter

Biggins provided the calm; and no one can put a bullet in something with more grace than Seetha Srinivasan. Peggy Whitman Prenshaw gave me the keys to get started, and over the long haul, there has never been a time when I am not beholden to Chip Arnold.

Of course, there is no way to sufficiently thank Ann Beattie for her fictional gifts and her extraordinary generosity—with information and hospitality. To be a part of the Beattie-Perry traveling cosmos is an abiding gift and pleasure.

DT

Notes

1. In a 1990 interview that didn't make the collection Perry said that there was nothing much to do in Charlottesville but kiss and work (Hubbard). On a related note, Beattie told interviewer Montresor in 1992 that she was unlikely to ever collaborate on an art project with Perry (Montresor 233). In 2005, however, Beattie wrote the introduction to and interviewed Perry for his book on Charlottesville. This happy reversal of fortune suggests the benefits of Charlottesville for kissing and work continues.

2. See Welty's extensive work as photographer in the WPA in her photography collection. See also her short stories, "A Memory" and "Kin." The narrator of "A Memory" offers an observation that can be usefully applied to much of Beattie's fiction and vision: "It did not matter to me what I looked at; from any observation I would conclude that a secret of life had been nearly revealed to me for I was obsessed with notions about concealment and from the smallest gesture of a stranger I would wrest what was to me a communication or a presentiment" (76).

Works Consulted

Beattie, Ann. Introduction. *As I See It*. By John Loengard. New York: Vendome, 2005. 6–11.

———. Introduction. *At Twelve: Portraits of Young Women*. By Sally Mann. New York: Aperture, 1988. 7–11.

———. "Essentials Get Lost in the Publicity Shuffle." *Writers on Writing*. Vol. 2. New York: Holt, 2003. 13–18.

———. "Find and Replace." *Follies: New Stories*. New York: Scribner, 2005. 111–27.

———. "It's Just Another Day in Big Bear City, California." *Distortions*. Garden City, NY: Doubleday, 1976, 232–48.

———. "Placing Lincoln." *Lincoln Perry's Charlottesville*. Charlottesville: University Press of Virginia, 2005. ix–xx.

———. "Spiritus." *Where You'll Find Me*. New York: Linden, 1986. 97–105.

———, and Andy Grundberg. "Agreeable Accomplices." *Flesh and Blood: Photographers' Images of Their Own Families*. Ed. Alice Rose George, Abigail Heyman, and Ethan Hoffman. New York: Picture Project, 1996. 7–11.

Bonetti, Kay. *Ann Beattie Interview with Kay Bonetti*. Audiocassette. Columbia, MO: American Audio Prose Library, 1987.

Gelfant, Blanche H. "Ann Beattie's Magic Slate or the End of the Sixties." *The Critical Response to Ann Beattie*. Ed. Jaye Berman Montresor. Westport: Greenwood, 1993. 21–29.

Hubbard, Kim. "For Writer Ann Beattie, Winters Are Anything but Chilly Since Her Marriage to Artist Lincoln Perry." *People*. 3 February 1990: 90–95.

McKinstry, Susan Janet. "The Speaking Silence of Ann Beattie's Voice." *The Critical Response to Ann Beattie*. Ed. Jaye Berman Montresor. Westport: Greenwood, 1993. 134–40.

Montresor, Jaye Berman. "This Was in 1992, in Iowa City: Talking with Ann Beattie." *The Critical Response to Ann Beattie*. Ed. Jaye Berman Montresor. Westport: Greenwood, 1993. 219–54.

Murphy, Christina. *Ann Beattie*. Boston: Hall, 1986.

Olster, Stacey. "Photographs and Fantasies in the Stories of Ann Beattie." *The Critical Response to Ann Beattie*. Ed. Jaye Berman Montresor. Westport: Greenwood, 1993. 117–28.

Pope, Kathryn. "An Interview with Peter Levitt." *ZinkZine*. Fall 2003. http://www.peterlevitt.com/currenttext.html.

Porter, Carolyn. "Ann Beattie: The Art of the Missing." *The Critical Response to Ann Beattie*. Ed. Jaye Berman Montresor. Westport: Greenwood, 1993. 75–89.

Romano, Carlin. "Author Ann Beattie, Demystifying Herself." *Philadelphia Inquirer* 29 July 1991: 8C.

Rothstein, Mervyn. "Ann Beattie's Life after Real Estate." *New York Times on the Web*. 30 December 1985. http://www.nytimes.com/books/98/06/28/specials/beattie-estate.html.

Sitesh, Aruna. "Her Testimony: American Women Writers of the 90s in Conversation with Aruna Sitesh." *Affiliated East-West New Delhi, India* (1994): 8.

Silverblatt, Michael. "Interview with Ann Beattie." *KCRW Bookworm.* 1 October 1998. http://kcrw.com/cgi-bin/db/kcrw.pl?show_code=bw&air_date=10/1/98& tmplt_type=show.

———. "Interview with Ann Beattie." *KCRW Bookworm.* 5 April 2001. http://kcrw .com/cgi-bin/db/kcrw.pl?show_code=bw&air_date=04/05/01& tmplt_type=Show.

Swaim, Don. "Ann Beattie Interview." *Wired for Books,* 1985/1991. http://wiredforbooks .org/annbeattie/.

Welty, Eudora. *The Collected Stories of Eudora Welty.* New York: Harcourt, 1980.

———. *Eudora Welty Photographs.* Jackson: University Press of Mississippi, 1993.

———. "Kin." *The Collected Stories of Eudora Welty.* 538–66.

———. "A Memory." *The Collected Stories of Eudora Welty.* 75–80.

———. "Old Mr. Marblehall." *The Collected Stories of Eudora Welty.* 91–97.

Yagoda, Ben. "Introduction." *About Town: The New Yorker and the World It Made.* New *York Times on the Web,* 2000. http://www.nytimes.com/books/first/y/yagoda-town.html.

Chronology

1947	Ann Beattie is born September 8, 1947 in Washington, D.C. She is the only child of Charlotte and James A. Beattie.
1965	With some effort, Beattie manages to graduate high school near the bottom of her class.
1969	Beattie receives a B.A. in English from American University.
1970	Beattie finishes M.A. at University of Connecticut.
1972	Beattie's first publication, "A Rose for Judy Garland's Casket," appears in the *Western Humanities Review*.
1973	Beattie wins an *Atlantic Monthly* "first" award for "Victor Blue." She marries musician/writer David Gates.
1974	After multiple rejections, Beattie garners her first acceptance in the *New Yorker*.
1975–77	Beattie teaches at the University of Virginia as a visiting writer and lecturer.
1976	Doubleday publishes Beattie's first short story collection, *Distortions*, and her first novel, *Chilly Scenes of Winter*. "The Story of a Bad Boy" appears in *Children's Literature: Annual of the Modern Language Association Seminar on Children's Literature and the Children's Literature Association*.
1977–78	Beattie teaches at Harvard University as the Briggs-Copeland lecturer.
1978	Beattie publishes her second short story collection, *Secrets and Surprises*. She is awarded a Guggenheim Fellowship. She publishes "Aunt Violet" in the *Washington Post Magazine*, and "Late Summer: Driving North" appears in *Story Quarterly*.
1979	Beattie publishes "The Cinderella Waltz" in the *New Yorker*. Joan Micklin Silver directs *Head over Heels*, a film version of *Chilly Scenes of Winter*, for United Artists, with a cameo appearance by Beattie.

1980   *Falling in Place* is published by Random House. "Warmer" is
        published in the *Washington Post Magazine*, and "A Biting Dog"
        appears in *Wonders, Writing, and Drawings for the Child in Us
        All*. Beattie receives the Distinguished Alumni Award from
        American University and the award in literature from the
        American Academy of Arts and Letters. Beattie returns to
        teaching at the University of Virginia. She also separates from
        her husband.

1981   *Jacklighting* is published in the Metacom Limited Editions
        Series. Beattie publishes "Afloat" in the *New Yorker*; "Mr. B and
        the Miraculous Christmas Tree" appears in *House and Garden*;
        "Journals" is published in *Film Comment*; and "What I'm
        Writing, What I'm Reading" appears in the *New York Times
        Book Review*.

1982   *The Burning House* is published. Beattie's story, "Weekend," is
        produced for PBS's *American Playhouse*. She also publishes
        "Blue" in *Vogue*; "Dancing" in *New England Review*; and
        "Moving Water" in the *New Yorker*. She divorces David Gates.

1983   Beattie is awarded an honorary doctorate from American
        University. She publishes "One Day" in the *New Yorker* and
        "Dazzling Retrospective Tours the U.S." in *Life*.

1984   Beattie publishes "A Shaggy Love Story" in *Ladies Home Journal*.

1985   Beattie's third novel, *Love Always*, is published. *Spectacles* also
        appears. *Harper's* publishes "On the Radio."

1986   Linden Press publishes *Where You'll Find Me and Other Stories*.
        Spectacles is produced as an audio cassette; "Honey" appears in
        Ploughshares. Christina Murphy's *Ann Beattie* is published in
        Twayne's United States Authors Series.

1987   *Alex Katz* is published, presenting Beattie's readings of the
        artist's paintings with attendant implications for narrative tech-
        nique. Beattie introduces and edits *The Best American Short
        Stories, 1987*. An audio cassette, *Ann Beattie Reads: "Desire,"
        "Learning to Fall," "Snow," "Skeletons,"* is produced by American
        Audio Prose Library.

1988   Beattie writes introduction for Sally Mann's *At Twelve: Portraits
        of Young Women*. She also publishes "The Sirens' Call: Joel

	Meyerowitz's Photographs" in *Architectural Digest*. Beattie marries Lincoln Perry.
1989	*Picturing Will* is published.
1990	Beattie publishes "Name Day" in *Antaeus*; "Such Occasions" in *New England Review*; and "Painterly Porcelains: Ceramicist Scott McDowell Impresses Images from Art and Nature into Clay" in *House and Garden*.
1991	Random House publishes *What Was Mine: Stories*. "Second Question" appears in the *New Yorker* and "The Point of It All" in *McCalls*. Beattie is awarded an honorary doctorate from Colby College.
1992	An essay by Beattie is included in *Flesh and Blood: Photographers' Images of Their Own Families*. *Americana* is published with photographer Bob Adelman. "Show of Hands" appears in *Mademoiselle*.
1993	Beattie is elected to membership in the American Academy of Arts and Letters. She publishes "It's Not That I'm Lying" in *Esquire*; and "Where Characters Come From" in *Mississippi Review*. *The Critical Response to Ann Beattie* edited by Jaye Berman Montresor is published.
1994	Beattie selects for *The American Story: Short Stories from the Rea Award*. She serves as writer in residence at Northwestern University's Center for the Writing Arts. She publishes "Fireback" in *Virginia Quarterly Review* and "The Infamous Fall of Howell the Clown" in *Antaeus*.
1995	*Another You* is published. "Peter Taylor's 'The Old Forest' " appears in *The Craft of Peter Taylor*. She edits special fiction issue of *Ploughshares*; "Coydog" appears in *Yale Review*.
1996	Beattie publishes "Buried Treasure" in *Ploughshares*.
1997	Beattie publishes *My Life, Starring Dara Falcon*. She judges the award ceremony for writers sponsored by the University of Iowa Press and the UI Writers' Workshop. She writes the introduction for *With This Ring: A Portrait of Marriage*. She publishes "An Inspirational Hotel" in *Attaché*; "Hiding Out in Mañanaland" in *Preservation*; and writes review for *Reader's Block*.

1998   *Park City: New and Selected Stories* is published. Beattie is
        elected Vice President for Literature at American Academy of
        Arts and Letters. Her story, "Stirring the Pot," appears in *Allure*.
2001   Beattie publishes *Perfect Recall: New Stories*. "Hurricane
        Carleyville" is published in *Ploughshares*, and she contributes
        an essay to *Maine: The Seasons*. She is awarded the PEN/
        Malamud Award for Excellence in Short Fiction. Beattie is
        appointed the Edgar Allan Poe Chair of the Department of
        English and Creative Writing at University of Virginia.
        "Melancholy and the Muse" appears in *Five Points: A Journal of
        Literature and Art* and"Reflection" is published in *Ploughshares*.
2002   Beattie's seventh novel, *The Doctor's House*, is published.
2003   Beattie's essay, "Essentials Get Lost in the Shuffle of Publicity,"
        appears in *Writers on Writing*.
2004   Beattie publishes "The Rabbit Hole As Likely Explanation" in
        the *New Yorker*.
2005   Beattie publishes her eighth short story collection, *Follies: New
        Stories*. She writes the introduction for John Loengard's *As I See
        It* and the introduction to *Lincoln Perry's Charlottesville*. "The
        Pleasures of Perplexity" appears in the Amazon Shorts (exclu-
        sively digital) series. The Rea Award is given to Beattie for a
        "significant contribution to the discipline of the short story as
        an art form."

Conversations with Ann Beattie

The Sixties: Where Are They Now? Novelist Ann Beattie Knows

Maggie Lewis / 1979

Ann Beattie was easy to find. She was the only one in the Algonquin lounge wearing Adidas. In that dark brown wood-paneled literary preserve, haunted since the Thurber and Ross days by denizens of the *New Yorker*, and filled the afternoon I talked to her with people dressed like, well, grown-ups—dresses and suits and grave looks—Ann Beattie sat in a chair waiting for me, one foot tucked under her, languishing back in her chair in that over-relaxed but cheerful style young, thin women sometimes have, and generally sticking out like a sore thumb, even though she, too, writes for that magazine.

Anywhere else, she'd look like everyone else, aside from the fact that she's pretty, with long blond hair. The Adidas, army surplus fatigue pants, and T-shirt she had on fit her comfortably and unobtrusively into that large increasingly amorphous group of those of us who grew up in the sixties.

Her writing reflects this belonging: Ann Beattie characters tend to wonder whether they should go to law school or not, and drive to Colorado in borrowed cars. A young romance is aptly encapsulated: "Both believed in flying saucers and health food. They shared a hatred of laundromats, guilt about not sending presents to relatives on birthdays and at Christmas, and a dog—part Weimaraner, part German shepherd—named Sam."

However, Beattie is not particularly writing about the sixties; she's examining vagaries and quirks of character. She says that the details of people's lives—which she admits picking up from friends—don't matter that much to her. In fact, she was genuinely surprised when she saw the rushes for *Head over Heels*, United Artists' adaptation of her novel *Chilly Scenes of Winter*, which opened last week, and noticed that everyone in it looked very familiar.

3

"It's so strange the way people look like me up on the screen," she said, leaning forward over the table, her eyes glinting, and her shoulder-length, straight-cut, blondish hair swinging forward conspiratorially, as if we were still living in the good old days and one could hide behind one's hair and murmur insurgent messages.

In fact someone in the movie looks exactly like her—Ann Beattie has a small part as a waitress. Even so, she said, "I'm not really used to seeing people walking around in jeans, saying things that I hear off the movie screen all the time. I usually think it's very irritating when people talk to me about, you know, being the writer of the seventies about the lost sixties kind of stuff. I keep protesting that's a horribly reductive approach to my work. It's unfair. I'd write essays if I wanted to make those kind of statements, like Jerry Rubin.

"But looking at the screen I was extremely surprised. . . . Whereas in the writing I tend to think that those specifics aren't terribly important, that I would rather have you understand something about characters in general rather than the way a thirty-year-old thinks in 1979. . . . Up on the screen that kind of immediacy is really shocking. And I do realize my stuff is different, having looked at it, whereas I never really looked at it that way on the page."

Other people do, though. If it's permissible to speak for a minute only as a child of the sixties and not as a concerned journalist, those characters are so familiar it's a little unnerving. Ann Beattie has an uncanny way of getting to the hidden reaches of human personality, the tiny person inside who is unsure what's going on or what to do about it, who has irrational fears and silly dreams and laughs at inappropriate moments.

Much as we'd all prefer that these hidden reaches *remain* hidden, she tirelessly plumbs them. Worse yet, she does it with a lot of humor and in public. Her jarring stories of the quaverings of recently-glorious sixties youths muddling through the seventies have been appearing in the *New Yorker* since 1974, and now *Chilly Scenes of Winter* goes on screen. It's almost too much for a respectable sixties washout to take.

Just as an example of the Beattie style of invasion of privacy, take the musings of Charles about his absent love, Laura, which are the essence, not to say substance, of *Chilly Scenes of Winter*. She was wonderful, kind, delightful, and beautiful, and he has no doubt whatsoever that he is utterly in love with her and that no one else will do. He only doubts that he will ever see her again. Most of the book is made up of his yearnings. And somehow, it is compelling. Almost suspenseful. But his thoughts are really his own—personal and awkward, with no comfortable clichés to tuck them into or make them less sloppy and alarmingly like one's own, and Beattie gets right in there, fishes around, and holds up to us the most awkward and intimate of them. For instance, he will be yearning along in a fine, noble, almost classically tragic vein, and he'll begin to think about a great dessert Laura used to make and wonder if he can find the recipe.

Sure, the dessert is a metaphor, a symbol of happier times, devotion and the sweetness of love. But it's so, well, *familiar* that you think of it as a dessert first. He wonders about it in such a down-to-earth way. He wonders what she put in it besides eggs. It might be in one of her left-behind cookbooks, he thinks, but he doesn't look it up. "He wants to think of it as magic," the narrator tells us, and just by that we are convinced that magic won't help. He thinks about the oranges, not symbolically, but as oranges, the way someone you know might think about a recipe.

In fact, maybe he is someone you know. He's someone Ann Beattie knows. I asked her if she got a lot of her material from friends.

"Yeah," she said, "I have no shame. I don't very often take something that happens literally and chronologically the way it happens and type it up for the *New Yorker*—life is not art, I don't mean that it is—but a lot of lines or a lot character traits are not necessarily taken from one person, but might be a fusion of two. A lot of times I'll name somebody a friend's name. It will be a different friend than the one I've got the personality of.

"I have a lot of fun writing. I like to put in a lot of jokes. Sometimes when I write a very serious story I give a public reading, and I'll be reading some very somber thing that I've written and just burst into laughter."

This is because, she said, she's making fun of some friend of hers.

Is she making fun of poor Charles?

Sure. She considers *Chilly Scenes of Winter* a funny novel. "It just got to be a game with me. I do know people who were obsessive the way he was obsessive, and partly it was an in-joke to kid the particular people that that character was modeled on."

This could get dangerous, I said, but she said she never betrays confidences, or if she uses a secret it's in a different situation or with a different character. "I like more to pirate the obscure dreams of friends of friends rather than to try to write something that's almost, like, biographical." Even this device comes back to haunt her.

"Years later I'll meet this friend who'll say to me, 'I have the most amazing thing to tell you. You must be psychic. This happened to me in 1975'!" She growled this out in mock amazement, demonstrating innocent confoundedness, and laughed. "I just sit there and look dumb."

Though at the end of *Chilly Scenes of Winter* Charles himself calls it "a story with a happy ending," and an optimist would agree with him, if cautiously, most of her stories have confusing, or, at best, precariously balanced endings. But never conclusive, resolved endings. Like life.

Somehow, though, they are more than tape recordings from the field. They are more haunting than one's own inconclusive episodes. She's not just spying. And perhaps she gets away with relishing other people's weaker moments and inner whimpers because she's so candid about her own. She'll describe everything, even her writing habits and technique—at least as far as she understands them. The mystique of the artist is going to be gone altogether if she goes on giving interviews.

"After a reading, somebody talked about some writer—I don't know who it was—who had all these very intricate things about writing: I mean, the paperweight had to be four inches from the tablet, and the tablet had to be imported from France, and I just said, 'Oh, how ridiculous. I'm very loose about it. For instance, I . . .'"—she lowered her voice and puts on a nonchalant expression—"'oh, I could only write on an electric typewriter, and I don't write till after midnight ever, and my mother *does* send me special typing paper from Washington, D.C., and I do edit with a particular kind of pen—it can only be a Bic with black ink, not blue ink—and I do like to wear my husband's flannel shirts when I write, and I have to have the desk in the same place. . . .' I mean, I realized when I started to get into all this explanation how incredibly neurotic it was, whereas I think of myself as [saying], you know, 'Oh, it's midnight, the . . . day is over' and just sort of running out to my study and starting banging out work. Unh unh." She shakes her head. She's onto herself.

I asked her if she was ever tempted to fix up happy endings for her characters.

"Boy, am I ever tempted to fix things up for everyone I know, me included," she said. "Literarily, you mean? I'm terribly sorry for my characters. I don't know how they got in these messes."

Of the happyish ending for *Chilly Scenes of Winter*, she said. "After, like, four hundred pages, I deserve not to have an unhappy ending. The book I just wrote [*Child's Play*, a novel Random House, 'I assume,' she qualifies nervously, will publish in 1980] has sort of a quasi-happy ending. I just can't do that in a book; it just gets me down too much. When I finished fifteen pages of 'Burning House' [a story in which a wife asks her husband if he's leaving her and he replies that he's already gone] I shoved the type-writer away."

If she is the one who is writing the stories, how, one might ask, *do* charac-ters get into these messes?

That's the one she can't answer. It's not so much that she takes characters from real life who have already gotten into messes beyond their control. It's more that she doesn't plot or plan her work. She just writes whatever comes into her head. She said she's afraid she sounds defensive when she describes her writing process. But that's the way it happens.

"When I sit down to write something it's very true that I only know the first line, or I only know one tiny part of some tiny event. I don't even know how that will turn out in the story. I don't know whether it will be a funny throwaway or whether it will be the crisis in the last line.

"It's just some small thing that makes me sit down to write a story, and then I realize the amount of garbage that I've been storing in my head. A cer-tain amount of that comes out on the page, and a certain amount of that sur-vives editing the story, but I really don't have ideas"—that is, discussable, bandyable-about ideas, ideas you can point to.

"A great number of writers—I don't know a great number of writers—of the writers I know, they can talk about ideas a lot more easily than I can. 'I'd like to write this,' and they know, rather specifically, what they'd like to write. I don't have a clue. If you forced me to sit down at a typewriter today, you'd probably get a letter to my grandmother."

This is not so much an admission of ineptitude as a whimper, in the true Beattie mode. She is reacting to the way other writers talk about their work. She mentions an article in the *New York Times Book Review* this summer in which various writers told what books they had in progress: "John Irving even knew the titles of the chapters of his novel!"

". . . Before I became a writer myself and realized that you could deviate from what at least my generalizations were about writers, I thought that was the way you wrote. . . . And I feel still sort of defensive, or I realize that I sound as though I'm kidding when I talk about, 'Oh, I don't know anything,' and 'Oh, it just comes to me' and 'Oh I just banged that story out.' But I can't think the way a great number of writers obviously think, if what the *Times* wrote was representative."

She figures her method must be subconscious. She confesses to putting whatever song happens to be playing on the radio as she writes in the background of her stories. Though she doesn't plot her stories out—"I don't know any plots,"—she said, "subconsciously I think I'm figuring all the time."

She often finds out how she feels about a chance remark someone has made to her by where it turns up in the context of a story. She'll note down the occasional title for a story, but mostly she keeps her ideas in her head until needed. Even then, she said, "Sometimes I'm just exhausted and I have a wonderful idea for a beginning of a story, and I just turn the light out and go to sleep. I probably shouldn't do that. I probably should write it down and file it under the first letter of the first word of the idea, but I can't. I really don't want to think of it that way. It's just sort of a fun thing that I do that fortunately I've been rewarded for."

"I keep my typewriter in good repair is all I do," she said. That and going out to her study and sitting down to work. Sometimes she works for sixteen hours, sometimes three. Sometimes the sixteen-hour days come three in a row. But it isn't regular. There's no strict schedule. "I can't do that. It wouldn't be fun. It's enough that I have to wash the dishes every day, let alone write every day."

She began to write in graduate school as an act of rebellion. "It was a real revulsion to how literature was taught in graduate school that made me want to do it instead of analyze it. For some reason I learned how to do it, and here we are."

Here we are, after the *New Yorker* turned down twenty of her short stories, with encouraging notes, and she kept writing them until they took one. "A friend sent the story off to the *New Yorker*, the first story that ever got sent in that they did something about, because I really thought it was terribly unlikely. I mean, for one thing, they're terribly disorganized, leaving aside the subject matter, which I wouldn't think would interest the *New Yorker*. But you can't outguess the *New Yorker*."

Her advice to young writers is to be thick-skinned and persistent. Considering her nonchalant style, it is hard to imagine her being earnest enough to submit twenty stories to the *New Yorker*.

I asked her if she had been in a big hurry to get her work published.

"I was in a big hurry not to be impoverished, and I was in a big hurry to get out of graduate school, and I was in a big hurry never to teach again.

Writing was just sort of a process of elimination. I don't have tremendous skills in a tremendous number of areas. I never really set out to be a writer. I just sort of backed into it," she said coolly.

The most she'd say for this career she backed into was, "I enjoy it as, you know, a playtime activity."

This was said in a friendly, confiding way, as it got later in the afternoon, and the cackles and honks rose in volume around us in the Algonquin lounge. Ann Beattie shrugs a lot. It's impossible to tell if she cares more than she will say about her characters, her writing, and what becomes of all of them. Her writing, too, shrugs a lot. She tells you a story and, strange, disturbing and funny as it may be, the narrative voice is even, to the point of flatness. It's a voice that won't shout or even explain much. Perhaps that is what makes her seem so peculiarly a writer of our time. It's not that her characters are wondering about the new Bob Dylan album; it's that she lets them wonder rather than pointing out that they're wondering. And she doesn't answer the questions they raise, either.

Sometimes the effect is alarming. If Ann Beattie pushed her typewriter away after writing "Burning House," there are also readers who probably felt like pushing the *New Yorker* away after reading it. But when that wondering is on target it makes you think. It's almost reassuring. What's compelling about Charles, an underachiever who doesn't clean up his room, eat enough vegetables, or have any hobbies is that he stays unquestioningly in love all the way through *Chilly Scenes of Winter*, wondering the whole time if it will work out. It's almost an act of faith.

Beyond that, it's very hard to say why it means so much to us that Charles misses Laura. You have to be there. Perhaps it won't strike you at all, and perhaps this is the fault of Beattie's work. She hangs it all together so gently that sometimes you don't look for meaning. When synopsized, her stories sound either glib or flat. Within the story or novel, there isn't much structure, only events that rhyme with each other and a flatness that has a resonance.

Even when nothing is going on in one of her stories, something is usually happening to the reader. Beattie has many shadings of nothing-going-on. Some are nerve-wracking, some are calming, and most of them make you wonder yourself. The fact that she listens to what's on the radio and what's on people's minds gives all her stories, even the ones where nothing happens at all, a vibrancy. If nothing else, they remind you that a song on the radio can offer an amazingly apt response to anything someone might say. They are stories full of speculation and full of possibilities.

Maybe she calls it a playtime activity because there's no point in trying to explain all this. Maybe there's really nothing there, and you just fill in the pauses—not to say chasms—with your own thoughts. If nothing else, she arranges chasms effectively, sometimes breathtakingly. Perhaps that's where her art lies. There's more than that, I think. But never mind, you'll probably explain it to yourself, in the puzzled silence after reading *Chilly Scenes of Winter* or perhaps her next story in the *New Yorker* or when *Head over Heels* ends up in some movie theater.

Ann Beattie Interview

Fred Sokol / 1980

From *Connecticut Quarterly* 2 (Summer 1980), 71–106. Reprinted by permission of Fred Sokol.

Ann Beattie, short story writer and novelist, has lived in various locales in Connecticut. As of this interview (February, 1980), she was living in the western part of the state. Her gracious home, filled with knickknacks and snapshots, is a few hundred years old. She, her husband, David (a bluegrass/ jazz guitarist), and dog, Rufus, are liable to move at any time. So speaks the track record.

Ann, whose short stories appear regularly in the *New Yorker*, has also published in the *Atlantic Monthly*, *Ms.*, *Transatlantic*, the *Virginia Quarterly Review*, and many others. Her stories have been anthologized in two collections: *Distortions* and *Secrets and Surprises*; she has written two novels: *Chilly Scenes of Winter* and *Falling in Place*. A film, *Head over Heels*, was adapted from her first novel. The movie, discussed at some length in this interview, has since circulated widely and drawn substantial audiences.

One who cares deeply for her friends, Ann keeps a ready supply of postcards nearby, and is a most reliable correspondent. Casual, warm, and witty, a drop-out of the doctoral program at the University of Connecticut, she admits to tossing fine dinner parties.

FS: First I'd like to ask where you're from and where you're headed.
AB: I come from Washington, D.C., and lived there until almost twenty-one, then left there for Connecticut. I've pretty much been in Connecticut, with the exception of a few years, ever since—different parts of Connecticut. I have no idea of where I'm headed.

FS: What about schooling?
AB: I went to American University in Washington and then I went to graduate school at the University of Connecticut. I studied literature and went

11

through the Ph.D. program but I didn't finish it. By then I was selling stuff to the *New Yorker*. I didn't want to be a teacher anymore, didn't need the credentials and always hated graduate school, so I split.

FS: And you have no idea of what is going to happen next or where you are going to be?
AB: I have no idea.

FS: Do you find yourself trying to live in places with some land?
AB: It matters to my husband a lot more than it matters to me. I don't like noise and we usually want protection from noise. Other than that it wouldn't matter to me if I lived on an acre. Anything less than a hundred acres makes him pretty nervous.

FS: How many acres do you have here?
AB: Around four acres. This is sort of like limbo. It's not really country. I mean you can see your neighbors. Before when we lived in the country we really lived in the country. We lived in Virginia and that was on a hundred-acre tree farm in a very small town that no one ever heard of called Cobham.

FS: Nobody except the people who've read the back cover of your book.
AB: Yes, we had what I thought was the most beautiful amazing house—this huge ten-room house with open porches, four bathrooms, gorgeous trees and things like that. Some interviewer came down and wrote about the humble cottage that Ann Beattie lived in.

FS: He probably looked at the back of *Distortions*.
AB: Yes, I know, but that's just a photo of the front door.

FS: What about the thing that was in the *Times* on Sunday? Did you read that you're slated to be the successor to John O'Hara and John Cheever as the "chronicler of suburban life" or something like that?
AB: I had it read to me on the phone.

FS: How do you feel about that?
AB: Well, I don't think that it pleases many writers to be compared to other writers in such broad sweeps as that. You know, I think that they're very fine

writers and if somebody were to say something more specific about our vision or even our sentences or something, I'm sure I would be very flattered, but that just seems like the usual attempt to try to pigeonhole writers. I don't know how many subjects there are in the world to write about. I don't think the suburbia that I write about has anything to do with the suburbia that Cheever writes about. I must say that while I admire both writers, I haven't read very much of their work at all, so maybe that's a more apt analogy the *Times* has drawn than I know.

FS: I don't know why they group O'Hara and Cheever together really to start with. When I think of that kind of grouping I think of Updike more with Cheever, and not necessarily with you. But I was even surprised that they used that.
AB: I certainly wouldn't see that. Obviously people wouldn't say anyone who writes about suburbia has moved into Cheever territory. I'm not quite sure what they meant by that.

FS: Do you feel like you write about suburbia?
AB: Well, I have since I've lived here again. I like to think I'm unique. I like to think it's not easy to categorize my writing. Somebody would say "you're a writer about suburbia," that's true; if somebody were to say "you write about dwarf houses," that's true too. To me, I try to think that I'm not very predictable. So I would block that out even if it were true. You might be able to go through my book and say this is about suburbia and this is and this is. You'd enlighten me that it was. I don't think about locale a great deal. The new book (*Falling in Place*)that I've just written that's coming out for Random House and the *Times* is talking about, certainly takes place largely in suburbia, although why not say I'm writing about the urban scene since the other half takes place in New Haven, Connecticut, and on Columbus Avenue in New York. It's just that there isn't a well-known writer who's done Columbus Avenue. So it's easier to talk about me and Cheever.

FS: It's easier not to live there to write about Columbus Avenue.
AB: That's true, too.

FS: Do you think about audience when you write? Do you think about the people who are going to read it?

AB: Yes and no. I think about and I realize that the audience is out there now. I don't think about pleasing them in any way. I'm not the sort of writer who could write to an audience even if she wanted to, as far as I know.

FS: So, who will read *Falling in Place*? I mean, besides the publisher. Would you predict?

AB: That I really never understand. Apparently, my opinions, because I move in such a small group of people, are not representative at all. I would imagine that people like you and me are going to read that book. My publisher hopes that it will have a more widespread appeal than my other work has. The publisher has read the book. Yes, the people at Random House have read the book. They think it will have a larger audience because I'm taking on suburbia. So I guess what is assumed is that suburbia will read it, and I do too. It won't kill them.

FS: Have you consciously written about the sixties and early seventies? Have you thought about that?

AB: I never did it in terms of thinking of what should be the theme of my work—"aha, it should be disillusionment after the 1960s." The way I write is really very much what's happening at the minute. For instance, *Falling in Place* takes place over a very short period of time. It takes place over at most a period of about a month. And in fact, the book was largely written in a month, so I'd look out the window and if it was a full moon that night, that's what I typed into the manuscript.

FS: It was largely written in a month. What do you mean exactly by that?

AB: That I wrote the book in seven weeks.

FS: Do you hand write it?

AB: Oh, no, I type it; I wouldn't have any fingers left if I hand wrote it. But I just take what's there at the moment and write about it. If a certain song is playing on the radio all the month I'm writing, that's the song that gets into the book. I just hate to do research and so I use and select from what's readily available.

FS: What about the novel as a form? Do you feel comfortable with it?

AB: Oh, no, not at all. I don't understand the form. I can't imagine how people write novels.

FS: And you're a short story writer?
AB: Oh yes.

FS: Why did you write this novel? Did Random House say, "Hey Ann, how about writing a novel?"
AB: No, that's what everybody wants as well. I mean that's what the literary establishment wants, of course, because they can point to facts and figures and show you that stories don't make money. To some extent, if you want to hit the reading circuit, which I don't, you are more likely to hit it because of novels than short stories. People just take novels seriously. People talk to me now about "your stories and your novel." Well, that's something that I wrote in three weeks, you know, seven years ago, that I think of as just being another story and not one of my best.

FS: What would you say is your best?
AB: I don't know. "The Burning House" that came out in the *New Yorker* and that hasn't been collected yet is one of my favorites of recent writing. Back in the distant past, I'm pretty fond of a story called "Wanderers" and another called "Colorado."

FS: What about "Milo and Venus?" No, that's not the title. Do you like that one?
AB: It's called "Cinderella Waltz." There's been a lot of interest in that— anthologies and people wanted me to do television and stuff like that. I don't have a great deal of feeling for that story; I don't think it's one of my triumphs.

FS: Do certain characters in your stories stay with you? I mean, how do they evolve? Are they people you knew? Do they pop up?
AB: That's a hard question. The answer that I usually give is that I switch heads. I'm perfectly apt to write about one friend. I never really take a friend and try to write exactly the way I see him in life or exactly the way we spent an evening together. But some little bits and pieces of that will come in and I'll even be consciously aware that it's friend "X" that I'm writing about. But if I give the friend a name in the story, I give it "Y's" name so that people who know me have to sort of go through the story like an acrostic, if they really want to figure out the literal level of it. But, I can think of only one or two times that a story has even predominantly been something that actually

happened chronologically the way it happened and factually the way it happened. I don't think I'm very good at that. I think journalists are good at that. I'm lucky that it comes out changed to begin with or I'm sure I would not have a friend left.

FS: Do you ever write about yourself?

AB: I'm sure I write about myself a great deal. Again, I try not to reflect on writing a lot because I feel that once I become self-conscious about it, it's going to become an inhibiting factor.

FS: Do you find that you have to revise a lot? The way you talk about your writing, it's bang, bang, bang. That's one, that's another one. Do you really have to go back and work on it?

AB: Sometimes it's bang, bang, bang. For instance, "The Burning House" was really just like once at the typewriter and word changes or a line struck here or there. It seems like I used to be able to do that much easier when I started writing, for instance, a lot of stories in *Distortions*. I don't mean that I just throw them into the typewriter and they come out into a manilla envelope which is already stamped and it goes by carrier pigeon. They seemed to come easier than they do now, for whatever reason. Maybe, I hope, it's because I know more now and so it's harder to write.

FS: Did you always feel that you were going to be a writer? When you were a little kid did you write things?

AB: I did. I was an artistic little kid; I painted and drew a lot. I did that a lot more than I wrote. But I always had a large vocabulary and always tested way above my grade level in reading. I always read a lot. But no, it really seems surprising to me that I became a writer. I certainly didn't set out to become one.

FS: As opposed to Joyce Carol Oates who has said that before she could write she painted to take its place. But she always felt driven to write.

AB: It is amazing, too, the number of writers who are also painters.

FS: Do you paint now?

AB: No, I make collages and send them to friends on postcards.

FS: What about the big business aspect of this writing? You're involved with Random House in New York, the big time, and you don't have an agent?

AB: Oh, sure I have one. Not for the world would I not have an agent. The agent arranges the deals and the business aspect of it. It's not as though I never set foot in the offices of Random House. There is still a whole lot that I do. But no, I wouldn't presume to operate without an agent.

FS: Some seemingly reputable source mentioned to me that you handled your own business.

AB: I assure you I've always had an agent. Well, I haven't always had an agent. I started selling to the *New Yorker* before I had an agent, but pretty soon I got one. I have a different agent now, but I've had her for many years.

FS: Does the *New Yorker* expect you to come up with a story every so often?

AB: Well, you know, they hope I'll come up with a story every so often. They don't put any pressure on me. Then again, I'm rather prolific so they don't have to. And it wouldn't do any good if they did put pressure on me. There's nothing really spoken between us about that. I do have a contract with them which is a first reading agreement. When I do come up with something, it generally means that they see it first. Then, in exchange for that, they pay me much higher wages than they would pay somebody who wasn't under contract. But if they don't want it they send it on to my agent and she can do whatever she wants with it.

FS: That's anything you write? Or exclusively short stories?

AB: It's just short stories. That's all I write. The *New Yorker* sees novels in case they want to excerpt them. I've only written one novel in the last five years. If somebody requests me to write something, I can do that—by simply asking the *New Yorker* if it's all right. But I never do that kind of work. People ask me if I want to write an article on this or that, but I just don't write articles.

FS: Getting back to contemporary writers again, do you have favorites? You said that you didn't group yourself with anybody else.

AB: I hope not. That may be self-protection. There are lots of writers I admire. I don't think that our work has anything to do with each other's.

FS: Who for example?

AB: Well, I think one of the finest story writers around is Raymond Carver. And I think that Joy Williams is an excellent story writer, too. And, I think that Ann Tyler often writes excellent stories. I think highly of Donald Barthelme's work. I can't imagine what I have in common with any of these people. I read a lot of non-fiction and I read a lot of small magazines. I read some of this and some of that, but I don't very often read books and sit down with them and try to figure out, "Gee, who's my favorite writer" and read all his or her work.

FS: Do you ever feel envious or jealous of other writers—of either their writing or their lives?

AB: I can categorically say that there are no other writers whose lives I envy.

FS: And writing styles?

AB: No, usually writers who do things like that I think of as being so far afield. If there are people who are a lot like me who are my contemporaries I am not aware of them. For instance, when I read *Blood Tie* by Mary Lee Settle, I thought, "If I could write a book like this, I would die happy." It's so far, though, out of the realm of possibility that I would ever have her view of life or sentence structures or anything else that jealousy couldn't enter into it. We're obviously just two such different perceivers and our methods are so different that jealousy just seems out of the question. Envy—that could be done, but not jealousy. I'm jealous of Mark Rothko; I wish I could have done that. The people that I most admire seem so far afield that I just can't imagine being jealous. Even with writers that I like very much, there are just *some* things that I like very much. I think you should judge somebody by the best work. You can't be jealous of somebody who pulls off one good story each year.

FS: You pretty much consider yourself Ann Beattie writing short stories and you won't type yourself into the category of say a realist or anything like that.

AB: I forget all that literary terminology. I deliberately obliterated all of that when I quit graduate school and I stopped teaching. I certainly am not a fabulist—I am a realist as opposed to that. I'm attempting realistic stories.

FS: I don't know what that means. What about feminism?

AB: Again, I don't consciously put issues into my work. Certainly, I would consider myself a feminist. I don't think that that means that I would always have to take a feminist line with every character that I put into my work, for instance. I'm sure that there are a lot of characters that the feminists would want to just shake by the shoulders and say "Ah, come on." But, then again, I don't think they're a stupid lot and that they only want to see politics, feminist politics, printed here and there and everywhere, too. It's something in my personal life that I'm probably a lot more aware of than what I do artistically.

FS: Do you find writing to be a lonely experience?

AB: No. Fun. If it weren't fun, it would be lonely, that's certain. But I really have a good time doing it when it's going well. Of course, I have a miserable time when it's going badly. I really enjoy doing it. I don't like to be analytical about it. I don't like to write book reviews about other people's work. I just like to go off by myself and write.

FS: A lot of writers say that "It's hard work, but I must do it."

AB: There are hard aspects of it; I find it grueling to go over galleys of a five-hundred page novel for the third time and have to go through endless revisions and things like that. The initial writing is a lot of fun and that carries over, too. I do write a lot and while I'm doing the tedious stuff, I'm probably doing something that pleases me on the typewriter at the same time.

FS: So you usually work on a few things simultaneously?

AB: Yes, but then often I don't write anything for six months. If I'm moved to write, I write.

FS: How do you occupy yourself when you're not moved to write? What do you usually do?

AB: It's a bad time to ask me that right now because if I were to give you a list of what I did last week it would mostly have to do with getting this book out with Random House. The movie that was made of *Chilly Scenes of Winter* is reopening in Boston.

FS: Why don't you talk about that a little bit. What happened to *Head over Heels*? All I know as a stranger to you is that *Head over Heels* opened in New York, at least I thought it did, and it got good and mixed reviews. I was intending to go see it and then it was gone.

AB: It actually played awhile, I'm sure it played for a month and what happened is that it picked up business. It had a horrendous first week. I don't know, again this is something that I was very much disassociated from, this whole project. I mean I simply signed over my book to these people. I didn't do that—that may sound more passive than it is. I signed it over because when the producers, Triple Play Productions, came to talk to me in Boston to first propose the project, I liked them a lot and I not only liked them personally but they read the book the same way I did. It seemed like if anybody could get this project going, these people could. I was just very enthusiastic. I didn't think it would be a piece of crap if they made it. So I was very supportive but there was nothing officially that I did for this. I mean I didn't write the screen play. What I did officially for this was to show up in Hollywood for a walk-on part as a waitress which I had asked if I could do and they said yes.

FS: Did you have fun?

AB: Yes, I got to wear two pairs of falsies and seventeen hairpins. I was the waitress of my dreams. A friend of mine who saw it toward the end of its run in New York said that when I came on for my four-second walk-on, the entire house just blew up. I did not look like myself; you really have to remember that the waitress is me. Anyway, I think that what happened to it was that it was a very small budget movie. It was $2.5 million which is what they spend on TV shows and it didn't just take off instantly the way, say, *One Flew Over the Cuckoo's Nest* did. That was low budget and nobody had the highest hopes for it and it was just an overnight sensation. This movie wasn't that and United Artists just stopped backing it and just plain lost interest. I think they decided to use it as a tax write-off. They brought it in at budget, they didn't lose any money so . . . if it didn't work, it didn't work.

FS: Who's reopening it?

AB: Well there were so many theaters in Boston who were wild to get this movie and a journalist up there put it on his "10 Best List" and then got them to send a print of it and finally UA is doing it. All the publicity is being done, I understand, by the theater. It's still not paying for ads in the *Boston Globe*. But they wanted it so much up there that they got it. So UA is flying one of the producers and me and, I think, Mary Beth Hurt and I don't know who else up there. I guess all the producers are coming up and there's going to be a new sort of opening in Boston.

FS: What about the business of the book *Chilly Scenes of Winter* now turning into *Head over Heels*?

AB: I think it's a horrendous title. I think that's part of the reason it didn't do well. It was a movie that was going to appeal to a larger audience than UA thought to begin with. I think it's a very good movie. I think what they were afraid of was that it would have such a limited audience of people our age that what they wanted to do was pretend that this was a general audience movie—which it isn't. So, it lost everything. Would you go to see a movie called *Head over Heels* if you knew Fred Astaire wasn't in it? I don't think I would . . . and I think the publicity campaign was horrendous; I mean the art work that was run in the *New York Times* I thought was very misrepresentative and very ugly and alienating in its own right. They're redesigning that now for the Boston thing and hoping, obviously, it goes on from Boston. I just think last minute things that are very important, like title and publicity, were just diametrically opposed to what the movie was. So they lost both the crowd that would have gone and the theatrical crowd.

FS: You're saying the script of the movie itself is quite different from the book.

AB: I think it's an excellent script that Joan Micklin Silver wrote. I really do. I think in many ways it's an improvement on the book. Put it this way, if I had my choice of seeing the movie or reading the book, I'd see the movie.

FS: Some Joan Micklin Silver films seem to suffer from this sort of thing. *Between the Lines* didn't have much of a run, though I suppose that *Hester Street* did fairly well. She seems to be pretty good at what she does. I wonder why this sort of thing happens.

AB: Again, I think she's at a disadvantage not operating on a super-million dollar budget and that's where they're going to put the weight. They can dabble in these things and then if they catch on—well, you know, then all the better. *Girl Friends* by Claudia Weil—I guess not that much was expected of it but suddenly it got to be a real cult movie. Part of what happened with *Head over Heels* is that it was reviewed in the *New York Times* and the headline the day after it opened was *"Head over Heels* Drama Opens." Believe me, if the script and the movie are true enough to the book you would not categorize this as a drama. If it was that badly misperceived, it was off on the most wrong foot it could have been off on. And then by the time Andrew Sarris got around to praising it in the *Voice* it was pretty late. It did O.K. in New York—it kept picking up. But it was just not such a staggering overnight success that they winged it out to Pittsburgh.

FS: Why is *Chilly Scenes of Winter* now reissued as *Head over Heels*?
AB: I have no idea.

FS: I saw it in a supermarket for the first time and I had to pick up the book and thought, "Maybe she's written another book."
AB: I picked it up in the supermarket, too. I was looking for a Christmas present for my mother's Christmas stocking and went down to Bethel, Connecticut, and there sits *Head over Heels*, formerly *Chilly Scenes of Winter* by Ann Beattie, and I'm enraged of course. It's ugly, it has the same ugly art on the cover that the movie has. I had no idea. Similarly, that same month, I walked into a bookstore in New York City and one of the women said to me "Your book is doing great." After all this time, I thought *Secrets and Surprises*? She said "No, no, no—*Distortions*." I found out that night they had issued *Distortions* in paperback. She gave me a copy so I went out wandering down 6th Avenue, looking at this paperback they had put out as *Distortions*. I frankly doubt whether it was legal to do what they did with *Head over Heels*, but I'm very busy and I just haven't worked myself up enough to look into that. I'll look into that. What can you do after the fact anyway? There it is.

FS: My assumption was that a theater like the Orson Welles in Cambridge would get it and then maybe someone in Northampton would get it and it would work its way around this way and that way and everybody would go see it. Well, what about the teleplay for Channel 13? How did that come about?
AB: I don't know. Somebody at Channel 13 wrote me a letter and asked me if I wanted to write for Channel 13.

FS: Anything?
AB: Yes. A piece of fiction. I don't know television language to use it with you. My idea was to change and adapt a story that I had written a long time ago called "Weekend" and they weren't terribly hot on that idea. I think they wanted flat-out original material, but they let me do it so that's what I'm doing. It's going to be for a one-hour whatever-you-call-it for TV. I don't

watch TV. I suffered through *Saturday Night Live* for the "Mr. Bill Show," but since it's almost never on, I stopped doing that.

FS: What about influences on your writing? Could you mention someone in particular?
AB: I don't think there have been any compelling influences on my writing. It's not as though I can say John Hawkes was my mentor or anything like that. I never met John Hawkes. I just pulled that out of the air. There was a man at the University of Connecticut named J. D. O'Hara who was never my teacher but who knew I wrote and was interested in my writing and I guess to the extent that anybody really served as an editor and encouraged me in the early days, it was O'Hara. He's a very keen reader, very sharp, and I still show him a lot of my stuff to this day. My husband was always very encouraging. He would send these things out himself and keep track of where they'd gone and was really certain that I was going to be a famous writer and I should keep after it. All my friends told me that's nice and people were always supportive enough about it. I guess really O'Hara was, other than my husband, the person who helped the most.

FS: How long have you known your husband?
AB: Ten years.

FS: So, he's seen you evolve through all this?
AB: Oh, yes, I wrote one story a year when I met my husband.

FS: Like me.
AB: You should meet my husband maybe. He'll have you writing novels in a week.

FS: No, I don't write novels in a week. That's why I'm astounded that you do.
AB: They're so unbearable to write that I think you should do it as quickly as possible and get it over with. You're going to have endless hours refining them and rereading them and stuff like that after that period. I just can't stay with it; I can't imagine it.

FS: Some people take years and years and profess to say that that's the only way that they can do it.

AB: I am sure that's true. I don't put that down at all or think I'm superior in any way. In fact, being honest about how quickly I write puts me in for a lot of criticism. People automatically assume you can't do it. But I think all of those assumptions are like putting down Blake for saying he didn't really hear those voices.

FS: Ann, you said you taught some.
AB: For eight years.

FS: College level?
AB: Harvard was the end of the road.

FS: I knew you taught at Harvard and at the University of Virginia, but where else?
AB: Yes, I taught full-time all over. I was a teaching assistant which meant two classes a semester at the University of Connecticut. (But when I taught at Virginia, I taught full-time and was teaching two classes a semester.) As far as I'm concerned that was just slave wages for full-time teaching. You know, I had forty students a semester and made $3,500 a year for doing it.

FS: You were saying you write at night and sleep late in the morning?
AB: When I'm not doing business. I've been commuting to New York City and back so often lately. Walking the dog is what I've been doing. Then before that it seemed like I was writing a novel and that was terribly unrepresentative. And now that things are finally starting to calm down I'm writing for Channel 13 and doing a few readings again because I'm feeling better.

FS: If things are O.K. you do a lot of sleeping in the morning and your heavy writing at night?
AB: Oh, yeah.

FS: How can you do that? Don't you feel exhausted by ten in the evening?
AB: I really believe in day people and night people. I really think people's bodies are on different clocks. I even feel now like I just woke up and I've been awake for three or four hours. And I'll feel this way until seven o'clock tonight when I'll start to pick up and then by nine it will be O.K. to start writing. My favorite hours are from 12:00 to 3:00 a.m. for writing.

FS: Then certainly "the most recommended method" of sitting at one's desk every morning trying to write from 9:00 a.m. to noon—that wouldn't make it for you?

AB: I could tell myself that until I ended up in the bin.

FS: Do you have scheduled hours for yourself? Do you say to yourself, "Well, I'm really going to write." Or is it chance?

AB: Once I'm working on a project (like now when I'm working for Channel 13) naturally when people want me to go to dinner four nights this week I'll say no to all four dinners. I schedule time that way. But I don't ever think, for instance, if I have an empty week, should I write or see my friend. I really don't adhere to schedules at all, and don't have the slightest desire to do that. The times that I've tried that, when I have been in a slump and I try to get out of it by saying, "Come on, Ann, sit down at that typewriter," I've gotten in a worse slump. It's better if I just let it ride.

FS: The anarchic writer, huh?

AB: Yes. Everybody's so different about writing and I don't think you can generalize about that. Well, I also have the leisure to sleep all day if I want. I'm very lucky. I'm sure that if I worked from 9:00 to 5:00 I wouldn't come home and write a novel. I wouldn't write at all. Also, I find that when I do something that's so much a routine, it does drain me. Teaching drained me particularly. When I read so much flawed material and spent so much time trying to think of how to help other people, at the end of the day I didn't want to do something spontaneously myself. I felt like I had done it for art for the day.

FS: Your own writing suffers. I can speak from experience. You forget what's right and what's you.

AB: And also after years of grading papers, I don't spell half as well as I did ten years ago. I'm always running for the dictionary. It really gets to you.

FS: What about fiction writing classes and workshops? Do you think they really do people any good? There are some would-be writers who every summer pack their suitcases and go off to Vermont or New Hampshire. Of course, they're trying to get to Iowa. They think that's the grail.

AB: I'm personally very skeptical about those things. Again, it depends upon the person. If you find a person who is talented and who needs a lot of support for that talent and who lives in an attic in Peoria, and the only way he's going to find some support for that talent is to go to the Iowa Writer's Workshop, I think if he knows himself well enough to think he should do that, then he probably should go to the Iowa Writer's Workshop. If you put me in the Iowa Writer's Workshop I would have been so rebellious, and I would have been so bummed-out by that kind of attention to the fact of writing itself, that I would have split Iowa in a week. That's why I didn't go into an MFA program. I just want to be left alone. That says a lot about my personality. I was very antagonistic to authority, so it's very hard for me to try to answer that in a sane way. I think, first of all, there are too many writer's workshops. There are too many bad writers and would-be writers teaching these workshops. My reservation is that usually people will be too influenced by wrong things said to them.

FS: You didn't do any of that?
AB: I wouldn't do that for the world.

FS: Do you feel like you have a lot of patience?
AB: Yes, I do. I'm sure I do to sit eighteen hours a day for many days running. On the other hand, I don't have the kind of patience that would let me make out a schedule. Then, I would get upset and just walk away from the typewriter. But if I'm involved in it and it's fun and going well nothing can get me away from the typewriter.

FS: Have you ever written poetry?
AB: Yes, I usually don't admit to it but the last poem I wrote was in 1970. Truly, the last poem I even attempted was in 1970. And I was a bad poet. I wrote in my school courses like everybody does and at the beach. I probably wrote maybe three or four poems that I tried to make really good in 1969 and 1970 but I haven't written any more since then. I think that's very hard. I think even writing a novel is easier than writing a poem. I couldn't tell you why.

FS: I found I was deceiving myself for the longest time that I had the potential to be a decent poet and I'm not sure that I understand poetry as well as I should.

AB: No, that's exactly it. It's a song and I don't understand music so I don't understand poetry. I read a lot of contemporary poetry. I read more of that than I do short fiction and I have a lot of faith in contemporary poets. I think there are some real geniuses writing out there now, Louise Gluck, for instance, Gregory Orr, Michael Ryan, Jay Parini. I just think those people are astonishing—they just take my breath away, and I very rarely feel that way about fiction writers. And, even in small magazines, it seems that the poetry is of a much higher caliber than the short fiction.

FS: I was going to ask you how you feel about small magazines. Do you read them quite a bit?
AB: Yes, as compared to the normal public. I probably read three or four a month. I read *Newsweek* every week and comparatively I'm doing a great job of it. But I pretty much keep up.

FS: What about the myth of the writer as a kind of tragic, mystical soul? Many people who haven't been exposed to a lot of literature really think that. They hear about a Poe and/or a Hemingway and they typecast. What do you think about all that?
AB: How can you generalize? I know some writers who are tragic figures all right, maybe not in the way that you're talking about.

FS: They have classically miserable lives, they have bad marriages and perhaps their kids do and so forth.
AB: But I'm not at all convinced that that doesn't happen to most accountants. I feel that the commuter train that I ride from Westport is more a ship of fools and more tragic probably than the gathering at P.E.N. in New York City [an international organization of writers, poets, playwrights, essayists, editors, novelists, and translators, whose purpose is to bring about better understanding among nations]. There are different levels of tragedy. Writers are really self-aware. I don't know if you can generalize in the same way about accountants going into their own minds for personal reasons. They're probably going in for a lot more functional reasons. I mean take it from the standard personality of what might make someone a writer versus an accountant. That kind of thinking about yourself certainly is going to produce a lot of melancholy because if you think about yourself a lot you get answers. Look at the world out there that you get answers from—just that kind of syllogism that

so many writers are involved in and the necessity to keep going in the face of obstacles. Most writers are not like me. Most writers do not get up at noon and do not have enough money to live without ever getting off their butts. That could end tomorrow too, but sitting here speaking today, I'm in an incredibly privileged position. I personally don't feel that I'm a tragic figure of melancholy, but I couldn't imagine what I'd think if I made a thousand dollars a year at this. It would probably be more anger than melancholy, but again it's very hard for me to generalize. It seems like more of the writers that I know are either vastly successful or don't have money to keep their houses in the winter. I'm odd—so I hate to speak from this position. Especially since I don't go after assignments and since I limit myself very deliberately to what I want to do.

FS: What about humor in your writing? I found myself laughing quite often while reading *Chilly Scenes of Winter*.
AB: An interviewer once said to me that this was one of the most depressing and sad books he had ever read. The first time I heard that comment it really took me aback. I said I was laughing so hard at the typewriter that sometimes I couldn't go on. At the end of his interview with me he said, "I was laughing too but not always with you." I think I'm funny. I think *Chilly Scenes* is essentially funny.

FS: The characters depicted are close, in a sense, to being a little bit pathetic.
AB: I think a lot of people started to read the book and thought it was a book about alienation and they're not used to a humorous perspective in works about alienation. People read *Catcher in the Rye* and don't understand that Salinger is being tongue-in-cheek about Holden. They think, "Here is this poor suffering protoplasm out there." People simplify and that kind of simplification leads to gross misreadings of books. They form a stereotype that once you've written a book like *Catcher in the Rye* you could not possibly be ever turning the barb against your character. When you write a novel like *Chilly Scenes of Winter* they wonder how you can make fun of Charles when he's an obsessed man, when he has nothing in his life. But I think there is a lot of humor in these situations and I think the people that I'm writing about are pretty self-aware characters so they would see the humor.

FS: Do people you know or others come up to you and say, "Oh, that Charles. He's like somebody I knew."

AB: Oh, yeah, particularly since the movie, people have talked a lot about *Chilly Scenes of Winter* that way, but I get letters all the time. When stories come out in the *New Yorker* people read them and I get a lot of mail and three-quarters of that mail is to tell me that this is exactly like my brother in Utah. If people write me a fan letter, I usually send them a post card and thank them for writing or reading. I don't really much care if it's like their brother in Utah, to tell you the truth.

FS: It seems to me that with your stories (and I've read a lot of them in the *New Yorker* and in the collections and have probably read them twice), I have a hard time remembering the plots. There are real things about the characters that stay with me, but I simply forget the plots. My memory isn't that awful. Do you have a negative or positive reaction to that?

AB: I would agree with you that they're not highly plotted stories. I don't know how to write a highly plotted story. I think that my stories circle: they keep coming around and around. You know they're kind of episodic stories. It's harder to remember those than something that has a linear line. But that's what gets me into trouble writing a novel. You can't write a novel that way. You can write a story, even a thirty page manuscript and get away with it once you're adept at it. But you can't do it with a novel.

FS: Do you think *Chilly Scenes* is too long? I say that because you said previously that it seemed like a great big story to you.

AB: What I meant was that I think everything as I write as a story that I tell. And to me it doesn't matter if that story comes out three-hundred odd pages or fifteen. I judge them all the same. I say, "What happened in that that made it good or interesting?" The page line never has anything to do with that. I don't mean to put down *Chilly Scenes*. I enjoyed it when I wrote it. I still think that it's interesting in a lot of ways, but I think in terms of what I can do artistically, that was the best I could do in those days. That was many years ago—in 1974. I've learned a lot in five years—I hope.

FS: What about writing about older people? Do you ever do that?

AB: No, hardly ever. I have one story about older people "Victor Blue" that was in *Distortions*. I guess I don't feel enough in touch with older people to make assumptions about them. You mean people in their sixties? No, very rarely.

FS: When you see people in situations, are you conscious that maybe you're witnessing story material? Are you constantly being an observer, first, and then a writer?

AB: People around me are conscious about that—even people who are close to me that I would *never* expose. People say to me all the time, even people who know better, people will turn to me in a situation when I am not being "Ann Beattie, The Writer" at all and say, "If you put me in the *New Yorker*, I'll kill you." And that's a very odd feeling for me because these people are not people who are saying this with ulterior motives meaning "I want to be in the *New Yorker*." A lot of people bring me stories. They say, "Ann, wait till you hear this one," and they tell me something over the phone. And it's fantastic. But once I've heard it, I have no interest, then, in writing it. But getting back to what you asked—a little bit more lately than in the past I sometimes realize that something's a story, but I would say that almost three-quarters of the time when I realize that, I never write about it.

FS: You write often in the present tense.

AB: Yes, because I don't understand tenses. I can't even remember what they're called. I keep getting into the *plus que parfait*. I can't get that into English.

FS: And here I was thinking she has such a grasp on language and she's chosen the present tense above all others because everyone else writes in the past tense. It's nice to see that. It's one of the things I like the best about your writing. Easiest, huh?

AB: I'm very bad when I get into the past tense, just talk to my editor at the *New Yorker* about that. Some of my sentence structures are unravelable.

FS: How do you get titles for each story?

AB: My husband titles them. I can't think of titles. Sometimes my editor at the *New Yorker* titles them. For instance, he gave my new novel its title. My husband gave *Chilly Scenes of Winter* its title because there was a song by Cousin Emmy that he'd always liked called that. And the song played nowhere in the book so he made me write in the book a place where Charles plays "Chilly Scenes of Winter," which I think is a good title.

FS: But they wouldn't keep it for the film.

AB: UA did a marketing research thing and they thought it was too long, that the word *chilly* would alienate people and *winter* was bad for titles. I think they paid something like $50,000 to come up with an alternate title. In fact, the first person that they paid $50,000 to, came up with *Chilly Scenes of Winter* and why that was right, but UA didn't like that and so they paid it out again and got whatever they got. When you think about what the author is paid to write this book versus what Hollywood pays for marketing research, it's really pretty amazing.

FS: Do you think you're going to have any children?
AB: I highly doubt it. Because of the obvious. First of all, I don't feel the lack of not having any children; second of all, I can't imagine myself fitting a child into my schedule—which I'm not unhappy with. Third of all, I don't have any reason to think I would be a good mother. I'm terribly impatient. It's just not something I feel a real interest in. Maybe I would turn out to be a terrific mother and just be wild about a kid. But it's a terrible risk to have a child when you feel the way I do. I can't imagine doing it with such little motivation as I have. Also, my life has been very unsettled and I am very pessimistic about the future and I do think that a year from now this could all end. I think these are very difficult times to bring a child up. The problems that I have with my dog are legendary! So I really don't even think about a child that much. I would really be very surprised if I did that. Other things I have done have surprised me. If you told me I'd own a Volvo and live in Fairfield, Connecticut, I would have laughed you out the door, too.

Visiting Ann Beattie

Joyce Maynard / 1980

The first one to appear at the door is a large enthusiastic dog of no special
bloodlines. Behind him—a good deal less frenetic—stands a tall, slender
woman wearing a sweater and jeans. People must often tell her that she
resembles Joni Mitchell. She leads me in (the dog has bounded ahead and
arranged himself on an antique sofa) and turns down the music, which is
rock, and loud.

It's impossible to visit Ann Beattie's house—off a highway in Connecticut,
not precisely rural or suburban—without thinking about all the houses in
Ann Beattie's stories, mostly in New Hampshire and Vermont, where Ann
Beattie characters have come for weekends, broken up relationships, fixed
themselves scrambled eggs, rolled joints, flipped coins to determine where
they should go next. Very often there are lots of extra mattresses or sleeping
bags lying around these houses, and a constantly shifting number of occu-
pants. There are likely to be interesting salt and pepper shakers in the shape
of alligators or handcarved cherry wood marionettes or soapstone bookends
or wallpaper covered with cabbage roses. Usually there is music playing—
Louis Armstrong 78s, or Bob Dylan, or some obscure blues singer. Nearly
always, there's a dog.

Inside this house there are objects enough to set up a shop on Columbus
Avenue: comfortable, unmatched second-hand furniture and antiques, good
Oriental rugs and a giant cardboard Land O'Lakes Butter sign. There are
books along all walls, except where there are records: rock, blues, soul, jazz,
country. Clusters of photographs from the twenties, a large head of Richard
Nixon and a formal framed portrait of LBJ, Lady Bird, Luci and Lynda, hand
tinted. There are tiny celluloid baby dolls, a tin kangaroo wind-up toy, shells,
a set of toy appliances still in the box, labeled "My Dream Kitchen." A 1940s,
dust-bowl kind of dress hangs from the ceiling with a bull-dog face mask

attached and a long scarf draped around the neck. Taped to the refrigerator are about thirty Polaroid photographs. These are Ann Beattie's friends. She and her husband, a musician, do not plan to have children, but their house is filled with pictures of friends' children. "When they come here," she says, "children always want to know where my kids are. They can't believe an adult would have all this stuff."

Ann Beattie is thirty-two. Born in Washington, D.C., she was not, she says, the kind of child everybody always knew would be a writer. She attended college in Washington and graduate school at the University of Connecticut. "I really cannot remember what I had in mind," she says, "and I think that's because I never had anything in mind." She entered a Ph.D. program, she says, because a personnel agency told her she wouldn't get a job without cutting her nails and she didn't have any intention of cutting her nails.

If some of what Ann Beattie says and what her house contains reminds one of elements in her stories and novels, there is also a distinct difference between this woman and much of the world she describes. It is hard to find more than a couple of characters in all of Ann Beattie's collected works whose relationships seem stable, whose careers matter to them, who eat dinner on time. But though it's easy to picture this house as the scene for one of those endless, complicated, somewhat messy weekend parties she describes, the fact is that the kitchen is immaculate, the shelves have been recently dusted, an electric typewriter sits on the desk and a small photograph of the *New Yorker*'s editor, William Shawn, is taped to the bulletin board. Things get attended to here.

I ask whether Ann Beattie would agree that her writing chronicled, perhaps for the first time, a particular counterculture world. And because it seems to me hard to fathom someone of that world also writing about it successfully, I wonder to what extent she sees herself as part of such a world.

AB: I've gotten very hostile to that response to my work. I mean, people never say things like, "James Joyce, he was pretty mired in Dublin, wasn't he?" He really stayed pretty close to home, didn't he. I mean, if that's what you have to say about Joyce, that's a pretty reductive approach to the work. And I feel the same way about my work. If people want to take that as a stepping stone for what I'm writing about, well, of course it's there. It's certainly true that people I write about are essentially my age, and so they were a certain age in the sixties and had certain common experiences and tend to listen to the same kind of music and get stoned and wear the same kind of clothes. I realize that it's all there, but what I've always hoped for is that somebody will then start talking more about the meat and bones of what I'm writing about.

JM: Isn't that partly because readers regard the group of people you tend to focus on—I hesitate to label it—as a particularly exotic one?
AB: People are still tremendously interested in either fancifying or romanticizing the 1960s, and they have it in their heads that I know more about that than they do. People like to romanticize writers, and I was a writer of a romantic period. Therefore, I must be romantic. Well. I was watching the 1960s on my parents' television. I wasn't out getting gassed every day. I never took acid.

JM: So you wouldn't say your fiction deals with any particular types?
AB: I don't think the people I'm writing about are ordinary people. But I don't think they're as extraordinary as most reviewers have thought. I move within a small, narrow circle, and these are some of the oddities of that circle.

JM: I get the feeling—looking at your friends' photographs on the refrigerator—that I must know some of their stories.
AB: Well, you do. And I've had friends actually pick up the *New Yorker* and throw it across the room. But I never expose something that is a real bitter wound in some person. And I give nice dinner parties to make up for it.

   Also, I hardly ever hear something from a person, and use it just the way I heard it as an anecdote for a story. What comes out is very scrambled. I do sometimes lift things, but I don't even have that kind of an ear that allows me to really correctly remember dialogue. In fact, I have no idea what's making an impression sometimes until years later. I am just chronically unable to look on anything as material: I think I probably talk as much as, if not more than, my friends on those evenings. People tell me stories now that I'm an established writer, and it's very frustrating to me because they tell me great stories and they have a beginning and a middle and an end and they're my kind of material and they fascinate me. But once I've heard the story I feel like it already exists and there would be no fun in my writing the story.

JM: It's a little hard for me to put together the image of the person who sits smoking grass and listening to John Coltrane with her friends and the person who gets dressed up and rides the commuter train to the *New Yorker* offices some mornings, and has lunch at the Algonquin.

AB: I guess it's also true that I am much more interested in alienation than I personally feel alienated. I mean, if I believed exactly what my characters believe, or if I looked at these stories as trying to teach me a moral lesson, I would say, "Well, the hell with it. Everything is useless." And stay here in Redding and not even bother to write stories. My writing is obviously some attempt to grapple with that alienation that I'm dealing with in the stories, while at the same time not giving answers, because I don't think there are answers to give.

JM: Your new novel concerns not only young people in their teens and twenties, but also a suburban businessman in his forties. In structure, too, the books seems very different from anything you've done before. Do you see *Falling in Place* as a departure from your earlier work?

AB: Yes, it's certainly different from anything I've written before. It's more a beginning, middle and end novel. It has something happen. At least for me it's a more ambitious kind of book than I would have been capable of in 1975, when I was writing *Chilly Scenes*. I don't know how to write a novel. That's why my novels are very different from one other. I would like to take a course in that sometimes, if I ever take another course.

JM: What would you like to have answered for you?

AB: Oh, how you can possibly wade in so deeply and stay with it for so long. When I write a story it's usually about fifteen pages and I write it all in one sitting, or two sittings. So with a novel, it's very hard for me to work on Monday and Tuesday, and on Wednesday I wonder what I said on Tuesday, let alone what I'm moving toward. And it's also a great risk because I've never written anything that I knew the ending of. And in fact, with the novel I wrote before this one I [never published], I wrote four hundred pages and still had no idea what the ending was. Which is why it turned out to be a total loss.

JM: So you embarked on the new novel not knowing. . . .

AB: I didn't even know who the characters would be. I just knew I wanted to write something about children. So I started with the character of John Joel, and I put him up in a tree. . . .

JM: And you saw that he was fat? That he was unhappy about his parents?
AB: Yes. I knew a certain series of facts about him. But I didn't know what to do with them. That's why Chapter Two doesn't also begin with John Joel. That's why all the chapters jump around. I can't think how somebody would move from one to the next, so I have to take a breather and hope that I come up with something.

JM: It interests me that, for someone who writes with such precision about the objects in a room, the foods being eaten, the music that's playing, you offer virtually no physical descriptions of your characters. Actually, I'm surprised that it doesn't bother me more, as I'm reading your work.
AB: It bothers my editor at the *New Yorker*. He's always asking me, "What does she look like? What is she wearing?"

JM: So that's an intentional thing you do?
AB: No, I guess I just see the person so clearly I don't feel any need to describe him. Whereas the other things in my peripheral vision are easy to seize upon and sort of bring into focus. Then too, I figure if they're playing John Coltrane records and are stoned, they're not wearing anything from Brooks Brothers. . . .

JM: Now music, on the other hand, is a nearly constant presence in your work.
AB: I certainly listen to records a lot. But if I write a story I tend to put in what my husband is playing on the stereo at that moment. I don't really rush over to my John Coltrane albums thinking, "Is this the perfect song to have playing at this point?" That's just what's on the turntable.

JM: And you can be writing successfully with John Coltrane in the background?
AB: I'm very good at dealing with background noise. I really did have a lot of crazies around when I started writing.

JM: In this new book, the song "Heart of Glass," by Blondie, is almost like a refrain. Could you play it for me? [She does, and one realizes it's a song that was playing on the radio at the beach all last summer.]
AB: I don't even know what the words are. But it was as though somebody had planted that song on the airwaves to go with what I was writing in the

book. The same thing was true for the business about Skylab falling, which is mentioned several times in my new novel. That's what was in the news when I was writing, and if I'd tried to invent something, it couldn't have been as good.

I really love the notion of found art. Warhol soup cans—that kind of stuff. When I write something, I like to look out the window the night I'm typing and see what kind of moon it was on July the fifteenth and put it in.

JM: Maybe this isn't a question you can answer. But I wonder what you see as the themes of your work.

AB: I never have a big subject in mind. When I start to write, it's usually with a single line in mind or some little image that I saw.

JM: You're not interested in larger themes?

AB: No, I don't think I've ever written anything about a larger theme.

JM: Relationships between men and women?

AB: I just assume that there are going to be moments. But when I start to write, it isn't with the thought that I want to communicate about the relationships between men and women. I think, "I'd really like to work that interesting ashtray I just brought into a story about men and women."

JM: Still, your stories are not simply assemblages of small details. I can imagine a facile kind of writer doing a superficially serviceable imitation of an Ann Beattie story, including an ashtray and a certain sort of very spaced-out remark and a lovable dog and some wonderfully good meal or some fascinatingly terrible meal—and not succeeding at all.

AB: Well, it's done—not just with me, but with anybody who is conspicuous in any way. I'm embarrassed and offended by anybody misperceiving and thinking that I'm just writing about how alienated everybody is, and how everybody has three odd objects on their table and a strange record playing.

JM: How do you know a work of fiction is over?

AB: If it sounds right, it's over. But I get into a lot of trouble with endings. They either come to me or they don't. They're very important to me—much more important than beginnings.

JM: Your two published novels seem to me to have surprisingly hopeful endings—considering the bleakness of the characters' situations earlier in the books.

AB: Yes, but then again, I could make a good argument that when seen in context, they may be isolated happy endings. If you had just the facts of the story, maybe so, but if you had the cumulative effect of the material that's gone before, it should somewhat alter your unmitigated joy in finding out the characters are going off together.

JM: You take a bleak view of the future of marriages?

AB: I take an ambiguous view. I think, for instance, of *Chilly Scenes of Winter*, Charles has pursued this woman all through the book and he does get her. But you should understand by that point that he's a strange enough character and that they're mismatched enough that the rest of their life clearly isn't going to be easy. It's not as though it's just a frieze for all time that you can do with a movie camera and really capture something. The characters presumably still walk and breathe after the last period, and who knows what's going to happen?

JM: I get the impression that *Falling in Place* must have been written in a pretty concentrated period of time.

AB: No one would take it seriously if I told you how quickly I wrote it. [She does tell, off the record. It's a very short period of time.]

JM: I guess you didn't take a lot of vacations during those weeks.

AB: I worked eighteen hours a day. My husband was going across the United States so I was bored and alone here, and I was terribly sick. But I had time on my hands, plus I had a deadline. I hate deadlines. People say, "Wow, look how well you responded," and that may be true. But I'm a complete wreck still—burned out—and this is nine months later.

JM: At this moment do you find yourself thinking about new subjects? Do you know what your next novel will be?

AB: You presume there's a next novel. That's great! Good for my morale. Could you write me twice a year and ask how things are going? I really do feel like a bumbler with the novel form. I can't envision ever writing another one. Then again, I didn't envision writing this one. I wonder if there *are* novelists who feel that they know how to write novels. I wonder if this knowledge exists. At least there must be people who are not petrified of attempting it, who think of the work they're going to do automatically in terms of its being turned into a novel. I say, "My God, is there any way out of this?" I mean, I've actually ripped up material because I just can't face getting into a novel.

JM: So you think of yourself more as a short-story writer?
AB: So far, that's what has brought me the most happiness. I just adapted a story of mine to be dramatized on PBS, but I don't have any burning desire to be a screenwriter. [Ann Beattie did not write the script for the film version of her first novel, renamed *Head over Heels*.] No, I'm basically lazy, and nothing pleases me more than sitting around writing for the *New Yorker*. But it's not as if they accept everything I write, not by a long shot. And I don't write that many stories any more either.

I wish I had a more organized life. What I envy is the writer who gets up every morning and makes a pot of coffee and if he can't write a poem, at least he revises the ones he wrote last week—while I may do nothing for three months except vacuum the house every four days and stare into space.

JM: The times when you're not writing must be very frustrating.
AB: Terribly. But I've learned I can't force it. I'm really at the mercy of just letting the impulse to write take me over, and when I can't write, I just create silly blockades for myself.

JM: Like what?
AB: Well, I read a lot—mostly modern fiction, nothing before 1960 if I can help it. And my relatives give me subscriptions to a lot of magazines: *Reader's Digest, Early American Life.* . . . My husband forced me to give up *People* magazine for my thirtieth birthday. I'm a great time waster. See what a shiny coat my dog has? I go buy him vitamins. I rap with him. I brush him.

JM: I get the feeling, from your work and from the photographs on your refrigerator door, that friends are very important to you. Does friendship in fact play the kind of role in your life that it appears to play in the lives of your characters?
AB: I think so. That may be true with most people my age—who associate more with their friends than they do with their families. I'm very fond of my

parents, but I have no brothers or sisters, so obviously the idea of a surrogate family is more interesting to me than someone who grew up with siblings. I think nothing of driving four or five hours to visit a friend. I'll drive to California—on maybe one or two days' notice—to see a friend.

JM: And did you actually know somebody who did what the two lovers in *Falling in Place* did, during the early days of their relationship—hold hands uninterruptedly for two days?
AB: Yes—four days. They've split up now.

A Conversation with Ann Beattie

Larry McCaffery and Sinda Gregory / 1982

From the *Literary Review* 27.2 (1984), 165–77. Reprinted by permission.

Since Ann Beattie's short stories first began appearing, in the mid 1970s, mainly in the *New Yorker*, she has quickly emerged as one of the most distinctive voices in contemporary American fiction. Her first two books, *Chilly Scenes of Winter* (a novel, 1976) and *Distortions* (stories, 1976), with their coolly dispassionate prose rhythms and their vivid portrayals of the disaffections, anguish, and boredom of middle America, were widely praised by reviewers. Her second story collection, *Secrets and Surprises* (1978), and her second novel, *Falling in Place* (1980), solidified her reputation and exhibited a growing maturity as a stylist. A third collection, *The Burning House*, was published by Random House in the fall of 1982.

Sinda Gregory and Larry McCaffery interviewed Ann Beattie in Los Angeles on January 27, 1982. Their questions and comments during the interview are identified SG and LM, respectively.

SG: In your interview in the *New York Times Book Review,* you respond to the comment made by Joyce Maynard that you are primarily a chronicler of the sixties counterculture by saying, "It's certainly true that the people I write about are essentially my age, and so they were a certain age in the sixties and had certain common experiences and tend to listen to the same kind of music and get stoned and wear the same kind of clothes, but what I've always hoped for is that somebody will then start talking more about the meat and bones of what I'm writing about." The "meat and bones" that you refer to seems to me to involve the difficulties involved in people understanding each other—the difficulty of saying what we feel, of making ourselves clear, of having the courage or honesty to say what we mean. Would you agree that this issue of the breakdown of communication is one of the meat-and-bones areas you're referring to?
AB: Yes, my fiction often has to do with that. A direct result of this breakdown of communication is the breakdown of relationships. I don't think the people

in my stories are representative, by the way—that's really off the point of what you just asked me, but it's behind Maynard's comment, and behind what a lot of people have said about my work. I'd say that the people in my fiction reflect some of my own personal problems and concerns, perhaps to an exaggerated degree, but I don't mean them to be taken as representative of the culture. So that's part one of the answer. As to part two, what you're saying sounds perfectly insightful to me—I'd agree that these breakdowns do have a lot to do with my work—but even this, I think, tends to generalize a great deal. I mean if I were to ask you to be specific and cite to me what the common denominator is between two different stories of mine, I wonder what it would be?

SG: I'd probably say that a lot of your stories that differ in many respects still seem to focus on relationships in the process of breaking down.
AB: Okay, I can see what you mean, but often the people in my stories are unstable in some way even before the relationship—their problems often predate the relationship we see, or there's no reason to think the breakdown is a consequence of the relationship itself.

LM: In quite a few of your stories you seem to imply that one of the reasons that people's relationships break down is because they can't express themselves. You don't always explain why they are unable to talk to each other, but often your stories have scenes with characters who are totally cut off from each other or who misunderstand each other.
SG: A good example of this is the scene in *Falling in Place* where the whole family is sitting around while John has taken them out for a Chinese dinner: at one line each one of them makes a gesture of generosity towards the others that is misconstrued and rejected, so they draw back; in that scene it seems impossible for anyone to express what they want to express.
AB: Yes, I'll have to agree that these kinds of scenes do appear in my work, in one form or another. But this is not something I'm doing deliberately. Personally, of course, I believe that many people have a lot of trouble communicating, but I'm afraid this sounds so banal that I hate to dwell on it because it's hardly something I originated. When I was working on that scene Sinda just mentioned, for instance, I was mainly thinking of the literary effects—the tension it creates—and not the general issue involved. I guess I feel that if you're mainly interested in showing people not communicating you ought to be at least as interesting as Harold Pinter.

LM: You know, what I really tend to notice in your fiction is not so much the issues you raise but the specific people you place into your stories. What interests you about your characters?

AB: I'm often interested in my characters because they can't break away from the situation they find themselves in. If they can't communicate to begin with, you'd think more of them would fly off than they do. Part of this interest is a reflection of my own experiences with people. I find it very hard to envy most of the couples I know. I can't imagine exchanging places with those that are together, even those that are happy, because it seems to me they have made so many compromises to be together. So I'm very interested in the fact that there are these personalities who have compromised in so many ways. On the other hand, there are so many people who are together because of all the obvious reasons: they don't want to be lonely or they are in the habit of being together, or this whole Beckettian thing—I can't stay and I can't go. This tug interests me more than the fact that they're not communicating—I want to find out why they're staying and not going.

LM: A lot of your characters are very self-conscious individuals—self-conscious about their roles, about the cliches they use to express themselves, about just about everything. Sinda and I notice this same sense of self-consciousness in ourselves and with the people we associate with—maybe it has to do with education or the kinds of people we have as friends—but we notice that this tends to intrude into relationships. It almost seems as if the more self-aware you become, this self-awareness gets to the way of spontaneity or whatever it is that is "natural" in relationships.

AB: Yes, I know just what you mean. This kind of intellectualizing or self-consciousness just allows you to hide from yourself forever. People can easily fall into the trap of thinking that to label something is to explain it.

SG: It's the same thing with the irony your characters often seem to have—it's a kind of defense mechanism. . . .

AB: Yeah, all these artifices assist in helping people delude themselves.

SG: —even though these artifices and intellectualizing are supposedly, on the surface, helping people develop insights about their behavior and that of others.

AB: These insights aren't very profound, though. If you notice, usually in my stories one person is insightful and the other person isn't. They end up in a tug-of-war when it becomes inconsequential whether they're insightful or not. In a story like "Colorado" Robert knows what the score is with Penelope, but so what? And she understands why they've ended up in Vermont and her understanding doesn't matter. Charles Manson said there was a particular voice telling him to do something, and David Berkowitz said that it was a dog, Sam, up in the sky motivating him. Don't people always say that what motivates them is logical? What matters is that they're getting through life and they're unhappy and there's something missing. If I knew what it was that was missing, I'd write about it, I'd write for Hallmark cards. That would please a lot of my critics.

LM: Yeah, I've noticed that some critics have complained that your stories don't offer "solutions" or resolutions to your characters' problems. How do you respond to this idea—championed recently by John Gardner—that writers need to supply answers and not simply describe problems or situations?
AB: I don't expect answers of anyone other than a medical doctor, so no, it wouldn't occur to me that writers should have to supply answers. I certainly don't feel that it's the obligation of any artist to supply answers.

LM: What about your trying other fictional approaches? Are you ever tempted to try, say, a detective story, or an historical novel, or something like that?
AB: *Falling in Place* was meant to be an "historical novel."

LM: I can see that, but what about writing about historical periods other than our own? One reviewer said, half-jokingly I think, that no tune exists in your work before 1968. . . .
AB: No, I've never tried that type of work because that would require research and I fear libraries. No kidding, I don't know if I could do it or not, so, in brief, the answer is that I've not been tempted in that direction. I'm very much interested in writers who are tempted and do it. Mary Lee Settle is one of my favorite writers, and the research she undertakes to find out background is amazing: she gets herself in a rowboat and goes down the banks of a river in West Virginia to see the way it curves at a particular point; and then she studies topographical maps, circa 1890, to see if that bend was in the river at that time or not; then she flies to Boston to listen to a speech JFK gave in a particular town in West Virginia to see how this relates to her material. I'm fascinated with this approach, but it seems like Perry Mason stuff to me. Sleuthing and trying to keep all that in one's mind would be impossible for

me. I hate writing novels to begin with because I can't remember what the
character did five days ago; so I write everything quickly, including novels,
which is why complexity fouls me up. If I can't remember in a fifteen-page
story what one of my characters did on page five, I can take a few minutes
and look it up and make sure that the X who walked in on page five was a shit.
But if I can't remember if this character is a shit or not and I have to take the
time to go through chapters one through nineteen to find out what his off-
the-wall comment was that showed he was a shit, then my train of thought is
gone. So for me it would be just agonizing to try to go back and write from
research and then imagine something, because at least with my own writing
I have a touchstone in that I'm writing out of what happened yesterday.
I could never assimilate things the way that Mary Lee Settle does and then
get them down into a coherent form.

SG: You just said that you work very quickly. What kinds of work habits do
you have—have you always worked in spurts like this?
AB: No, at first when I found out there was something I could do—I was
learning, teaching myself, mostly, how to write—I wrote a lot more than I do
today. Those stories were more speculative and funnier than what I write
now. I don't think I have as much to say today. Some of the things that interested me when I was starting out don't interest me as much now—or they
interest me in a different way. I've always had what people call "writer's
block," but it's never scared me because I never thought of it as that. My total
output is pretty large and I can't be too frightened about deviating from
work habits that have always never been a routine. So my work habits have
been erratic.

SG: What about the mundane details, like whether or not you work at a typewriter, or during the day, and things like that?
AB: I always work at a typewriter. I can make some revisions or do fine editing in longhand, but if I'm revising a whole page I always go back to the typewriter. When I lived in the country I usually worked at night, although this
isn't true any longer. I find that I'm very lethargic during the day, and everything seems distracting and it's very hard to concentrate. Of course, now I do
different kinds of work—when a revised script for PBS is due in forty-eight
hours, what are you going to do? Explain that you don't start writing until
after midnight? I get in there and start writing right after breakfast. I'm also

very neurotic about my work habits. To this day I have my mother mail to me, from Washington DC, a special kind of typing paper—which isn't even particularly *good* typing paper—from People's Drugstore. It costs about $1.29 a pack. I used to always work in my husband's clothes. He's not my husband any longer, but I still occasionally put on the essential plaid shirt.

SG: Are you a coffee-drinker while you work—or do you go more for the straight gin or dope method?
AB: Not coffee, but I find writing is surprisingly oral—when you're not talking you need something. But I never take drugs when I write and I never drink either. I have gotten really out of it to remember what something feels like, and then managed to crawl to the typewriter two days later. People will say to me, "Boy, you must have been really stoned to write that stoned scene in *Falling in Place*." They forget that writers have memories. When I wrote that scene I had probably had two aspirin and a glass of water. There's such an energy rush when you do it cold.

LM: What seems to get you to sit down at the typewriter in the first place? Do you have a specific scene or character or sentence in mind?
AB: My stories always seem to begin with something very small, whether it be one or the other of those things you've just mentioned. If I were to say I usually begin with a character, that wouldn't mean that I would know the character's occupation or whether the character is happy or sad, or what the character's age was. I would know that the character is named "Joe," and, yes, sometimes the idea that the character's name is "Joe" has gotten me to the typewriter. More often it's really a physiological feeling that I should write something—this feeling doesn't always work out. Many times I'm wrong about it.

LM: What do you mean by a "physiological feeling"?
AB: I don't know how to talk about this without sounding like Yeats saying that the "Voices" were driving him into a room and dictating to him, but it's almost like that, almost that crazy to me. Something in me has built up and this is a compulsion to go and write something at the typewriter. And, yes, it's not totally amorphous, there is something in the back of my mind: it's a name, it's a sentence, it's a sense of remembering what it is like to be in the dead of winter and wanting to go to the beach in the summer, some vague

notion like that. It's never more than that. I've never in my life sat down and said to myself, "Now I will write something about somebody to whom such-and-such will happen."

SG: What you're saying is very interesting because I think most people assume that because your characters are so particularized and real-seeming that they must be based on people you've actually known. Does this happen very often?

AB: I probably shouldn't answer that because, given the nature of most of my characters, it wouldn't be much to my advantage to admit it if I did. It's interesting to me, though, that there have been some instances when I thought I've come very close to capturing the essence of somebody even though I've made some little change in their clothing or in the location of the story. These changes are made subconsciously, it's not something I do deliberately, but these changes are always enough to throw people off. That's what interesting to me—I don't think someone has ever said to me, "Hey, that's me," and been right.

LM: That's never happened?

AB: Not even when I thought it was most obvious. On the other hand in places where a character I've created has nothing to do with anyone I know, people have insisted that a particular line is something they've said. I had a sentence in a story called "Like Glass" and I was showing it to a friend; the woman who's narrating the story says of her husband that when he talked about his dreams his dreams were never full of the usual things like symbols but were summaries of things that had happened. And the friend of mine who was reading the story stopped and said to me, "This isn't true of my dreams!" So there you have it.

SG: You said somewhere that when you began *Falling in Place* that you had no idea of where it was heading, that you only knew you wanted it to be about children.

AB: That wasn't quite true. I knew the beginnings of the first sentence. "John Joel was high up in a tree . . ." and then it occurred to me that if somebody was up high in a tree, it would probably be a child, and if it were a child it was likely that there would have to be a family surrounding him. So then with that as an idea I proceeded to write the novel. I had seven weeks to go with this deadline at Random House. I understand that in the real world people don't come after you with whips that say "Random House" on the handles; but it still makes me very nervous to have deadlines because I don't like to have deadlines—and I've organized my life so that I don't have deadlines very often. But in this case I had this deadline that was making me very nervous, and I looked out my window and there was this wonderful peach tree out there. That's what started *Falling in Place*.

LM: But despite being written in seven weeks under the pressures of these Random House whips, *Falling in Place* seems to me to have a much greater sense of structure or "plot" in the traditional sense than, say, *Chilly Scenes*—that is, it seems to be working towards that climax, the shooting of Mary by John Joel.
AB: I was so surprised when that shooting happened.

LM: How far in advance had you realized that this is where the book was heading?
AB: Never. I was totally amazed to find the gun in the kid's hands. But then I remembered there had been that odd box which belonged to Parker's grandfather.

SG: So you hadn't planted that box there with the gun in it?
AB: No, in fact, after the shooting happened I thought, "Oh, my God, we're only three weeks into the book and here Mary is dead on the ground—what am I going to do to resurrect her?" So I resurrected her. Really, I was very upset when that shooting happened.

LM: But despite these kinds of surprises, wouldn't you agree that *Falling in Place* is a more "writerly novel" than *Chilly Scenes of Winter*—that it has a tighter structure and is governed by a more coherent set of images and metaphors?
AB: Sure. Remember *Falling in Place* was written several years after my first novel. I wrote *Chilly Scenes* in 1975, and it was all dialogue, basically; it was really more like a play than a novel. And that book was written in three weeks. I hope that I did know more about writing in the summer of 1979 than I did four years earlier. And, of course, things happen to you that also help create a focus for your work. I was living in Redding, Connecticut, when

I wrote *Falling in Place*, and I had been living there about a year. While I was actually working on *Falling in Place* I didn't really realize how much of Redding had gotten into my head. Actually I guess I had grown very hostile to Redding and was very upset by being there, so in a way it was almost a relief to write something like *Falling in Place* and sort of purge myself of these feelings. We had had more than a year of very bad times and total isolation living in this wealthy commuter community that had nothing to do with us. And I was watching the people at the market and it was like when you're sick and have a fever and everything seems in sharper focus. I went around with that kind of fever for about a year, and then I had this deadline, so I wrote *Falling in Place*. I don't think that it follows that this is the way I always work—if you put me in Alaska for a year I'm not sure I'd write about igloos—but it did happen that way in Redding, Connecticut. There was so much more I had subconsciously stored away that I wanted to get out than there had been about anywhere else I've lived before.

SG: I have a question about the structure of *Falling in Place.*
AB: Yeah, what is the structure of that book? I've been wondering about that myself.

SG: Why did you have every other chapter take the form of those brief, italicized sections?
AB: You want to know the truth about those chapters? I started out that novel by writing chapters—I would write a chapter a day. But after I wrote the first chapter—it was the opening chapter that's there now—I realized that I had forgotten to put any background information in it, so I made notes to myself of what I had to go back and include in the first chapter. The second day I wrote a chapter and then thought, "Here's what I left out of this one." The third day I thought, "I wonder if anyone has ever written a whole book like this. I wonder if this isn't too artsy?" Then I thought, "Who cares?" Eventually I went back and made these lists a little more articulate and they became the italicized chapters. If I were teaching this book, I could imagine myself making any number of pretentious guesses about why the book is structured this way, but in point of fact the book is structured this way because I left in these notes and comments to myself. Another thing I should mention is that I'll do anything to trick myself into thinking that I'm not writing a novel—it's easier if I just think in terms of chapter one, chapter

two, chapter three—I can deal with that. So I thought of the italics at the end of Chapter One in *Falling in Place* as being a kind of coda. And of course the chapters in that book don't all function in the same way: some of them repeat what you already know, some of them tell you what you know is an absolute lie, some of them tell you what to anticipate later on. I think Random House was a little baffled and wondered, "What do we call these?"

LM: One of the things I like about your fiction is precisely the thing that some critics seem most troubled with—that is, your work often seems to recreate a sense of modern life's aimlessness, its lack of coherency and resolution. Is this a conscious strategy on your part—a desire to suggest life's formlessness, that life isn't shaped like most well-made stories and novels suggest—or does, this sense emerge mainly as a function of your writing habits? In other words, does this "aimlessness" result from your view of the world or mainly from the fact that you don't know where your works are headed?

AB: There are at least two honest answers to that question. One is to repeat what I've said before that I've never known beforehand what I'm setting out to write, so that even when I write the ending to a piece it's only at that point that I know how it ends. I do agree how you characterize my endings—the sense of them is "aimless," but the language used to create this sense isn't. I imagine, though, that subconsciously this is aesthetically what I believe in. . . .

LM: You mean that you can't wrap things up neatly with a nice climax and denouement?

AB: Not the people and situations that I'm writing about. I don't hate books in which this happens; in fact, I rather admire them. One of my favorite books is non-fiction, *Blood and Money* by Thomas Thompson. The last page is so apocalyptic and satisfying. If I could do anything like that—see things with such an overview—I would wrap things up neatly. But it's not the way my mind works; it would seem inappropriate to what I've done, and I've never been able to overhaul a story. In fact, stories often get thrown away in the last paragraph, even the last sentence, because I don't know how it can end. It seems to me most honest personally to write something that still implies further complexity. I'm not writing confessionally. If I want to do that I can write my grandmother and say, "The day began here and it ended here." It wouldn't occur to me that this approach would be pleasurable or meaningful in a story.

SG: You've mentioned how *Falling in Place* started. Do you recall what the opening image was in *Chilly Scenes of Winter*?

AB: No, not really. All I remember about that is that I had an idea in mind about the friendship between two men, Charles and Sam. I wrote quite a bit of background about them, and I showed it to a good friend of mine who handed it back to me and there was only a little shard of paper left—the remains of page 51 with Charles saying, "Permettez-moi de vous presenter Sam McGuire." And everything about how Charles came to meet Sam, what town they lived in, everything else had been scissored away. And I thought, you're right, just jump in. So whatever had been my original intention as I began the book was gone. The book that now stands is what took over. My friend had done the perfect job of editing. When the book came out I was amused when reviewers would talk about "Beattie's amazing, stark beginning," when in fact my friend had actually taken the scissors to it. My friend J. D. O'Hara, to whom *Falling in Place* is dedicated and who teaches at the University of Connecticut, used to take the scissors to the ends of my stories. Maybe I'm just a victim of my friends' Freudian obsessions, but in both cases they were right. It was really O'Hara who, in literally taking the scissors to my pages, suggested that more elliptical endings to my stories might be advantageous.

LM: I've also noticed that you seem to almost be deliberately refusing to provide the kinds of background and psychological information that most writers do— you just put your characters in a situation and show the reader that situation.

AB: I don't think that my characters are what they are because of interesting psychological complexities. They're not clinical studies to me. That would be a mind that worked in a different way than mine works. It's like: I like *you*, but I don't care about your childhood; if we know each other for the next ten years I would no doubt be interested if you were to tell me about your childhood, but to think that having known you at some point in time would change my impression, help me in any way to uncover what I'm looking for in our personal relationship, isn't true for me. For whatever reasons, I just seem to react to what is right there in front of me. So that's usually the way I write. There is often background information—though I supply it late in the story.

SG: Your prose style is one that most reviewers have called "deadpan" or "emotionless." Are you consciously aiming for a certain kind of effect in relying on this kind of style?

AB: I think that's the way people talk. I know I think that way—in short sentences. If I didn't describe things neutrally I would be editorializing, which is
not at all what I mean to do. It may be that I have gone too far with my prose
style in this direction. It's a very mannered style, really—or the effect of it is
very mannered—but that effect is no more conscious on my part when I sit
down at the typewriter than these other things we've been talking about. I
write so fast that I couldn't possibly think about whether or not I'm putting
compound or complex sentences into my prose, or whether I'm writing like a
dope, or whatever. I mean, we're talking about writing a whole story in two
or three hours.

LM: But from what you just said I take it that you are conscious about trying
to eliminate an intrusive, editorializing narrator?
AB: Usually, but not always. There's a story of mine called "Greenwich Time,"
which was in the *New Yorker*; it doesn't exactly have editorializing but it does
have what is purple prose for me. So I won't say I never change my prose style
or point of view. I don't think you would even recognize that "Greenwich
Time" is by me, except maybe in terms of the characters—it's full of analogies, it's constructed like a prism, the language is extremely deliberate and
insistent; it's ostensibly seen through the main character's eyes, but the
author is so completely and obviously there that you couldn't possibly
remove her.

SG: Is this kind of different approach something you've been doing more of
recently in your stories, or is it just an isolated incident?
AB: It's something I realize more that I can do now. But it certainly would be
so damn hard for me to do it all the time that I avoid it. And, of course, the
most important thing is that this different approach seemed appropriate for
that story, whereas it wouldn't be in others.

SG: When you say that you write the way you do because it's "too hard" to
write in other ways, what do you mean?
AB: I don't think I have an overall view of things to express.

SG: So you focus on trying to observe small things. . . .
AB: Not so much small things as small moments. I wish that writing these
stories would suddenly lead me to some revelation that could help me as well

as existing as art, as well as pleasing others. But don't think I've ever written anything that's allowed me to put pieces together; or maybe I have a psychological problem that makes me resist putting pieces together, that's the flip side of it. But one or the other is true.

SG: It's interesting that you relate this to your own psychological makeup because I noticed that your characters often seem to have moments where they seem unable to put the pieces of their lives together, unable to understand their own or others' motivations.

AB: This particular problem may indeed be particular to me. Based on what I've experienced, even with the people I'm closest to, I can't predict or always find consistency to others' behavior—and I don't think I'm especially bad about reading people. What I'm perceiving, though, is probably correct I suspect: people are unpredictable. What I tend to think about someone is not something like, "X will always be cheerful on a given evening; therefore I should call X and we'll go out and get a pizza." Rather, I think, "I'll call X—anything might happen." I think this way even if I've known X for fifteen years. Obviously this attitude works its way into my fiction in all sorts of ways because I can't pretend to project myself into any other position.

LM: What other contemporary writers do you especially admire?

AB: This is a hard question for me to answer because it makes me seem like a fool to like so many. I do read a lot these days, whereas years ago I didn't. If you asked me. "Who do you think is always good?" that would be really hard—I'd say "Almost nobody, me included." But for individual moments or books or stories, there's so many. Obviously one writer I like is Mary Lee Settle, whose name seems to have come up several times tonight. Barthelme—I think he's the true genius of our time. Ann Tyler is really good. Joy Williams is one of the best short story writers in America; she has a collection out called *Taking Care* which is great. I just read a Tobias Wolff collection called *In the Garden of the North American Martyrs*, a terrible title but the first story in it is absolutely magnificent and the whole book is really first rate. Raymond Carver. If there's one story I could die happy having written, it's "What Is It?" by Raymond Carver. If there's one novel I could have written, it would have been Steven Millhauser's *Edwin Mullhouse*. Stanley Crawford, whose last book, *Some Instructions for My Wife*, is a bitterly witty book; my favorite book of his is *Log of the S.S. The Mrs. Unquentine*. I also read a lot of poetry. I'm a great admirer of Louise Gluck, Jay Parini, Gregory Orr, Michael Ryan, Sidney Lea.

LM: In your story "A Reasonable Man" one of your characters points to all the books lining his walls and then wonders whether or not any of them were written by happy people. Has writing made you happy, or does it tend to aggravate things, open up wounds, the way it apparently did for Sylvia Plath?
AB: Writing doesn't open up wounds for me; during the writing of them it has made me happy. There have been a couple of times, only three I can think of, where I have finished a story—and remember that when I start to write something I don't know what it is I'm going to write and have gotten to the end of it and thought, "I really wish I had never had to put these pieces together." These were "The Burning House," a story in *Vogue* called "Playback," and a story that will be out in the *New Yorker* in a few months called "Desire."

SG: Why did you regret finishing these?
AB: Each of these made me realize that I had kept at bay and deliberately misinterpreted painful truths. But it is worth the price of discovering what you don't want to know because you can also have the sheer pleasure of writing something absurd like "It's Just Another Day at Big Bear City, California," and deciding to have spacemen take pornographic pictures. I mean, that's fun and I basically write because I think it's fun. There are a few things I wish I never had written only because I wish I hadn't found out the things I found out.

LM: So at least occasionally you feel that the process of writing allows you to discover things about yourself.
AB: Yes, but always only in retrospect. I don't ever sit down thinking that. I just do it, the way I get my groceries.

Ann Beattie

William Goldstein / 1986

From *Publishers Weekly* 230 (19 September 1986), 120–21. Reprinted by permission.

Leaned against a window in Ann Beattie's kitchen is a family portrait of President Lyndon Johnson, his wife Lady Bird and their daughters Luci Baines and Lynda Bird, an official photograph taken (it is obvious from the clothing and hairstyles) during the White House years. Why is it there? In the late 1950s Lady Bird was Ann Beattie's dancing teacher at the Wesley Methodist Church in Washington, D.C.

Beattie, now thirty-eight, lives in Charlottesville, VA., little more than two hours from where she grew up in D.C., and she writes short stories and novels that have been variously criticized and praised for including such extraneous or telling details as the above. Her fourth collection of stories, *Where You'll Find Me*, has just been published by Simon & Schuster.

"My writing is full of things seen, not heard," Beattie says. "I get more material staring out at the world, not overhearing things." She is a "specific" writer. "I focus on detail, but that's not what my work is *about*."

Beattie is fascinated by "reflective people in a mess," she says, offering her own partial and generalized view of her work. "What catches my attention are situations that are ironic. Look what everyone takes for granted. Look at how that makes everything ironic. The subtext, the detail, the telling gestures that reveal it," mesmerize her. Her characters, as she understands them, "are not forthcoming. When they say something 'emphatically,' I believe they believe it emphatically." Writers, the author says, "don't trust surfaces because they're so used to making things. . . . Writers are deciphering."

Seeking meaning in fiction seems, to Beattie, somehow beyond the point. Fiction describes, fiction depicts; it is its own world. "Writing communicates a lot. But not answers to direct questions. I just want to make [a story] satisfying in and of itself," Beattie says. "I don't want to explain it to someone. Writing is not a corrective activity. . . . You either get it or you don't," she adds, not coy or evasive. "It resonates or not." After all, the writer "only knows the world he knows," Beattie points out. "And he has any number of attitudes—critics fixate on the *details*, trying to dismiss them; readers fix an author thematically—but he doesn't have one attitude. There are fluctuations and complexities in fiction."

Beattie says the "ambiguity is what I want in writing," her own and others. "I don't read fiction for answers. I like writers who imply questions. Complexity is really consoling. . . . Put life out as a puzzle and acknowledge it as a puzzle."

Beattie began writing "seriously" when she was in graduate school at the University of Connecticut, in the early seventies. Her first stories were accepted for publication by the *Atlantic* and the *New Yorker* within "about ten days of each other" in 1972 or 1973. After the *New Yorker* took two or three more stories, she signed a first-read agreement with the magazine, under which they have first refusal of any story she writes for publication. And the *New Yorker* does reject her often, she says; ironically, her income for the stories they do run has also been diminishing, since the magazine pays by the word and her stories, be design, have become briefer. There is rarely any correlation between what she expects will be accepted and what is.

But sending stories to the *New Yorker* has at least one advantage for Beattie, who often can't come up with titles and submits them untitled. Roger Angell, her editor at the magazine, titles stories he rejects. "Letters come back to Lynn [Nesbit, Beattie's agent] saying, 'We are returning *X* . . .,' and the title is almost always perfect."

Beattie is seized by "the dramatic moment that radiates in a story. Remembered moments, something happening, and remembering or anticipating at the same time. Hopefully, always, the moment means more than the moment." She "types fast . . . if a story is going to work. It's a wonderful way to get out of control." If she doesn't come up with a rough draft "fairly quickly, if I'm not two or three pages into it fast," Beattie throws it away. There will be no undiscovered Beattie manuscripts—Beattie also throws away completed stories if she can't come up with a last line, because if "a zinger" doesn't come naturally, she feels she either didn't have a story or she hasn't gotten to the story she wanted to tell. Her short narratives are much revised, though, and "take a long time" to sharpen, Beattie says. She sometimes will leave a story for as long as a month before she can understand it enough to revise it.

In assembling her tales for publication in a book, she is selective. "Tonally it's nice to pick up a book with coherence," she believes. *Where You'll Find Me* contains about two-thirds of her work since *The Burning House* and three unpublished stories that fit in with the "sensibility of the collection."

In novels, though, "you have to deal with chronological time," which Beattie says she finds difficult to do. In *Love Always*, her most recent novel, "I didn't want to tell a story chronologically." Beattie wrote that novel in pieces, and when all the chapters were finished she spread them on her living room floor and reassembled them "like pieces in a puzzle." She was "foiled by having to fix it technically, to go back and revise the chronology." Novels are "episodic," and though they, too, tell "stories" and "have many moments. . . . People are always waiting for a distillation, and answer," which Beattie avoids stating. "This whole syndrome of looking for truth," as she calls it, confuses her.

So writing another novel is not something Beattie is thinking about right away—she has written three, *Chilly Scenes of Winter*, *Falling in Place*, and *Love Always*—and she prefers to write stories. "The forms are radically different. Who can say why my proclivity is for one or the other? It's like being in a store where there are all these beautiful things you can touch. Of course, it's perfectly nice if you don't *want* to touch something. Choosing a form somehow demonstrates a tactile relation with the world. . . .

"The writer knows what he wants to write about. You wonder about private things and figure out how to present aspects of what you are thinking about," Beattie says. "You find very easily what part of you is the actor you're positing" for each emotion or each scene. "You're the basis," she adds, quickly qualifying that "that doesn't make it autobiographical. . . . But you don't want to pretend you're a machine. . . .

"You make educated guesses," Beattie says about characters. "The writer's subconscious makes a distinction" between self and them. "You put a character out there and you're in their power. You're in trouble if they're in yours," Beattie feels.

Beattie does not "lead a very structured life. If you don't allow time to write, how do you know you will?" she asks. She no longer teaches (although she did for eight years), and now, thanks to a lucrative contract with S&S (rumored to be around $500,000 for a collection of stories and a novel), she does not have to, though teaching was not really a drain on her. She writes better at night, she says, "and it didn't matter whether I was teaching during the day or, now, vacuuming, or running errands." But "I have a lot of freedom," Beattie admits.

"This is the life I've chosen. But I've paid a price, I've given up a lot," she says, referring vaguely to marriage, children, *other* lives she might have had. Beattie was married once, is divorced, and she lives with someone in Charlottesville, but for a self-described "specific" writer she is not forthcoming about her personal life. Even the spare biographies on the back flaps of her books have been "incorrect by the time the book gets published," somehow "foiled" by chronology, as Beattie says she is in her novels.

"I have a lot of leisure," she says, although that is not at all the word she wants to describe what she's doing when she does not seem to be doing anything. "It's not an ideal life, necessarily, but I'm not sorry I figured this life out for myself. I have a lot of worries, crazy hectic things. People say writing is a lonely life, but that's not what occurs to me.

"I truly have so much free time that it's hard to explain how other things psychologically pollute that." Beattie pauses. Even a week on a beach, "something that's leisure for someone else . . . I can spend a week of my life fairly bored or depressed, thinking, 'What a life!' I can float around (although I don't know any writers who work nine to five), but I find out about the world by observing."

Beattie is "always storing things up," she says, although she doesn't "save things" for her writing. "The process of transformation is what amazes me."

She compares herself to a photographer: "Writing is not a 'hands-on' skill," she says. "It's all in your head. Private. There isn't anything you can do if you feel helpless. I imagine that at least as a photographer you can strap a camera around your neck, go out and *get* into it. Maybe I'm wrong. But I can't go out and find a story. And I can't just sit at a typewriter tapping keys. It would be the best thing in the world if that worked." Painters, she suspects, may face her problem. She has been working for the past year on an essay about Alex Katz for a book of his work Abrams is publishing in 1987.

"I've been girl journalist, going around with a tape recorder, interviewing people about Alex Katz, being analytic, trying to tell the truth about his paintings." This is her first nonfiction project. "In fiction," Beattie says, the goal is a little bit different: "you just have to be right," she says.

"The subtle ironies of [Katz's] work," attract her. "He does a lot of diptychs and triptychs. They're essentially narrative paintings. Our work is different, obviously, but as a story writer I'm drawn to how he implies things visually that we do tonally. I write about what I see. We [both] start with a visual image." Beattie says that Katz "has been simplified by people who haven't caught his tone."

Wearing shorts, her very tanned legs swinging over the arm of a beige leather chair in her sun-drenched, domed-ceiling living room, she combs a barrette through her medium-long blond hair, drawing the separated strands up into the air and letting them fall back down to her shoulders. She could be talking about herself.

An Interview with Ann Beattie

Steven R. Centola / 1988

From *Contemporary Literature* 31.4 (Winter 1990), 405–22. Reprinted by permission.

Born in Washington, D.C., in 1947, Ann Beattie is most recently the author of the critically acclaimed novel *Picturing Will* (1989), a moving and often disturbing account of fragmented family life in contemporary American society. Establishing her literary reputation in 1976 with the publication of a novel, *Chilly Scenes of Winter*, and a collection of short stories, *Distortions*, Beattie has since published the novels *Falling in Place* (1980) and *Love Always* (1986) and three collections of short stories: *Secrets and Surprises* (1978), *The Burning House* (1982), and *Where You'll Find Me* (1987). She has also written a children's book, *Spectacles* (1985), and commissioned books on painter Alex Katz and photographer Bob Adelman. In her fiction, Beattie deals mostly with relationships, as she tells us below. Whether she writes about relations between parents and children, husbands and wives, or men and women in general, she accurately records the little joys and sorrows that are daily experienced by members of her generation—the flower children of the sixties grown into the yuppies of the eighties. But her faithful depiction is often unflattering and critical; she holds a harsh mirror up to her troubled society and reveals with disconcerting clarity its imperfections.

Beattie has taught as a visiting writer-in-residence at many institutions. Among these experiences, two stand out: she was a visiting writer and lecturer at the University of Virginia from 1975 to 1977 and a Briggs-Copeland Lecturer in English at Harvard University during the 1977–78 academic year. Her awards include a Guggenheim Fellowship (1978), an award for excellence in literature from the American Academy and Institute of Arts and Letters (1980), and a distinguished alumna award and honorary doctorate of humane letters from American University (1980, 1983).

This interview took place on September 17, 1988, in Beattie's Charlottesville home. Although she claims not to have much interest in critiquing her fiction, Ms. Beattie's comments are always astute and insightful.

Q: Everyone seems to go after a tag when discussing a writer's work. Do you think any tags are particularly appropriate in describing your achievement as a writer?

A: I'll have the nasty word rear its head even before you ask it. Certainly I've been grouped with other writers as being a so-called minimalist, and I'm not sure that I like the definition of that very well. It's been interesting to see my colleagues articulate what's wrong with categorizing them that way, and I feel quite bonded to them in terms of going against that label. I'm most pleased when people don't use "minimalist" in the pejorative but speak about the specifics of my work and how the particularities establish emotion.

Q: Some writers—I'm thinking of Toni Morrison, in particular, who takes pride in the fact that she is a black female author—want to identify themselves as female writers. Do you want readers to view your fiction as the product of a woman writer?

A: My best guess is that people who read my writing would know that it was written by a woman. I can't prove that, but I know when I read students' stories and see the initials and don't know if it's written by a man or a woman, probably ninety-five percent of the time I guess correctly, and I would say that other people guess correctly too. So I'm not quite sure that there's anything to hide even if you want to. I mean, finally the writing *does* have to do with your identity as a woman. On the other hand, it does have to do with my identity as a woman that I drive a car and that I cross the street.

Q: What, in particular, do you think people could notice in your writing that would identify you as a female writer?

A: Jung takes a lot of bashing for talking about the difference between the male and female psyche; you get into a lot of horrible stereotyping, obviously, by going along with the generalizations of Jung or of anyone else. I'll admit that some women who write seem more concerned with domestic life than male writers. You could find exceptions to everything, but most of what I write is about relationships, and beyond that I'm not sure there's anything that demonstrates an old stereotype of the female sensibility.

Q: I've always been impressed by your ability to capture the private thoughts of men in your fiction. In fact, it's hard not to be conscious of how well you bring your male characters to life—I'm thinking specifically of John in

Falling in Place, Nick in "A Vintage Thunderbird," and even Charles in *Chilly Scenes of Winter*. These characters could only be men. Do you find it easy to characterize men, and do you think there is any difference in your handling of male and female characters?

A: It depends on the character, really. Certainly there are female characters that can be incomprehensible, and there are male characters that can be incomprehensible. I like problems; I mean I like to get in there and try to figure them out, but I suppose the limitations I have in life are going to be the same limitations I have in fiction. One of those limitations does *not* seem to be that I can only befriend women or that I can only befriend men. And, similarly, when I write, it doesn't seem presumptuous, it doesn't trouble me, it actually seems natural since I spend so much time talking to men, to feel that I understand things from the male perspective.

Part of the answer to your question has to do with image; I don't mean "image" as in what the media think of as a writer. But I think people have notions of what writing is even if they don't articulate them very often, and they do have pretty strong notions, too, of how they want to appear. And sometimes it seems important for those people to explain themselves rather directly—that is, to say women should have a female protagonist and that that female protagonist would, ideally, be an extension of the writer, or a stand-in for the writer, or whatever. As far as I know, it isn't necessary for me to think of myself as a "writer," period. So I'm not drawn to talking exclusively about women *just* because I am a woman and want people to understand me as a woman who writes. And because I do think of myself in some larger sense, or of writing as being only a particular thing I do, I suppose I'm not drawn to exploring myself and my feelings exclusively in what I write; in other words, a male character I create might function quite well as an exploration of certain feelings because characters are never just a continuation of my own identity.

Q: So you enjoy a degree of detachment as a writer and don't see yourself as working through your personal problems with your characters.

A: No, or at least not personal problems per se. I mean certainly the characters may embody some variations of my personal problems, but I'm not writing autobiography.

Q: Do critics try to suggest that a specific character in your fiction is really you?

A: Not convincingly—that would be very hard to do. While it's sometimes assumed that these may be autobiographical pieces, I've never experienced the corresponding autobiography. I write a lot of stories in the first person, which leads some people to make the mistake that the "I" narrating is the author. More often I've had people understand that these stories must be the world I move in rather than that they're some episode that really happened in my life, and even about that they're right and they're wrong. A lot of these things are only things that I've observed, things that I've seen that seemed problematic—not perhaps the most likely things to have explored because of the region or the people that I hung out with, or anything like that, either. The fiction obviously does have to do with me, but it has more to do with what's captured my attention, what seems possible to transform into art.

Q: Earlier you said that a lot of your stories deal with relationships. One of the relationships that stands out is that between a parent and a child. You often seem to suggest that parents are in some way responsible, if not primarily responsible, for the problems their children face. Would it be accurate to say that in your stories children often have to deal with problems that they haven't created but have more or less inherited from their parents? Do you see that as a problem in American society?
A: Quite simply, yes and yes. I don't think anything is going to change in a hurry.

Q: Is that an eternal situation, or are children in American society nowadays growing up with certain kinds of problems that they didn't have to deal with, say, fifty years ago?
A: The nuclear family has broken down, so there's a different set of realities. I think adults often make the mistake of thinking they understand their children. I think children are always watching and understanding but may not be quite as comprehensible to the parents as they think.

Q: In a novel like *Falling in Place*, then, John and Louise have allowed Mary and John Joel to grow up too fast because they assumed that their children were older mentally or emotionally than they actually were?
A: Yeah, sure, partly. But they've also had to acknowledge that the children are just out of their control. How they got out of their control has, I think, as much to do with social forces as with anything else. I think the book is probably a pretty accurate picture of particular aspects of suburban life. It's hard; it's not as easy as just pointing the finger and blaming somebody.

Q: Your stories also deal with the problems that men and women face in their relationships. Once again, I'm wondering if you're dealing with a timeless situation, involving the battle of the sexes, or if you're showing new problems in male-female relationships that may not have occurred previously.
A: They were covered up previously. Increasingly, people have moved out into the workplace. Society might define people by their jobs, but I don't think people necessarily think of themselves only as worker bees. When there's such a division between public and private identity, there's going to be a fair amount of anxiety and chaos.

Q: Are your female characters more conscious of their opportunity to express their feelings—feelings women have always had but have never before been allowed to verbalize?
A: I'm not sure that many of my women characters verbalize their feelings, though, even now. What I see in the stories are attempts that both parties have made to adapt, or the failure to find some sort of cohesive way to live, rather than what you've just said.

Q: But how about the narrator in "Where You'll Find Me"? She strikes me as a woman who knows she is confused and knows she is in a relationship that she's uncomfortable with because it isn't right for her. Doesn't she express her feelings when she tells her brother, Howard, about her momentary contact with another man, and her realization of their mutual attraction?
A: Howard reveals himself first, and then he starts that game of falling dominoes. Presumably, what she's doing—part of the mistake that she's making— is that she only reveals things, really, on the defensive, not on the offensive. That's part of why she's lacking the energy she's lacking in that story. He says, "Well, okay, let's turn the tables; let's play truth." And then she tries to top him. And he goes on to top her, and we end up with people who have topped each other but still not escaped their distance or their problems.

There's a level of discourse men and women can, and sometimes do, have. But I also think that what you see on the surface can be quite misleading. The clothes people go out and buy for themselves can have more to do with what they hope to express than their modes of conversation. There can also be a kind of extremely disembodied way in which people relate, at least the people I'm writing about in a story like "Where You'll Find Me"—New York City people, of a certain social class. There can be a terrifying veneer; people can exchange words but actually not talk much. What some of my stories demonstrate is not much different from theater of the absurd plays in which people don't communicate their Pinteresque point and counterpoint, or something like that.

Q: Don't your stories suggest that people really lead, or want to lead, secret lives? A lot of your characters either have clandestine affairs or harbor within themselves secret desires. Aren't your characters essentially torn between their public selves and their private selves?
A: Yes, that puts it very well.

Q: So, first and foremost, they cannot connect with themselves, and as a result, they cannot connect with anyone else.
A: Yes, but I think that they realize it's condoned that they not make this connection. A lot of the stories are about moments when people get tricked into revealing something that they didn't mean to reveal, or something happens and there's a kind of epiphany. It's about when those worlds get shaken up a little bit.

Q: Is that why your characters often seem to use drugs, alcohol, or casual sex as a way of escaping from their problems? Would you care to comment on your characters' use of these means of hiding from reality?
A: I think people are often very unhappy. I also write more often about what troubles me than what pleases me. If someone wanted to assign me to write about the cat show at the armory, I probably could go off and write a nice piece about the cats. Or maybe not. But such an assignment wouldn't interest me.

Q: So your characters do use sensation as a way of escaping from their problems?
A: Well, even if they aren't, they have to interact with people who are. The woman in "The Burning House" has a brother-in-law who is smoking grass in the kitchen when the story begins, but *she's* not alcoholic or out of control, laughing and screaming like Tucker, who runs the gallery. She's certainly not as pathologically devious as her husband. But those people's worlds are the only world she lives in.

Q: Since we're talking about the world your characters live in, let me ask you a related question. Are you aware of how frequently you refer to cars like Volvos and Thunderbirds, to schools like Harvard and Penn, and to a lifestyle that is generally associated with the more affluent members of American society? Do you deliberately deal with this particular class of people to show that the rich have a more difficult time giving their lives meaning than the poor because the rich devote almost all of their lives to the pursuit of materialistic goals?

A: I don't think that at all. Rich people are individuals, too. Though, in point of fact, I think poor people are worse off than rich people. If I had to have problems as a rich person or as a poor person, I'd rather have them as a rich person. I'm writing about what I observe, though I'm uncomfortable with my writing being deciphered only in terms of social class. Some of these stories are urban, some are not. Does social class really matter in a story about, say, spacemen who come to earth and take pornographic pictures?

Q: I asked that question at least partly because of a difference I've observed between the fiction of white and black writers in America today. This may be oversimplifying matters a good deal, but I think it is generally true that black female writers dealing with a black community give more emphasis to spiritual matters and are more likely to celebrate the communion among souls that can be found in their community. White writers, on the other hand, seem to focus more on an affluent society characterized almost exclusively by people's alienation and disintegration.

A: Well, look, rich people have more time to be alienated; I mean, it's as simple as that. You can sit around and not have health insurance and not have food on the table, or you can run out of white wine and be sorry you were never given an honorary doctorate from Yale.

Q: Which is the more serious problem?

A: Not having food on the table. I'm not writing what I write because I think I'm solving problems. I would be the first to admit that I don't think anything I write is going to stand society on its ear. I think that there are quiet and personal forms of desperation that can be very meaningful, regardless of social class, and that maybe the black writers writing about spiritual matters are often implying that that may *not* be the path to salvation. Certainly, such writing is not only being done straight, any more than John Updike's writing means to extol the virtue of being able to have an argument and jump into your brand new car and roll off into the suburban night.

Q: I don't know whether you believe that people have the freedom to mold their lives, but in some of your stories your characters lack that freedom. They try to grapple with overwhelming forces that they ultimately fail to control, and because they struggle and fail to give their lives meaning, their situations can justifiably be described as tragic. I'm thinking of a story like "In the White Night" and the novels *Falling in Place* and *Love Always*. Would you agree that there is a tragic vision of the human condition in these works?

A: Well, you've said it, and I guess I would have to agree with it. Again, though, it's interesting that I don't tend to think of those ideas as being united in the way you just said. On the other hand, I don't think that what you said is wrong, though the works you've named all seem very different to me. I hope that the people I'm writing about have different sensibilities. Personally speaking, it seems to me that people often have more free will than they wish to exercise, but I think that you really have to talk about the stories case by case.

Q: In "Spiritus," there is a striking scene where the male character seems to register mentally a litany of facts to ground himself in an existence that, I thought, at least temporarily held off absurdity.

A: Let's put it this way. You asked a question before about secret lives, and I do believe everyone has them. I don't think that they're necessarily titillating. Certainly there are variations, and I don't mean to say that I think that people are inevitably and only bizarre in their secret lives. But I do think that people have certain yearnings, and in this culture there are not necessarily many out- lets for them. I like to create characters to try to see if I can locate their secret lives, but once I've done that, I like to look at the secrets within the secrets. The character in "Spiritus" is vacationing on the Cape, worrying about his wife versus his mistress, and he has a nice life in Boston, on some level. His are perhaps not the worst problems in the world. But the nagging thing is that he has to say his own litany because there really isn't anybody for him to talk to. In spite of all the talk about bonding and sharing, America has become, for a lot of people, a silenced community.

Q: So it's almost as though the public existence is a type of charade and the real existence is the private one.
A: Then again, if nothing gets enacted, the word "real" can become very problematic.

Q: Isn't everything, then, reduced to absurdity?
A: It doesn't seem that clear-cut to me; it's not just that people close their doors and then the charade ends. It seems more that people have to both enact the charade and at the same time find ways to accommodate other people who are doing some other charade.

Q: Is this a particularly American situation?
A: As far as I know. For instance, in Italy, you rarely see the breakdown of families you see here; it's the exception rather than the rule.

Q: Often in your stories, there is a nostalgic remembrance and sad acceptance of the loss of some past experience; in works like "Winter: 1978," "A Vintage Thunderbird," and "Jacklighting," you seem to suggest that we long for an irrecoverable past. Is that an accurate way of summing up how some of your characters respond to the past?
A: Yes. The people I know miss things a lot. I think that's another thing that doesn't get articulated in this culture. You know, it's become a joke: the psychiatrist who says, "Was yours a happy childhood?" That's the clichéd joke of our time, right? And so much humor turns on that. Well, was it? I mean, clichés exist because they're based on something that's transpired over and over.

Q: Is the past that's longed for real, or does it inevitably become somewhat distorted simply because it is the past?
A: *The Great Gatsby* should have taught all of us the answer to that question.

Q: In an interesting exchange between Garrett and Nancy in "Skeletons," Nancy asks him if he is afraid that "somebody might know something about [her] that [he does not] know." Isn't it always the case in relationships that one person fears somebody else will know more about his lover than he knows?
A: I guess it's usually the case in fiction. That's how the writer can be convincing: by raising the right questions, more than by answering them if you

manage to convincingly demonstrate that you know all aspects of that character well, usually you can pull off the story. And if you don't, you're lost.

Q: In that same story, Garrett tells Nancy, "Everything is a competition." Do you think a lot of people approach relationships with the same notion?
A: No, I don't really think that. Again, they're particular characters. Also, you can't necessarily take him at his word when he says that everything's a competition. When he's announcing that, he's not speaking to her as though he's broadcasting an opinion to the world; he's not sitting on a panel and saying this is his personal philosophy. He's used to gaining power in his relationship with her by seeming to be self-effacing. And probably on some level what he is saying is true, but on another level, the problem is more complex. And, of course, it's always a good trick as everybody knows at the age of five—to pretend to be your own worst enemy, because then people console you. He's maneuvering.

Q: And she ends up marrying him and having his children, yet, ironically, Kyle has this beautiful vision of Nancy at the end of the story and almost seems to glorify her or give her immortal status because of her embodiment as a romantic ideal in his imagination.
A: But, of course, she never knows it. She really does have no idea that on the particular night when his car goes out of control, he suddenly remembers her again. He had even started to forget before that skid happened and jarred the memory. I hope everybody's secret life is implied in Kyle's sudden vision of Nancy Niles. When they don't expose themselves in that story, I expose them— even quite literally, by making an analogy and holding up an x-ray. At the end of the story you're left with a visual image of a swirling car, while people are marching down the street somewhere in another city, not knowing that the car is going out of control. So, on one level, you have an image of motion and action and so forth, but what the story is about is people who have drifted and never taken any action. Obviously, she didn't make the most intelligent decision. Obviously Kyle lost out, and her husband lost out, and she's lost out.

Q: The feeling that is evoked reminds me of the end of *The Great Gatsby*.
A: At the end of *Gatsby*, when Fitzgerald writes the famous "boats against the current, borne back ceaselessly into the past"—I think he believes that. I think that at least for the moment of that book, Fitzgerald did have an expansive ideal he wanted to mention. But he doesn't end in such a way to eulogize

his characters. He wants readers to be complicitous in his hopefulness but skeptical because of what history has—or should have—taught them. When he put that particular ending on *The Great Gatsby*, he was assuming that his readers could be enlightened and even seduced.

Q: Do you have any specific audience in mind while you are writing your stories?
A: I don't, but I certainly have traveled around a lot, and it seems to me the audience is so diverse that I couldn't pitch something to "the audience" if I wanted to. The thing that's so surprising to me is that I meet people who have read me very carefully and who understand the complexities, whereas when I read reviews, even positive reviews, forget negative reviews—they might like it but they often don't understand what I've written.

Q: Why do you think some critics have problems understanding your works? Take, for example, reactions to the conclusions of both *Chilly Scenes of Winter* and *Falling in Place*. Several reviewers have criticized the happy endings of these novels, but these books obviously do not have happy endings.
A: I'll tell you, those people must get along in their daily life better than I do; they must be philosophical when they don't get the correct change at the car wash.

Q: All the details in *Chilly Scenes of Winter* point out that it is impossible for Charles and Laura to live happily ever after in the kind of fairy-tale romance Charles imagines. Even without the last scene, everything suggests this is an impossible relationship. So why do you think they complain about the "happy" ending?
A: Maybe they believe that there are snowflakes that are "just alike."

Q: I find the story "Snow" to be very powerful. I especially like the way you convey abstract ideas with evocative images in a series of sentences near the end of the story: "Who expects small things to survive when even the largest get lost? People forget years and remember moments. Seconds and symbols are left to sum things up: the black shroud over the pool. Love, in its shortest form, becomes a word. What I remember about all that time is one winter. The snow." Can you talk about how you came upon these lines?
A: The thing I like about writing is that I write things that I haven't thought of before in another form. In other words, I could be sitting with my dearest

friend in the world, and there wouldn't be any reason to explore some of the things I have explored in the stories. What you just quoted is something that occurred to me at that moment in that context, which is a fictional context. There are things in that story, as a matter of fact, that are true, but as a narrative and as an explanation, they're a fabrication. I also like it that I can believe things that I discover in particular moments of fiction and not think that they apply in any larger sense, or that they sum things up for me either.

Q: So you wouldn't say that seconds and symbols sum up your experiences?
A: They may be things that rivet my interest, but I wouldn't say that they necessarily sum everything up. Also, we're talking about fiction and narrative tone, rather than the way I function in my daily life. I have to keep drawing the distinction because I really don't exist only in various fictional modes.

Q: So when you're writing and creating your fictional universe, you have to enter your characters' bodies, minds, and souls to bring them to life.
A: The writer is the person who's creating the persona, so some of you gets into that—your preoccupations or your despair or your whatever gets into that—but the conclusions you come to are arrived at in terms of the narrator's mind; you're answering for someone else.

Q: I found it curious that "The Lifeguard" opens with a joke, yet the events that occur are some of the most tragic that have ever appeared in your writing. Was there any particular reason you chose to open the story that way?
A: I suppose I wanted to make things as discordant as possible because that's what tragedy does.

Q: When you create something as tragic as the events in that story, are you hoping that by watching somebody else's destruction or self destruction the reader might gain an awareness that perhaps would never have been experienced without some involvement in your story?
A: I guess that if I really felt I had that power, I wouldn't exercise it obliquely. I think that if I did want to take the responsibility and did presume to think that I could enlighten people, I wouldn't couch it in fiction at all. I don't feel superior to my characters or to my audience, and I don't have the answers either.

Q: So you're basically saying to your reader: "Here it is. This story presents you with a situation involving these people. Do with it what you will."

A: They don't have to learn any lesson. Every experience—and diction is just another experience,—doesn't have to instruct people. Though you hope the work gives them pause. It's just beyond my comprehension that stories are written to legislate to anyone. It seems to me that what you have to do is be very faithful to complexities, and if you've done that (at least I want to let myself off the hook here), that's where the obligation ends. To articulate something complex, it seems to me, is all you can ask for.

Q: Let's talk a little bit about technique. I like the way you use interchapters in *Falling in Place*; I think you call them codas.

A: I should have known you when I was turning in the book and had to explain to Random House what they were.

Q: I was struck by the ease with which you could modulate viewpoint with this technique. Of course, the novel is centered mostly in John's consciousness, but the interchapters allow us to penetrate the minds of other characters, thereby providing us with additional perspectives and insights.

A: Well, it was very convenient; I have to admit that. I was very happy when the idea occurred to me, but it didn't right away. They started out being notes to myself about things I'd have to remember to include, later, in the chapter. And then I liked the immediacy, and I could see they were a good way both to augment and to undercut the main narrative. And I decided, "Well, just write your sentences a bit better and leave them there as is." I began to see that they could function as an undertow. They also seemed appropriate to a book in which I wanted to suggest that something was always going on underneath the surface or on the periphery.

Q: Is there anything that you do over and over again in your fiction?

A: I look at short stories and see other people find a way around using dashes for punctuation, but that dash—as though you're connecting quickly and making one thing contingent upon another in that direct a way—is something I do time and again.

Q: Is that idiosyncratic in the sense that it is part of your unique voice or your distinctive style as a writer?
A: I certainly don't feel very comfortable not calling myself into question in some way in the text.

Q: Would you say it's your signature?
A: It's not that methodical. When I read Don DeLillo's *Libra*, which is a great book I picked up because there's a character named Nicholas Branch who is writing a purported history, for the CIA, of the "real" story of the killing of Kennedy. It's very hard not to imagine that DeLillo is closely allied with Nicholas Branch. I probably ally myself with some character or position, too. I admit that I'm somewhere in the text. The italicized sections of *Falling in Place* were an obvious admission of that. The novel I just finished writing [*Picturing Will*] includes a text different from the body of the text you're reading: essays on the subject of childhood. Actually, it's a different fictional device than in *Falling in Place* because, as it turns out, there's a real necessity to have them there. It's not my voice at all. It's very hard for me not to call the assertions of the main text into question because I certainly don't believe that there is any one story or any one way to tell a story. If you think about it, although they're sort of intermittent, the crazy letters of *Love Always*, just dropped into the text and so badly written, do remind you of that larger world of lunacy outside the text of my book—and outside every other book. A counternarrative provides breathing space.

Q: In a lot of your stories, you use the third-person limited omniscient point of view. The ones I'm thinking of are "A Vintage Thunderbird," "Dwarf House," "In the White Night," and "Distant Music," in particular. Is there any reason why you chose this particular point of view for these stories?
A: Because they would never succeed if they seemed at all sentimental.

Q: Did you ever start a story with one point of view and decide it just wasn't working right, and then start over again using a different point of view?
A: No, although there certainly have been a lot of stories that never got finished, and sometimes that might have been the problem.

Q: You once mentioned a connection between Hemingway's "Cat in the Rain" and one of your stories.
A: "The Big Outside World," which is kind of a deliberate variation on "Cat in the Rain."

Q: On occasion your prose reminds me of Hemingway's writing for example, I was rereading "A Vintage Thunderbird" recently and found one scene particularly striking: where Nick is on the telephone listening to Sammy tell him everything that's wrong with his life, and Nick's response is simply to look out the window. Your description of Nick's looking through the grim window conveys nicely, without any commentary or unnecessary details, exactly what he is feeling at that moment. The objective correlative here reminds me of Hemingway's use of the same technique in "Soldier's Home," when Krebs simply looks at the bacon hardening on the plate in response to his mother's harassment about his finding a job. Is letting some detail speak for the character something you learned from Hemingway?
A: I probably learned it from Hemingway; it was probably done by osmosis before the age of sixteen—truly.

Q: So you're conscious of his influence in your development as a writer?
A: Yes.

Q: Despite that influence, though, your writing has a voice all its own I'm not sure I could accurately describe it, but I know I wouldn't confuse it with the writing of Raymond Carver, Anne Tyler, Bobbie Ann Mason, or other contemporary writers. Do you think about your voice or style of writing?
A: I'm more interested in writing and revising than doing a critique of myself, even though there's always an implicit critique in the revision process. This is probably not the most important thing to remark upon, but when I did start writing, I think I had very little sense of what other people were doing. I didn't read much contemporary literature and I had very little sense of what other writers sounded like. I knew what Jane Austen sounded like and I knew what Hemingway sounded like, but I didn't really know what contemporary writers (with a few exceptions) sounded like, and I wasn't trying to approximate anything.

Q: You seem to be suggesting that to be a writer one has to have a voice.
A: I don't see how anybody could ever write without a sure voice.

Q: So you wouldn't say that creative writing is something that can be taught?
A: Does anybody ever say, "Here's X; I taught X how to be a creative writer"? There are certainly writers who have helped other writers, or teachers, I should say, who have helped other writers. I would imagine how far you could go would depend on how good the combination was between teacher and writer. When I teach writing, I feel lucky because I don't have the fresh-man class assigned to me. I'm sure it would just not work. I wouldn't care if they wrote or not, for starters. But if there's something there to begin with that I can relate to, I'm usually able to be helpful. There may be very good science fiction writers. I just tell them, categorically, "I don't know the genre; I don't have any feelings about it; you could turn in something great or something terrible; I would never know. Don't take my class." But since I don't teach beginning writers, what I tend to do is line edit. I think they can learn even if I just hand the stories back with scribbles all over them, even if they don't talk to me. I think you can inspire people. There's also some-thing to be said for going into a classroom as a real-life rabbit.

Q: Have you ever felt after seeing something published that the story would have worked better if you had done something differently?
A: My revision tends to be that if the story emerges with a beginning, middle, and end to begin with, it's declared itself, and then I work within the parame-ters of what is given as best I can. If I can't do anything, I throw it out, and it never emerges at all. Some of them are personally meaningful to me in ways that others aren't, or I'll do something that seems different from what I've done before, and just for that reason, I'll like it.

Q: How long does the composition process take you?
A: Longer than it used to. It took me three years to do the rough draft of *Picturing Will*, and I threw out at least fifteen chapters.

Q: In what ways do you think your writing has changed from your early sto-ries to what you're working on today?
A: There are things that indicate a change in style to me that would sound funny if I talked about them with somebody who was not a writer.

Structurally, the stories have changed. I think that they flow in a different way than they used to. If you look at *Distortions*, you'll see that the book is full of asterisks. That's because I was jumping around in time. Now I think that method seems a bit intrusive, or just too easy, or more suited to the randomness I was grappling with then in the lives of the characters than what I tend to write about now. I can't imagine relying on asterisks anymore. The recent stories tend to be more of a piece; they don't quite cover as much territory as some of the earlier stories. And then I'm usually fond of beating myself over the head and saying, "Yeah another difference is that I've lost my sense of humor." I just can't imagine that I would ever again be as loose as I was when I was writing those early stories. They were very speculative stories; they were "Let's pretend" stories. The stories I write now are more claustrophobic. The stakes are higher.

Q: As I was rereading your short stories, I was struck by the tonal consistency of those in *Where You'll Find Me*. What seems to me to be the most meaningful way of describing the essential difference between the early stories and the later ones is to say that the recently published stories are much more poetic. They are much tighter than the early ones and more consistent in tone. "Imagine a Day at the End of Your Life" seems to fit in with the stories in *Where You'll Find Me* too because of its powerful use of evocative images that help to create a strong tone.
A: Also a lot of them are about storytelling now, as is *Picturing Will*. It just occurred to me that "Imagine a Day at the End of Your Life" asks you to listen to stories. Somebody tells a story at the end of that story. In *Where You'll Find Me*, the brother and sister tell each other stories. And then a story like "Coney Island" becomes a real volley in which each person comments on what the other is saying as though they're demonstrating storytelling techniques: "You forgot the part about X," or something like that. I'm conscious that people tell stories; it's not just writers who tell stories. I'm absolutely amazed at how perfectly lucid the elevator operator is.

Q: Now that you've finished *Picturing Will*, what projects will you be working on?
A: I'm going to write a text to go along with my friend Bob Adelman's photographs. There's a book that Aperture just published of photographs by Sally

Mann—it's called *At Twelve*—that I wrote the introduction for, and I might do some more of that. I like to write about visual things.

Q: It seems appropriate for you to be working with photographers; your writing is remarkably visual. Does writing about photographs affect your fiction writing at all?
A: I like to think I'm pretty sharp to begin with in noticing detail, but it's funny: when you work with somebody who really is purely visual, you realize you're not very sharp at all. It keeps me on my toes. It's also nice to have somebody to discuss things with because I do respond to things that are highly visual. Dialogue in fiction comes rather easily to me and is never as meaningful for me as getting something going visually. Or it isn't as mysterious, I should say, as beginning to establish a visual motif in the story. Sometimes I like to talk about visual images more bluntly; I like to be able to say, "Look at this photograph; this is what I think is happening;" instead of masking things in any way—being as subtle as I need to be to be convincing in fiction.

Q: Do you ever think about how you would like to be remembered by future generations of readers? What would you hope people would see in your fiction?
A: The same thing I always hope now: that it's moving; that it makes you think; that it makes you wonder about something. Certainly I would not care to be thought stylistically innovative, or anything like that.

Q: Would you want people to be able to say after reading your works that they had an idea of what American society was like in the 1970s and 1980s?
A: Not American society—no, I would really hope that whatever I said might describe human nature in a larger sense.

Q: Is that your ultimate goal as a writer?
A: I would be very pleased if the stories were thought of as moving.

Picturing Ann Beattie: A Dialogue

Neila C. Seshachari / 1989

From *Weber Studies* 7.1 (Spring 1990), 12–36. Reprinted with permission.

Ann Beattie was born in Washington, D.C., in 1947, the only child of James A. and Charlotte (Crosby) Beattie. "I'm from a middle-class family," she told me, "and, for whatever reasons, I was always a very autonomous person. . . . My parents gave me a lot of self-assurance . . . I've spent my life supporting myself. It didn't ever occur to me that I wasn't going to be out there [in the world] totally taking care of myself and orchestrating my life. . . . I deliberately didn't make choices that I thought might limit me. I decided not to have children, for instance." Beattie has indeed "orchestrated" her life most satisfactorily through writing, even though she has said that she first started writing because she was "bored with graduate school."

After the publication of her first story, "A Rose for Judy Garland's Casket" in the *Western Humanities Review* in 1972, Beattie became a frequent contributor to the *New Yorker* and a number of leading magazines. In 1976, Doubleday published *Distortions*, a collection of short stories, and her first novel, *Chilly Scenes of Winter*, both of which immediately established her critical reputation not only as a writer but also as the voice of the "Woodstock generation" of the 1960s. Her published works include three other novels, *Falling in Place* (1980), *Love Always* (1985), and *Picturing Will* (1989), and three more books of short stories, *Secrets and Surprises* (1978), *The Burning House* (1982) and *Where You'll Find Me* (1986). *Alex Katz*, a commissioned book on Alex Katz, the painter, was published in 1987. She has held prestigious lectureships at the University of Virginia and Harvard University. Her awards include one in literature from the American Academy and Institute of Arts and Letters (1980), Distinguished Alumnae Award (1980) and Honorary Doctor of Humane Letters degree (1983) from her alma mater, American University, and a Guggenheim Fellowship in 1980.

Ann Beattie lives in Charlottesville, VA, with her husband, Lincoln Perry.

The present interview was arranged when Ann Beattie visited Weber State College campus as one of the featured writers at the National Undergraduate Literature Conference in April 1989. She not only agreed to give the interview but graciously offered to come to Washington D.C. in December, so we could meet during the MLA convention. The following interview took place at the Sheraton Washington Hotel on 28 December 1989. I had sent her a set of thirty-two questions earlier but, as expected, the interview took on spontaneous turns, even though we did cover most of the questions sent earlier.

Seshachari: "The Sweetest Songs" deals with some ideas and themes that recur in your fiction often—tenuous relationships between lovers, or husbands and wives and, of course, music. Let's start with music first. How deep is your interest in music?

Beattie: Well, a few years ago I think I could have given you a more enthusiastic answer about that but in the last few years, for the first time in my life, I really haven't listened to much music. I used to work with music on and now I don't. I don't have any one reason for that; sometimes music seems suitable, almost as if you're selecting a soundtrack to a movie for what's going on in your character's life. When I wrote *Falling in Place* in the summer of 1979, a lot of things happening in that book were really taking place.

Skylab really was falling. How can you improve on that in fiction? I don't think I've ever heard a song get as much air time as "Heart of Glass." It's a rather haunting song but if I hadn't been writing that book, I wouldn't have kept the radio on. I wouldn't have been, in a sort of bemused way, listening for the next play of "Heart of Glass." So, I was just doing the thing that writers do all the time. I had my tentacles out, and I saw what was out there to grab, that would be appropriate to that particular kind of book. *Falling in Place* was meant to be very much rooted in a place and time, and music was a part of that.

Seshachari: Do you think that in the 1960s and '70s people listened to music a little more than they did in the '80s?

Beattie: I'm not sure they listened in the same way. For instance, my parents, who grew up in the Big Band era, are very moved by many of those songs and have particular memories. I could name a few songs and say exactly what summer they came out and what boy I thought I was in love with when I was fourteen years old, but I think that music used to be really more a part of the culture when people went out dancing in a different way than they do now. My parents' generation probably listened less, but the experience might have been more personal. When I lived in New York, not only did I have safety locks on the door but I had the music going, keeping the city at a distance, trying to find creative time and peace and so forth. I live in a small town now [Charlottesville, VA]; it's very quiet, and there is no commanding reason to listen to music all the time.

Seshachari: Perhaps also because you were married to a musician then, you might have listened to music more. . . .

Beattie: Oh yes, that's true certainly. I heard a lot of music that I never would have been aware of. In fact, he titled *Chilly Scenes of Winter*. It's a song by Cousin Emmy, and I'd never heard it. After he read the entire manuscript, he said, We should call it *Chilly Scenes of Winter*. I said, What does that have to do with anything? and he said, You know, the song, and he put it on. That's how the book came to be entitled *Chilly Scenes of Winter*.

Seshachari: It brought you recognition. You were even given a small part in the film version.

Beattie: I begged for it.

Seshachari: And did that lead to *Love Always*?

Beattie: No, I don't think so.

Seshachari: When you get into film life, and you see the actors and director. . . .

Beattie: Well, when *Chilly Scenes* was being made into a movie, I was out on location for a couple of weeks—very unofficially. But many years ago, I went to school with Tom Shales at American University and for a long time— before he was TV critic of the *Washington Post*—he did all kinds of arts and entertainment. I used to tag along when he went to Hollywood. I would stand around and watch what he was writing about or meet the people that he was meeting, so for several years of my life, I was in California quite unofficially. I was picking up things by osmosis. Much of what happens in *Love Always* is really from overheard conversations in the Russian Tea Room. It's an improvisation of the way certain Hollywood agents think and talk to each other.

Seshachari: I admire your extraordinary ability to absorb the sights and sounds of everything that's going on around you.

Beattie: It's interesting, though, that in daily life, I think of myself as being relatively unobservant. A number of my friends are in the arts, and they are visual people. I'm married to a painter. I know many photographers. Compared to them I never feel like I'm really focusing on what's interesting. However, when I sit down to write, I find that things that didn't even seem to impress me at the time come into sharp focus. I would be perfectly capable of going away from this interview and five years later, when I was writing about a character who was not in point of fact based on you, remember exactly the way your earrings look. If I weren't writing, I would have no reason to remember those lovely earrings. That is the strange thing; I don't know if you want to call it the subconscious, but things that I don't seem to notice are getting stored away.

Seshachari: Did you ever paint or sing?

Beattie: Only when I was a little girl. If I had had any creative talent in that direction I think that's what I would have loved to do—something visual. When I was teaching at Harvard in the 1970s, I went to Project Incorporated in Cambridge and took photography classes. I didn't even know how to aim the camera in those days. It started me looking at photographs in a different way. I think photography rather than painting is a more direct influence.

Seshachari: I could have guessed that because of the way Jody in *Picturing Will* handles her camera.

Beattie: I didn't know what those photo booths where you put the dollar in to get the pictures were called. I called up my friend, Bob Adelman, and he said, Photomaton, p, h, o, t, o, m, a, t, o, n. I put it in the book, but later found that I had no need for it because it was a technical term and I had to take it out. It just broke my heart not to be able to refer to that in the text.

Seshachari: Minimalism in literature is said to have borrowed heavily from the fine arts, both music and painting. Even if, as you say, you have no creative talent in music and painting, have they influenced your writing at all? Did you make a conscious attempt to bring their techniques into your writing?

Beattie: No, I didn't make a conscious attempt to bring them together. People could look at my interests in music and painting and say, Aha, doesn't it figure that she would work that way? But again, I really wasn't very informed at the point at which I started writing. I think it's more that these things coexisted than that they provided a conscious framework. I can't deny the influence. You mentioned things specifically [in the questions sent earlier]—the rhythmic pauses in music, or the way space opens up in a painting. I think they're perfect analogies, but I think they're probably analogies that could be applied to many writers. Also minimalism is a term that all of us who share so little in common and who are lumped together as minimalists are not terribly happy with. I like the notion that people are appreciative of the fact that my work is sometimes allusive and that there is an interrelationship of the arts. I'm not at all sure that this is restricted to minimalism though. People mean different things by the word, but I don't think it is that there is less there because things are being referred to. The things are simply there, transpiring, and sometimes people miss what's right before their eyes. I don't find, for instance, the conversations in Raymond Carver's stories oblique; I find them entirely comprehensible. I must admit that I read Carver very early on; also, for years and years I went to readings by Carver. I found that once he started to read, the humor became very apparent. I never sat in an audience where the people weren't entirely converted by the time they left—they were no longer frightened of his writing, once they heard him read. It was also true of Donald Barthelme's readings, although he was considered more of a postmodernist than a minimalist. He was a great friend of mine, and over the years I went to many of his readings. More often than with Carver even, people were actually coming out saying, My God, I get it!

Seshachari: Your own humor comes through too in your readings.
Beattie: It's gratifying that it does; I love to give readings. It's often been said that I'm an extremely depressing, cynical writer. I've never known what to make of that. My audiences have always laughed at the parts that are humorous. I think that I'm serious, but I don't think that I'm inordinately bleak. For instance, I think that Beckett is funny. If you read Beckett to children, who have no inhibitions, they'll giggle away. I think also that the question of intonation is one that a lot of American critics have not been educated for.

Seshachari: In a society that is fast losing its communicative powers—where individuals talk incessantly about things that mean nothing, while they circumvent the important things that are on their minds—minimalism as a technique for both writers and artists can be very effective. Let's go back to "The Sweetest Songs." Like much of your work, this story too reflects a male center of consciousness.

Beattie: I think I write about things that are mysterious to me. I don't write about things that I have the answers to or things that are very close to home. It just wouldn't be any adventure. It wouldn't have any vitality.

Seshachari: Are you saying you use male protagonists because male consciousness operates in a mysterious way and you want to probe it? Do you do that consciously?

Beattie: I think because I have done it repeatedly that on some level I must always have been intuiting that that was where my interest lay. Quite often my narrator or protagonist may be a man, but I'm not sure he's the more interesting character, or if the more complex character isn't the woman. You have to figure out who the right person is to tell the story. And often, people who are very self-aware will only sound as if they are pontificating if they tell the story. In terms of the dramatic thrust of these pieces, I tend to think a lot about women's consciousness is revealed in many of them, even though the man is ostensibly the center of attention.

Seshachari: I do discern latent feminism in your early work. It reaches its incremental peak in *Picturing Will.* In the 1970s critics called you a writer of the generation of the '60s and in the '80s it almost appeared as if you were going along and writing about your growing generation. But in *Picturing Will* you're really not writing about that generation anymore; you're writing about the present times.

Beattie: I hope so. I always would have argued, though, that my material transcended the setting. My friends and I make great fun of the fact that I was labeled the so-called spokesperson for the generation. I don't think many writers write from that perspective. I'm sure John Updike doesn't sit around thinking, Boy, have I got the number on suburbia. He'd be horrified if he thought that was all he was up to.

Seshachari: F. Scott Fitzgerald was happy that he "cut the ribbon" for the Jazz age and ushered it in.

Beattie: Yes, but then again you pay the price of being Scott Fitzgerald. There was an extremely insecure, highly neurotic individual who, yes, really did write about his times, but of course I don't think his writings have survived only as period pieces. I still think of *Gatsby* as being a very complex work that isn't at all merely rooted in the 1920s. That's what I mean; if your writing doesn't transcend the era, then it would really seem to be only of very limited sociological importance.

Seshachari: Tell me about your continued fascination with Fitzgerald.
Beattie: So often he thought he was an extremely sophisticated writer and actually the thing that was so appealing about him was a kind of childlike confusion. He was certainly smart enough to be quite skeptical about the people that he wrote about, though I suspect the perspective he presented to the reader did not necessarily emerge as what he intended. I also just think that he was capable of writing beautifully—sentence by sentence his writing can be simply wonderful.

Seshachari: He did have a dual perspective on everything he explored.
Beattie: That's the fascination about exploration. There is some reason, obviously, that you are drawn to your material, but the way in which you explore it might come to be quite different from what you would expect. In other words, if you were meeting all these people at a party you might have one frame of reference about them but once they were in a work of literature you might find, much to your surprise, that you had quite another perspective.

Seshachari: And also, when a book is published and goes into the public domain, critics are likely to interpret it differently.
Beattie: Yes, yes. People have isolated whole motifs—like the "jungle motif" in my story, "Dwarf House." I was sitting in a friend's class when that story was being discussed and I was absolutely amazed. I don't deny that those things are there. I think they can stay unarticulated in the subconscious of the writer. I do think that after you have written a draft of something, then you have to be your own literary critic and make sure that it functions as a piece of art, but that's not to say that what you've written is definitive and the only thing about the subject that could have been said.

Seshachari: Critics, like most people, see what they wish to see. I see *Picturing Will* as a wonderful contemporary feminist novel.
Beattie: I must say I was taken aback by that [question sent earlier]. My problem with thinking of it as a feminist novel is that Jody really seems to me

to be potentially a rather cold, unattractive person. She certainly isn't the kind of spokesperson for women's rights. She doesn't seem to be any kind of person you'd want to invoke as a representative feminist. She just doesn't function all that well. For instance, when she's on the highway photographing after the accident when her friend, Mary Vickers, hits the deer . . . what I at least wanted to show with that scene was her absolute detachment. The human impulse would be to embrace your friend in a moment of crisis, but instead, what she's thinking is, Thank God for the autowinder. It may not, at the moment you hear it, make her an absolute villain; she is not to be simplified quite that easily. But in many places in the book I tried to anticipate the ending in which she had more or less dissociated herself from her family and made a life for herself in which she was the queen bee around whom all the students and admirers hovered. This was fulfilling to her, but really it was Mel who was left to take care of the child.

Seshachari: I didn't think of Jody as a cold person, probably because, as I was first reading, I associated Jody with the idolized parental voice all along.
Beattie: I see, that certainly would temper your views if you assumed that that was Jody.

Seshachari: There is no reason to believe it's either Jody or Mel at that point. It's a parental voice of concern. But I somehow thought of both Jody and Mel as nurturers.
Beattie: I think she was, up to a point, but when she found Mel to come in and take over, certainly she shifted the burden of responsibility.

Seshachari: I think of *Picturing Will* as a feminist novel in a genuine sense— not as a novel which is a disguised political tract on feminism, but as one in which womanhood has come into its own, where a woman appropriates to herself the human right—and it's not a male right or a female right, it's a human right—to be oneself. Jody manages to reconcile her profession with her child and her marriage. Even though you do not talk about it, there is no reason to believe that her family life was unhappy.
Beattie: She's highly functional.

Seshachari: In the United States feminism is often pigeon-holed into radical feminism; I don't look at it that way at all. For me, feminism is a social ideal where a woman finds her own level of comfort in society as a male finds his own level.

Beattie: I do agree, but I think women have to fight harder. Women are obviously much more discriminated against than men in many ways. Given that that's going to be the case, you just have to decide individually how best to operate. I must say also that it's never worked to my disadvantage that I have long, blond hair. I'm not proud of that, and I don't send my pictures to the newspapers and say please print them. But if they have their druthers about whose picture to print, it's not because it's me, it's because some photo editors think it's more enticing to print the picture of some woman who has long, blond hair.

Seshachari: And high cheekbones. . . .

Beattie: And high cheekbones (laughter)! Also, just one more thing to explain my own success such as it is—you know I was pulled out of the slush-pile of the *New Yorker.* I had never personally met another writer at the point at which I published. I didn't study writing, I didn't know any other writers and much to the *New Yorker*'s credit, they read the unsolicited manuscripts. Many national magazines did and still do, and I was pulled out almost everywhere and none of those people knew what I looked like. Later, I think there was no way to keep people, who thought in certain ways, from capitalizing on that. It's not as though I volunteered to do ads. I refused to appear on television.

Seshachari: It's just good to have a writer who looks like one. Which women writers do you admire?

Beattie: I admire many, actually. Mary Lee Settle, who has come to be a very good friend of mine. Her newest novel, *Charlie Bland,* is really a very beautiful, poetic book. She's someone who is always willing to take risks in her work. There are a number of good short story writers—in particular, Elizabeth Tallent. I think her story called "Ice" is really one of the greatest short stories of our time. I'm also very fond of Deborah Eisenberg's work; Joy Williams is in a league by herself. Mary Robinson's "Mine" is a masterpiece. I like a lot of Margaret Atwood, I like much of Alice Munro. Again, if you were to ask me about male writers, there's often a novel I admire, but not all of their works.

Seshachari: Tell me about the genesis of *Picturing Will.* Who is Will?
Beattie: Ah, that's a hard one. That book went through three years of revisions. Initially, my only desire was to write something about the kind of bonding that a parent feels with a child. I wasn't even clear that it was going to be a mother, who was alone, who was raising a son. But that emerged fairly quickly; that imaginative projection was easier for me than beginning from a male point of view. I also thought, stylistically, I would like to do more of something that I've done from time to time in my stories, but that I've never done in a sustained way, in a longer work, which was just to write a different kind of prose. And when the book was first written, the first draft ended up being five sections done in terms of geography—Charlottesville, New York, Florida, etc. Later, I realized that I wanted only mother, father, and child.

Seshachari: A trinity.
Beattie: Exactly. I wasn't at all sure what Jody's background would be or who the child would be. They took on their characters rather early. In fact, I had to temper my judgmental tendencies toward her because I figured I wasn't going to write about some perfectly benign, pleasant professional. She was, at least in my mind, someone other than that. She was quite driven and quite conflicted in a lot of ways. That was the only thing that made her interesting to me. Again, all that may not have been demonstrated in the book, but it was the notion that got me into it.

Seshachari: In your previous works you don't talk about or describe sex at all, but in *Picturing Will* there is at least one explicit sex scene. Is that also a new departure?
Beattie: Again, that was not premeditated. Once I created Haveabud, that seemed inevitable.

Seshachari: How did you come to choose the name Haveabud? Did you do it deliberately?
Beattie: No, no. I realized after I had written it, but I thought, Oh, just leave it, it sounds amusing. It did start out as Haverford, which is his formal name.

Seshachari: I thought Haveabud was suggestive as in "Have a bud [boy]."
Beattie: Other people have said it sounds like an ad for Budweiser beer. I thought, Let people think whatever they want; it's just the way it came out.

Seshachari: Do you ever sit at your typewriter and say, Now I've never done this before. . . .

Beattie: Only with the prose style. From time to time I've sat down and thought, Oh, I'm going to do this differently. For instance, when I wrote *Falling in Place*, I didn't know I'd have those italicized sections. I was writing at least a chapter a day and I started to make notes to myself about other material I needed to include, and finally I realized, Why not let the notes stand? A kind of coda to each chapter—just write them a bit more coherently. So then I had the task of writing a chapter each day and making coherent the notes at the end of the chapter. The form was appropriate to the content. These are characters who keep things from one another. It seemed a perfect system: characters won't give the reader a complete picture, but an author will (ostensibly) fill them in later. That's sort of analogous to what I did in *Picturing Will* too, because it has no one story. Even if the characters think they know the story, we as the readers know they are simply mistaken. What I'm telling people in both these books is, Don't believe what you're told.

Seshachari: You were talking about taking risks. What kinds of risks did you take in *Picturing Will*?

Beattie: Well, the writing. I've never tried three hundred pages of compound, complex sentences in fact (laughter). I decided to let some of the complexity of the story come into the prose itself rather than just being referred to, as I do sometimes in stories. The endings of my stories draw people's attention because they do shift very much. I work on the endings a lot.

Seshachari: I remember Laura sitting on Charlie's lap at the end of *Chilly Scenes* and asking myself, Where do they go from here?

Beattie: That's an interesting case. I wrote those pages of *Chilly Scenes of Winter* when I'd only written about a hundred pages, and I didn't know where the scene would fit in. I put it to the back of my desk and I kept writing and then when I got to the pages preceding the end, I suddenly felt, Hey, wait, I've already written the ending of that, and I just shuffled it into place.

Seshachari: How do you plan your endings?

Beattie: I don't plan endings per se. I don't think I've ever known an ending in my entire life, even with a short story. And some stories or books fail simply at that point. They have to be thrown away if the ending doesn't reveal itself to me. When I was writing *Picturing Will*, the first two sections turned out to be pretty much the same number of pages, but when I got to section three—it was in section five initially—I thought. Well, now I probably have about another seventy-five pages of manuscript to write, but I felt very ill at ease. It took me a long time to realize that a long section would be quite inappropriate to my purposes, that really I wanted to write about childhood when it had disappeared. Will's been in the book, the focus is still on him, but we flip forward into the twenty-first century when he's a man in his late twenties, married, with a child of his own at the point at which he's called "child." And of course that had a lot to do with the book, because the book is, in part, about untold stories.

Seshachari: I was impressed with the detail with which you focused on the child's growing up. Where did you ever have opportunities to observe a child?
Beattie: Myself. I think that really is the thing about being an only child, that you do realize you are in a strange condition compared to most of your friends. I don't know that I thought about that as a kid—I certainly didn't have any perspective or any long view of my life, but I think even at that time I probably realized this was a strange position I was in. There were two adults in the house and then there was me. I was shorter, I didn't get my way as much. I think I reflected on that more than I might have, had there been several other children going around the house. My position vis-a-vis my parents was mysterious even at the time and, because I like to write about mysteries, I'm still writing about that many years later. Also things interest me that aren't right under my nose and clearly understood, and so if I spend an afternoon with a kid, I'm sure I tend to file away almost every second and almost every nuance, where clearly you just couldn't proceed with your life and do that if you were the child's mother.

Seshachari: Didn't you once tell me that the original Will is Jay Parini's son?
Beattie: Jay Parini and his wife, Devon Jersild, have a child who was born on my birthday—September 8—who is named Will, and I must say I have always been entirely charmed with him, but I don't mean to say that I've tried to capture his personality in the book or anything. And in fact, had they named the child Luca, my book would have been *Picturing Luca*.

Seshachari: So you love the kid.

Beattie: I love the kid. As I start to write something, I need some touch-stones. I need some familiarity. I did an approximation of the geography of Charlottesville, Virginia. It doesn't figure that strongly in the book, but the playground that I'm writing about is close to my house. I pass by it every time I take a walk. Real visual things like that have to get me going even if they get edited out later.

Seshachari: I like the little, crisis situations in the book which often wither away as they do in real life. For instance, in *Picturing Will*, do you remember the scene where Mel and Jody are about to go for a walk at ten in the night and Will and his friend . . .

Beattie: . . . are playing mole?

Seshachari: Right. Mel sneaks upstairs and opens the door to see they are still wide awake, not asleep at all. Jody and Mel go away. I thought, Oh no, now these two kids are going to get into trouble, and Mel is going to feel terrible. Fortunately, that doesn't happen.

Beattie: I'm trying to create tension when I do things like that. It is very much my sense of life that that wouldn't be the moment the kids would burn down the house, but when Jody was in the room, something like that would happen. It's being true to the way life is rather than to a fictional mode.

Seshachari: True. But being true to life also includes some violence. You are a realist—by reading any book of yours, one can pinpoint the time when it was written because of social and political events that are mentioned in it. But you steer clear of any genuine violence. Sure, John Joel shoots his sister Mary in *Falling in Place*. . . .

Beattie: But it's not dwelt upon. It's not dramatized. Really, the drama is simply the sentence that he does it.

Seshachari: And it's not the focal point.

Beattie: I read about violence. I watch it on television. Whatever the reason, it isn't something that seems a mystery to me. The lives that I'm writing about don't seem to be dramas that take that form. They have dramas that take other forms. It wouldn't be correct to say that there is a violent marriage in *Falling in Place*, but the discord in that marriage and the kind of coercion that the characters exert on one another is certainly very unpleasant. It's as erosive as violence might be aggressive. "Where You'll Find Me" doesn't have anything to do with human suffering in the same way a truly violent act would produce human suffering, but there is one line in the story when the brother turns to the sister—and this is a complete non-sequitur—and says, "I fell in love with somebody." Well, what that does emotionally to the sister—and I hope to the reader—is just make her heart fall into her heels. It is a kind of aggression that in my mind is comparable to violence. Domestic tragedies can have an effect comparable to violence.

Seshachari: There is plenty of similar violence in *Picturing Will*, as there is much stability as well. All the marriages in your previous books are, in a sense, marriages that peter out.

Beattie: Well, I get into trouble with my husband [Lincoln Perry] now if I do that. He reads the rough drafts of my stories and says, I hope these people don't get divorced. I feel intimidated now (laughter). You'll read no more about divorces in my work.

Seshachari: I am impressed with *Picturing Will* for that same reason. Here are two people who make their marriage work. Will we see more fiction where the marriages do work out?

Beattie: Well, at least temporarily; it's my current view of life (laughter). Also I think that people have found different ways to adjust to the complexities of their lives. There was a long transitional period in which that was very diffi-cult. Everyone would say now that we were sold a bill of goods with the implication that everything could be done, that you could have children, jobs, career success, a romantic marriage, and you could travel. In one way or another people found out that simply wasn't the case, that they couldn't have it all. People have made a lot of adaptations. I think people are living improvisations.

Seshachari: And I think too that couples don't make the kinds of demands of each other which endanger a marriage. Today's woman does not want to achieve through her husband's successes anymore. She's on her own.

Beattie: Yes. That's entirely true, at least in the world I'm writing about.

Seshachari: What do you think of Tom Wolfe's article, "Stalking the Billion-Footed Beast," in the November [1989] issue of *Harper's Magazine*? Do you agree with his claim that the only novel worth writing is the sociological, realistic novel?

Beattie: Anyone who makes a pronouncement that grand is certainly entitled to make it but I don't think anyone should be persuaded by it. I don't think there is any one kind of novel that should be written. You're in terrible danger of being an autocrat if that's what you think. I see his point. I don't think it's an unintelligent point; nevertheless, I think people have various talents. Indirection can reveal something just as well as confrontation. Take something like Bobbie Ann Mason's *In Country*. There isn't any one ultimate thing to say about the Vietnam War. I'm equally illuminated by Tim O'Brien's *The Things They Carried*, or Michael Herr's *Dispatches*. We know about the Vietnam War as part of our shared consciousness. How you want to speak about the repercussions of that war seems to me to be up to you as an artist. By the way, I think *The Bonfire of the Vanities* is a wonderful book. I had problems with the ending; I thought the ending was a bit expedient and possibly orchestrated to instill fear in the liberal reader, but leaving that aside, it is wonderful.

Seshachari: You enjoyed reading about New York!

Beattie: I'm not sure. I don't think Wolfe really had to put me in Sherman McCoy's apartment. We've all seen those doormen, we all know what that apartment looks like outside and inside, we all know what the Bronx is like. If people don't already know it, they're not going to get it very vividly from the book to begin with. That book, it seems to me, is about the tragedy of people's insecurities and the horrible price we pay for ambition and about a society that has accelerated out of control. It comes down to simple truths about human nature. I don't remember it because Wolfe made me see what it was like to have your car break down in the Bronx. I remember it because of Sherman McCoy; his cowardice has trapped him and made him pathetic, in his way.

Seshachari: Wolfe scoffs at minimalists as those who write about tiny situations, "very tiny domestic ones," and he calls them K-Mart realists.

Beattie: He's entitled to call them anything he likes. But again, I have to say that I see his point: often what writers are doing is not expansive in the sense of implicating society directly. Indirectly, I think the society is implicated. Trying to legislate form and toss writers out of the field, or the K-Mart parking lot, is simply folly.

Seshachari: Minimalists, by the nature of their aesthetic vision and practice, tend to write poetic descriptions and dialogues. Many scenes in your novels read like poetry.

Beattie: I don't think that that's necessarily true of minimalism. Remember that the painters who were minimalists had a philosophy that what you see is what you get: no more, no less. But this has nothing to do with the so-called minimalist writers. Frederick Barthelme clearly believes that the whole is greater than the sum of the parts. And the reader who understands that something is unstated—sometimes tragically unstated—between the characters would have to realize the connotations, the implied complexities. Also, Frederick Barthelme is funny. Bobbie Ann Mason can be quite funny. The minimalist painters were not funny. Minimalism in painting was a term of approval. It was a way to discuss a movement that was a responsive movement to a previous movement in art: Abstract Expressionism. When critics began to talk about literature in these terms, they were using it in a pejorative sense, saying that there were empty spaces. Bad empty spaces, not good empty spaces.

Seshachari: I think of them as suggestive spaces. I don't think negatively of minimalism at all.

Beattie: My problem is, I don't even see the empty spaces. They're filled with visual cues, tonal changes, and have far-reaching consequences. Perhaps what people really want to say is that there are a bunch of bad writers. And I certainly agree. Also you have to read the tenor of sentences. Readers need to be educated. If they don't think in terms of nuance, then perhaps they are not getting what is going on at all.

Seshachari: You once said that literature is not being taught in the universities as it should be. How should it be taught? What is wrong with the teaching as you see it?

Beattie: I haven't taught full-time since 1982. I don't know what's going on in the universities now. I just don't think there are many good teachers. I feel that teaching has to be done somewhat by indirection. You do have to pick the right works to subject people to, you have to know how to work with people individually. Part of the problem everywhere is that you have one teacher and anywhere from ten to fifty to one thousand students being taught by a television, and of course no knowledge is going to be imparted.

Seshachari: How did you teach when you did teach?
Beattie: I bullied them, that's how I taught (laughter). Actually I liked teaching literature much more than I did creative writing. Very few people want me to come and teach literature. They want to grab me and have me talk about my trade, which isn't of much interest to me. It's part of the reason I don't teach any more. I read the material very closely. If, for instance, someone told me, Well, this is just a dead head, or Nothing happens in this story, I would say "Turn to page forty-one." I ask students' opinions when I'm teaching literature, talk for a while in sort of general terms, talk about the approach the author makes, what the intent is of the piece and so forth. And then, as you were saying about my book, I find that people have quite differing perceptions. In many cases that's fine; in some cases they're having perceptions simply because they haven't read the text at hand. That's classifiable as an error. It has to be pointed out to them.

Seshachari: Many of your short stories and *Chilly Scenes of Winter* are written in the present tense. *Falling in Place, Love Always*, and *Picturing Will* use the more traditional past tense. What do you think are the artistic and fictional uses of the present tense as opposed to the past tense?
Beattie: In retrospect, I can say something about that, but at the time I wrote, the tense wasn't premeditated. I didn't sit down and say I'll now write a novel in the present tense. In fact I was so oblivious of having done it that when I was interviewed after *Chilly Scenes of Winter* and asked that question I said, It's not written in the present tense. So there's an answer for you. I think that the advantage of the present or past tense is that one sometimes is more appropriate to the material. It's what emotion you want to put into the material. You decide. It's not as though the material is an objective thing you're writing about. Sometimes it's better to hear about things as though they are currently transpiring. Other times, I think the advantage is that you can be somewhat more analytical when you're using the past tense. I think that you can interpret with the past tense in a way that you can't interpret using the present tense. Present tense has a more staccato effect too. Also, as I'm writing at the typewriter, it's sometimes easier for me to say, This is happening,

rather than, That must have happened. It really is just creating your own drama as you go along. I've never switched tenses at the beginning. But when I'm doing rough drafts, I often start out in the present tense and end up in the past, and then I have to decide.

Seshachari: Do you think the structure of the novel is undergoing subtle changes? Writers like Charles Dickens, for example, used such complicated strings of plot that came together only in the last few chapters. You had to read all the eight hundred pages to know how things happened. Novels in our century have tended to be more or less complete short stories strung together loosely. How do you plan the structures of your novels?
Beattie: The form doesn't precede the content in my mind. I don't have any particular model, and I don't think it would do me any good. Obviously Dickens was a genius.

Seshachari: Dickens was also writing for serialized publication.
Beattie: . . . as Tom Wolfe was writing *The Bonfire of the Vanities* for *Rolling Stone.*

Seshachari: So you've never experimented with structures in writing?
Beattie: Well with short stories I have. For instance, I wrote a very short story called "Snow." I was teaching creative writing at the time, in 1982, and I wanted my students to write a "you" story, so I thought I'd write one along with them.

Seshachari: Is that the one about the woman going back to the house that she used to live in with her husband and she recollects what the winter was like?
Beattie: And then there's a break in the text and she says, You remember it differently, you remember that the moon had a bit shaved off every night. It does occur to me that one of the things that makes prose interesting is that so much can be done with it, and if you lock into a predictable style, even for yourself, that's not terribly gratifying. I was particularly pleased with the ending to a story called "Skeletons." It took me a long time to figure out what I was doing there and how to layer that story.

Seshachari: You read that at Weber—it is about Kyle Brown, a Mormon.
Beattie: Yes. When I started with the rough draft, I didn't even know that Kyle would be the center of that story. I thought that it would be about Nancy Niles and her boyfriend, Garrett. And then I found myself quadruple

spacing [on the typewriter] and moving forward in time and telling myself that Kyle wanted to stay in touch with them, meant to stay in touch, but years intervened, and then I thought, Wow, what territory am I in now, what have I done, flipped forward twenty years? I couldn't tell you what gave me the impulse to do that but once I did, I realized Kyle had been more important than I had thought. Even though consciously I couldn't have articulated to myself why I had put Nancy Niles in a skeleton costume, I suddenly realized what every bit of it meant and I thought, Well, how am I going to get this across to the reader without doing it in a didactic way? So I tried to write about emptiness by invoking an image that was three dimensional.

Seshachari: Sometimes, didacticism works well in the authorial voice.
Beattie: Yes. I can't claim always to be hiding behind my characters. I do say things overtly sometimes, but the story never ends with those pronouncements. Even in a story like "The Burning House," the husband turns to his wife and says, in effect, would you really like a perspective on your whole life, here's the perspective. Though I did not end it with a profound, clearly articulated revelation because nothing ever ends at the moment at which some dramatic revelation is made.

Seshachari: It's the memory sometimes. . . .
Beattie: Exactly. The last line of that story had to be "I'm looking down on all of this from space, I'm already gone." That brought it right back to him and to the larger perspective I wanted the story to have. It doesn't seem to me that any fiction is about making or announcing a revelation.

Seshachari: What was the occasion for a limited edition of 250 copies of "Jacklighting," especially since the story was already published in *Antaeus?*
Beattie: For collectors, frankly. Someone from Metacom Press got in touch with me. People are always interested in having something everyone else doesn't have. And a pretty little book too.

Seshachari: Tell me about the role of the author and the reader. What is their relationship in terms of understanding and interpreting a work of art? Who is your ideal reader?
Beattie: Donald Barthelme. I was always very happy to publish something and send it off to Donald or send him something I didn't publish. . . . Who is

my ideal reader? I think somebody who is keen in the way that he was keen. I suppose somebody who isn't predisposed to like me. Also, someone who knows how to read. Readers have to give you the time to really read what you have written and to allow themselves the time to imagine that fictive world. I think it takes more patience and more willingness to suspend disbelief than it does pure intellect.

Seshachari: Your work demands slow reading.
Beattie: Well, I think of it as being sneaky work.

Seshachari: Critics have spoken of your gift for intimacy, which enchants readers like the "whispered secret" you speak of in your introduction to the *Best American Short Stories of 1987*. I think life is partly about being interested in trivia.
Beattie: And the cumulative effect of trivia is quite different from what Wolfe implies with the term "K-Mart realists." You've got to admit that Wolfe is being very judgmental when he implies that the writer is unsophisticated because he or she can't envision more than K-Mart. What he does not understand is that it's only a cultural talisman. Writers are really doing exactly what Wolfe wants them to do—talking about that external world we live in.

Seshachari: Let me not forget your book on Alex Katz. Was it really the editor who lured you into writing the book?
Beattie: Yes. I approached it as an assignment, one that I found pleasant because I admired the man. Some people thought I was writing about Alex Katz because I saw a great similarity in what we were doing, that I was explaining myself by way of explaining Katz's painting, but I think we're quite different. I approached his work psychologically. Possibly I could have approached it sociologically. I could have talked about the lifestyles of the subjects or whatever, but it did seem to me, after I had looked at his work for a long while, that what was of greatest interest to me were those relationships that were articulated so subtly in the paintings. I'm not equipped to discuss somebody's brushwork or painting style.

Seshachari: You do that very well.
Beattie: Thanks, but it wasn't meant to be a book an art historian would have written.

Seshachari: While you are both interested in portraits, he paints them in very broad strokes, while you go for little details that eventually illuminate the character.

Beattie: I put in a lot of details, and when I'm editing, I strike them if they turn out to be extraneous. One telling detail, as we all know, is going to be much better than six throwaways.

Seshachari: How often do you revise your work?

Beattie: Oh, constantly. *Picturing Will* went through five major changes, and fifteen chapters were thrown out.

Seshachari: Did the story change too?

Beattie: Sure. I revised the third section of the novel seventy-five to one hundred times.

Seshachari: What do you mean by changes? Do you mean a few words here and there, or do you mean massive changes?

Beattie: I wouldn't say that it was only a few words here and there, but I don't know that I could call them massive changes. A line that might appear to be a throwaway is really a huge cue to the novel and I really had to revise that section numerous times before that sentence came to me about the child who is jumping up and down; do you remember that?

Seshachari: Let's pull the manuscript out.

Beattie: "The child's knees bend as he does a skitterish little dance. Then, holding his arms stiffly, fists behind his hips, he jumps high and lands slightly crouched"—well, here's the punch—"looking something the way penguins did before they became extinct." A friend seized upon that and said, My God, I thought I'd die when I read that. Other people have said they didn't notice it—I mean, good readers.

Seshachari: When I came to the end, I sat and cried. I mean, I cry easily, and I don't mind crying.

Beattie: There, you're my ideal reader (laughter). I've written individual sentences that have made me feel ill because, had I not been writing the story, I would never have had to articulate something that was so painful. A lot of times you fight not to type the sentence. You fight to do something a little cooler. There can be an awkward second in which you decide you'll be a coward and compromise, too.

Seshachari: I was very touched that Mel had—it came as a surprise—that he had written all those monologues. It seemed perfectly logical. *Picturing Will* is, in a sense, picturing Mel and Jody too. The characters—as indeed the novel—get defined through vivid pictures.
Beattie: I didn't want to hit that too heavily, but there certainly is a motif of photography. Well, she's a photographer. At the end, even Will himself is thinking in terms of photography.

Seshachari: Portraiture. Was *Vogue* happy that you mentioned it by name in the book?
Beattie: I'd be very curious to know whether they sent Gene Lyons to interview me before or after having finished the galleys. They may not have known I mentioned *Vogue.*

Seshachari: Let me ask my final question. What plans do you have for the 1990s?
Beattie: Back to writing short stories. This summer, I wrote a very long short story called "Windy Day at the Reservoir." A friend of mine named Rallou Malliarakis did an oil on paper with the title "Windy Day at the Reservoir." She lives in New Hampshire, and it's the reservoir near her house. It just stuck in my mind as an image. I never knew I'd write a story with that title—I've never even seen the real-life reservoir, but that's where it turned out to take place.

Seshachari: It might turn into a novel?
Beattie: No. It's eighty pages. Since publishing *Where You'll Find Me*, I have at least a dozen short stories, and then this long one, which should make another book.

Seshachari: Have you written anything else like "The Working Girl," which you read at Weber and which is more post-modernistic in style—where you openly consult the reader and ask, Now what shall I do with this character?
Beattie: In some ways "The Working Girl" was a sort of forerunner of Mel's monologues. That kind of volley within one voice was something that I did

in "The Working Girl." There is also another story called "Spiritus" in the last collection which is told in a very staccato, matter-of-fact narrative.

Seshachari: Have you ever tried writing a story which actually suggests two or more endings?
Beattie: I've never done that exactly, but I've thought I've written the correct story and then suddenly, something has clicked and I've realized, No, I didn't write the right story at all. "Skeletons" was actually part two of another story about the same character, Nancy Niles. Part one was called "Taking Hold." I was in a plane on my way to Florida; after we taxied to the end of the runway, we were told we were about number one hundred one for take off and instead of being angry, I thought, Great! I can write another story about Nancy Niles, and then I wrote "Skeletons," which I think is a far better story. It's a variation of what you're talking about. In other words, I sometimes feel that the material is very ambiguous even to me, that it's still there to be explored.

Seshachari: What did you write the story on?
Beattie: On the air sickness bag! (laughter)

Seshachari: Something like Habe did in "The Sweetest Songs."
Beattie: Exactly. Just ordinary life. "Our sweetest songs are those that tell of saddest thought."

Seshachari: Ah, Shelley!

Novelist Focuses on Childhood Isolation

Josh Getlin / 1990

From the *Los Angeles Times*, 18 January 1990, E1, 14–15. Reprinted by permission.

As an only child, Ann Beattie spent hours observing adults at work and play, usually with her parents and often apart from other children. It proved to be excellent training for a woman who has become one of America's premier short story writers and novelists. "I probably saw a lot of things that other kids didn't see because I was alone," she says. "Being integrated into an adult world happened very early on in my life, and it made me a watcher. I saw things as being wrought with significance, in one situation after another."

Now, that experience has become the focal point of Beattie's latest novel, *Picturing Will,* a haunting study of a young boy and the adults who make up his world. Unlike her earlier works, in which thirtysomething refugees from the 1960s drift through an emotionally desolate landscape, this book features a more lyrical and psychologically direct style by the forty-two-year-old author.

Beattie, who has chosen not to have children, says her book is an "extended meditation on childhood" and represents a bold new direction in her writing. More important, the author of such well-received short story collections as *Where You'll Find Me,* and novels such as *Chilly Scenes of Winter,* hopes her new book will put an end to the notion that she is somehow the voice of her generation, as more than one critic has suggested.

It is a sore spot with Beattie, whose unsettling stories offer glimpses of moody, egocentric young adults stumbling through the seventies and eighties. Her brief, darkly written pieces are filled with middle-class people who tune in the Beatles on their car radios and are tormented by failing marriages, divorce, unhappy affairs, and separations. Like the suburban characters in John Cheever's stories, they are prisoners of ennui.

"What a lot of writers ignore is that I'm not a sociologist," says Beattie, relaxing on a sofa in her two-story brick home. "My test in writing these

101

stories was not, did I get it right about the sixties, but, is it literature? What I care about is whether my writing succeeds."

To her colleagues, that is no longer in doubt. Novelist Margaret Atwood, commenting on Beattie's distinctive writing style, wrote that, "if Ann Beattie were a ballerina, you could sell tickets to the warm-ups." Critic John Leonard praised the brooding tone of her stories, noting that "she seems to have jumped out of the head of an autumnal Samuel Beckett."

Thin, composed and cerebral, Beattie comes across in person like the prose that has won her such a wide audience. Initially reluctant to talk much about herself, the author gradually reveals more personal nuggets until, by the end of an interview, something of a portrait emerges. Dressed in a black sweater, black pants and black cowboy boots, she looks younger than her years and periodically brushes a shock of long auburn hair out of her eyes.

"For me, *Picturing Will* was something of a mystery, because I had no idea how it would turn out until the very end," Beattie says. "I've spent a lot of time hanging around with kids, but all I knew is that I wanted to write a book about children, about childhood."

"The rest, how it turned out, how it developed, is something as mysterious to me today as it was when I first started writing more than twenty years ago."

Looking back, Beattie says there were no early clues that she would become a writer. Born to a middle-class family in Washington, she was an indifferent student in high school and attended American University chiefly to satisfy her parents.

At first, Beattie flirted with journalism but then switched to an English major. About 1965, she began writing her first short stories, usually three-page vignettes about eccentric characters drawn from her own generation.

Friends praised the work, but it was strictly a hobby. When Beattie later entered graduate school at the University of Connecticut, she dismissed the idea of writing for a living—or doing anything for a living.

"I've never had a job in my life," Beattie says with a laugh. "I never wanted one then, and I don't want one now. I stayed in school not because of a love of the academic life or even because I wanted to buy time as a writer. I stayed in school because I didn't want to work."

The turning point came when Beattie's short stories were noticed by J. D. O'Hara, a professor and writer at the university. Without meeting her in person, O'Hara began suggesting editorial revisions in her works, leaving revised copies of the stories in the author's mailbox.

It was all very flattering, but when O'Hara managed to sell several of her pieces to small college magazines in Utah and Texas, Beattie had a change of heart. Especially when the first checks arrived.

"Well, I said, it's time to pursue that hobby!" she recalls. "I thought, you know, this might not be so bad after all."

During the next several years, Beattie sold stories to the *New Yorker* and *Esquire* and began attracting attention in literary circles. Her reputation soared when *Chilly Scenes of Winter* was published in 1976.

The story of an obsessive love affair, the novel focuses on a group of young adults in their twenties and became something of a cult classic. Many readers saw themselves in Beattie's post-college characters and her re-creation of the mid-seventies cultural scene. The book was eventually made into a movie, and Beattie had a cameo role as a harried coffee shop waitress.

"It was great, great experience," she says. "I got to wear the largest falsies of my life. It's true. They didn't have anything big enough in the costume department, so they put socks in."

In the coming years, Beattie would publish several collections of short stories, such as *The Burning House* and *Secrets and Surprises*, and novels including *Falling in Place* and *Love Always*. After living in New York, New England, and the South, she divorced her first husband and moved to Charlottesville, where she had once taught English at the University of Virginia. In 1988 she was married to Lincoln Perry, a painter.

Although her work has evolved, certain hallmarks of the Ann Beattie style are apparent. The openings tend to be abrupt and confused, there is little physical description and the setting is often irrelevant. Readers who begin one of her short stories may feel like they've walked into the middle of an enigmatic play that started hours before.

"These are not good movie beginnings," Beattie explains. "But I think that, because of the way the characters speak, and because of the narrator's tone of voice, you can pick up what kind of a world it is. I'm not trying to make it vivid visually, I'm trying to do it more through dialogue and through sentence cadence."

When they work well together, these ingredients produce powerful results. In her masterful short story "In the White Night," Beattie builds from an ambiguous party scene to a shattering human tragedy in less than seven pages. In "The Burning House," she lays bare a crumbling marriage and concludes with a chilling, unforgettable farewell from a man to his wife.

On occasion, Beattie has been able to write short stories with amazing speed, and reportedly finished the first draft for the novel *Love Always* in less than six weeks. But she says *Picturing Will* took more than three years to write and was her most exhausting project.

"I don't know why exactly, but I had to struggle with this novel. Maybe it's because there was something very different about it, a story about childhood and a real departure for me."

On the wall opposite the front door in Beattie's home hangs a large oil painting of a little boy. An adult is holding him protectively, while he stares at an abstract black and white shape behind a wire fence.

The boy, whose name is Will, is the child of one of Beattie's friends, and the painting was prompted by a family photograph that was never properly developed. It is a fitting symbol of the author's latest book, which blends disturbing snapshots of childhood with meditations on parental responsibility.

"I think that (Will's) character is somewhat similar to mine, as an only child, by saying that he's something of a watcher," she says. "But it also came out of the writing process—where you create characters that embody some hidden aspect of yourself that you're not very often in touch with." As the book begins, Jody, a single mother, is raising Will, her six-year-old son, in Charlottesville. The book focuses primarily on the boy and his thoughts, but eventually offers portraits of his mother, his friends, his stepfather, Mel, and his father, Wayne, who abandoned him years ago.

Gradually the barest threads of a narrative emerge: Jody's career as a photographer takes off and she moves with Will to New York to be with her lover. During a trip to Florida, Wayne makes it clear that he will not be a caring, nurturing person in his son's life. Will, who is shunted off to the sidelines by one adult after another, remains lost in a world of toy dinosaurs and playground outings until the very end.

The element of surprise in *Picturing Will* is key, because characters who start out as sympathetic turn into selfish, distant adults. People who at first seem bumbling and ineffective become the real heroes in Will's life.

"For me, the scheme of the book is that any character is going to be more complex than any initial assessment that can be made," Beattie says. "At first, it's exactly what you see, and then, as with any life, whether it's a child or an adult, it's more than what you say."

As Will's world gradually comes into focus, readers sense the impact that a six-year-old boy has on adults, and their often-callous treatment of him. But the book's real power emerges in a series of diary entries about parenthood that periodically interrupt the story. They feature some of Beattie's most evocative writing.

In one passage, the narrator reflects on a young boy's rapid growth and the bittersweet knowledge that childhood is fleeting:

"It becomes difficult to remember that he ever was (vulnerable). That the dog snapped at him, and he was afraid. That the cut got infected. That night after night, the same blue-bodied demon flicked its tail in his dreams. Sticky fingers. Wet sheets. A flood of tears. As you remember him, the child is always two."

The author of these passages is not revealed until the end of the book, and it comes as a genuine surprise. But for Beattie, the real surprise was the way her characters took on a life of their own as the writing progressed.

Before completing her final draft, for example, she discarded fifteen chapters and was uncertain where the book would begin. She had trouble developing the characters of Will's father and stepmother until their names were changed from Duane and Cory to Wayne and Corky. Then, magically, the problem disappeared.

"Usually, at some subconscious level. I catch on a little bit earlier than I did here," Beattie says. "But that's the good thing. I think most writers will tell you that once someone runs away with the material, ultimately, the writer is very thankful."

Asked about her upcoming projects, Beattie mentions several short stories in progress and a book about photography. But she sidesteps questions about how her work—and outlook—will change. Asked if she will once again draw on her own experience, Beattie finds that impossible to predict.

"It's just so hard to know," she says after a long pause. "I mean, all I can consistently say is that I write about what seems mysterious to me."

An Interview with Ann Beattie

Patrick H. Samway / 1990

From *America* 162.18 (12 May 1990), 469–71. Reprinted by permission.

Ann Beattie is a fiction writer who lives in Charlottesville, Virginia. Her works include *Distortions* (1976), *Chilly Scenes of Winter* (1976), *Secrets and Surprises: Short Stories* (1978), *Falling in Place* (1980), *Jacklighting* (1981), *The Burning House* (1982), *Love Always* (1985), *Where You'll Find Me, and Other Stories* (1986), and *Picturing Will* (1990). This interview focuses on her thoughts about writing fiction and her latest novel.

Patrick H. Samway: Since *Picturing Will* deals, in part, with childhood, I am sure our readers would care to know something about your background and, in particular, what situations in your early life you tend to put into your fiction.

Ann Beattie: First of all, I was an only child. While it is not necessarily peculiar to only children—but it is often true of only children—they become watchers because they belong to small families and are tightly bonded to those units. At the same time, they are just little kids and so they can't really quite function at their parents' level. I think that from early on I just wasn't up to a lot of things that I was experiencing; I was taken along and hovered over. It made me a watcher. Thus it is logical that I might attempt a profession like writing, but I have never written a story that was "A day in the life of. . . ."

Second, what keeps me so interested in writing, and still makes that storage of information in the brain seem so vital, is that I am continually squirreling away situations that I don't consciously realize are registering. Only when I write do I ever bring them forth again. They are not necessarily momentous things (I am not talking about witnessing a mugging on the street or something like that): it can be the smallest gesture, yet a real one, that I, at least, think I saw, yet the character that I am writing about has nothing to do with the flesh-and-blood person and is a kind of automatic process in the subconscious, or whatever, of blending and fusing things. Remembered people and events

106

just spring forth. What I remember is not inherently dramatic; it is just that when I write all those events and gestures become fictionally appropriate.

PHS: Do you find that you return often to your childhood?
AB: I return often to the emotions of earlier days, to that sense of wondering, of being an outsider. I was an extremely shy person back then. Though there has been a good deal of continuity in my life (my parents, for example, still live in the same house they moved into the year I went to kindergarten), much of my childhood is still a blur to me. My early stories were written when I was living in New England—I was in graduate school at the University of Connecticut for a number of years—and to some extent I was writing about the life around me in New England, but those stories were not autobiographical. I tended then, as I still do, to write about things that puzzle me. When I started writing I tuned into the life around me at that point and thought of it as fiction; I can't say that I returned to childhood memories back then per se.

PHS: What writers have been, and continue to be, important to you?
AB: Certainly there are writers that have been great inspirations, but there is no direct relationship between what they do or did and what I do. There are so many writers I can think of, Don DeLillo, for example, who is, as far as I am concerned, the best American novelist writing today. He is consistently looking at the dark underside and what he sees is absolutely fascinating. Ray Carver was a terrific inspiration too. Also, I like Updike's stories very much. It's funny, but when I first started writing I didn't have the money to buy literary magazines, but I did get the *New Yorker* on occasion. I like particularly the way Updike brings his stories around, but I never tried to appropriate his style or technique. Hemingway taught me about indirection and allusion and the correspondences of the external world to the emotional state. I acquired a good deal before I could articulate what it was.

I think, likewise, of F. Scott Fitzgerald and other writers of the 1920s. And, later on, Virginia Woolf became important to me. In fact, in *Picturing Will*, I had in mind trying to do something with the surprise revelations about Jody at the end of the novel that were not exactly analogous to, but certainly were inspired by, the death of Mrs. Ramsey in *To the Lighthouse*. In a parenthesis in Woolf's novel, you find out that Mrs. Ramsey has just died—and the world changes completely after that. So when I flipped into the twenty-first century in my own novel, and suddenly Jody was not the person the reader probably would imagine her to be, I was definitely paying homage to Virginia Woolf.

PHS: Your stories tend to be rather short, often six to seven pages in length. Why do you write using this minimalistic form?

AB: I have often asked myself that and I honestly don't know the answer. It is almost like asking somebody why green is his or her favorite color. I think of the various forms and genres as all being quite distinct from one another; I don't think that short stories have all that much in common with novels, nor poetry with short stories. I like each form or genre for what it inherently possesses. I do not write poetry and could never really express my world through poetry. A story re-creates for me more directly what my sense of the world is; a short-story writer has to use language differently from a novelist. Visual symbols are very important to me, and I try to have something visual in a story other than direct exchanges between the characters. And often that's what excites me to sit down and write. I can begin, for example, by looking out my window and seeing a real maple, and I might ask myself about a child who might sit in the tree. But I tend to see the tree before I see the person. Often it is not important for me to clarify my characters physically but to clarify the world they are living in. The sense of detail energizes me to write—like being a photographer or a painter.

PHS: In *Picturing Will*, I found the italicized sections philosophically quite moving; they reminded me of the prologue to James Agee's novel *A Death in the Family*. Were you thinking of Agee's novel when you were writing *Picturing Will?*

AB: I read Agee's novel years ago. It certainly is possible that Agee influenced me; that's all I can say. No one has ever asked me that before. I am not sure if I will ever know what impelled me to write this novel. I do know, however, that I had a lot of hidden anxiety in writing *Picturing Will* because the novel form is not the one that comes to me most naturally. I normally rev myself up by having some complex idea, not in terms of plot exactly, but in terms of how I'll approach writing the book. This novel went through many revisions. Initially I had all kinds of ideas about how to write it, and the italicized sections emanated from the narrator—they became the narrator's voice—and thus these sections, I can say, would not necessarily be my thoughts at all. As the novel developed I tried to make them more free-floating, and once a reader understands these sections in retrospect, definitely, I believe, open up the character whose views they finally are.

I wrote these sections as a kind of frame for the novel. Yet, I find it interesting that there are a number of chapters where Will does not appear or is referred to only in passing. The novel is not just about Will. I think children, in general, influence a person's life even when they are not present. I deliberately wanted to shift the focus from Will to the other people, who, in turn, would lead the reader to reflect on the power of childhood. In general, too, I believe these sections stabilize the text.

PHS: In Chapter 15 of *Picturing Will*, Haveabud and Spencer take Will through a shocking initiation into adulthood. Since you are often cited as being a comic fiction writer, how does this scene fit into your imaginary world?
AB: I believe that we go along in life, often with a smile or a laugh, and then BOOM, something happens unexpectedly to us. Samuel Beckett felt that in almost everything he wrote. I really didn't know I was creating a child molester. I was just writing about a type, about a troubled person who might prosper in certain large cities. But, as we all know there is a really dark side to those people just when they are really flying. Yes, I'm making a moral judgment here, and it's put there to surprise the reader precisely because it is ghastly. It could have been the climax of the book, but rather I consider it a kind of throwaway, while at the same time not a throwaway. The reader does not know exactly the repercussions of this on Will. This scene represents my notion that fiction never does tell you certain things even, paradoxically, if it tells you those things. I was completely shocked myself when I found out what went on in that motel, but, of course, I knew that Haveabud was not completely just a buffoon. He was evil. I think, from that scene on, there is more anxiety even if the reader tries to put it out of his or her mind. The scene serves as the last real reference point.

PHS: Eudora Welty has written about the importance of place in fiction. I notice that Charlottesville is becoming more and more important in your work. Will you continue to write about this city?
AB: It is hard to say. I know that when I have lived in cities, I have written about the country and vice versa. So I am not so sure that I will write about Charlottesville while I'm living there. In *Picturing Will*, Charlottesville is

mentioned, but I don't think it is too important as a specific locale in the novel. I wouldn't be surprised if I wrote about Charlottesville more in the future.

PHS: Let me pick up on something you mentioned before about the visual nature of your work. Since Jody, Will's mother, is a photographer, how do you view the relationship between taking photographs and writing fiction?
AB: I don't have any trouble at all composing. I am not one of those people who walks around a still-life six times to see what it looks like. I instantaneously know what picture it is I want to take. And that is analogous to the way I write. It is clear to me right from the beginning who is a major character and who is a minor one. If that hasn't worked itself out, if it hasn't impressed me dramatically enough, then I haven't seen the picture yet. Maybe I am just being imperious. Mel does say in the novel that we put a border around our world. In this novel, I am not saying something definitive about childhood, but only putting up borders around this particular child. And any border should be distrusted. There is nothing that can be taken at face value; people always use various postures when they tell you who they really are.

PHS: Do you read the type of criticism that Jacques Derrida and his confreres write about framing and other such literary devices?
AB: No, but my husband does. He often says, "Hey, you'd like this!" I think quite a few fiction writers do not want to know that some concept like framing has been written about exhaustively. It can be counterproductive.

PHS: Do you think that you will write essays about the nature of fiction?
AB: I doubt it. I think others have said it very well. I, at least, need to have a "presumed innocence" about writing. I would be afraid that writing such essays would encroach in some way on my fiction, and that once I expressed such critical views they would be chiseled into my mind and inhibit me in future writing.

PHS: How would you like your peers to remember you?
AB: Certainly not as a chronicler, a quasi-journalist or "The Voice of Her Generation." I would like my fellow fiction writers to see the larger implications of what I do and to judge me as being astute about human behavior. I am always very happy when people see the humor in my work and the precision that I think is there. I guess I would just like my peers to read my work carefully. What more could any fiction writer ask?

Counternarrative: An Interview with Ann Beattie

James Plath / 1991

From *Michigan Quarterly Review*, 32.3 (Summer 1993), 359–79. Reprinted by permission.

Book tours have a way of turning writers into gypsies. After Ann Beattie finished reading from *What Was Mine* at a Chicago-area book store, I drove her to her hotel, where, upon finding cold champagne and a fruit tray, compliments of her publisher, she expressed the same measure of surprised delight as a tourist might. Her appearance was equally down-to-earth. Beattie wore a loose tunic, patterned stretch pants, and bold socks. Nothing matched, she explained, because she purchased them on the road because her others were dirty. "My Reeboks," she said, lifting one foot above the coffee table, "I recently bought in Key West. On sale."

Born in Washington, D.C. in 1947, Ann Beattie enjoyed the early support of the *New Yorker*, where a great many of her stories of failed and failing relationships appeared. Her first novel, *Chilly Scenes of Winter* (1976), and *Distortions*, a collection of short stories published that same year, established her as a spokesperson for the hippie-turned-yuppie generation. Other books quickly followed: *Secrets and Surprises* (1978), *Falling in Place* (1980), *The Burning House* (1982), *Spectacles* (1985), *Love Always* (1986), *Where You'll Find Me* (1987), *Picturing Will* (1989), and her latest collection, *What Was Mine* (1991).

During the reading, Beattie sat in a chair on a small platform, rarely looking up from her book to make eye contact with the crowd of sixty or so. Once finished, however, she received the line of autograph-seekers and well-wishers with reception-line enthusiasm, asking each person a question or two, and personalizing every book. By the time she finished, it was well after 10 p.m. Yet, in the hotel room, relaxing somewhat with shoes off and a glass of champagne in hand, she was still gracious, still full of energy, full of interest—and seemingly eager to talk about her work.

JP: Like Raymond Carver, you tend to write what I'd call "fictions of aftermath," where most of the conflict or turning points have already occurred, leaving the characters to cope with or work through resultant problems. I think you've moved even more toward this now than perhaps you did in earlier collections. What is it about recovery and coping that strikes you as being infinitely more interesting to you than the cause and effect process leading up to it all, a process you seem to deemphasize?

AB: Well, I think you have to get the cause and effect process in the story. I don't think you can omit any mention of that, but I'm not sure that it needs to be the beginning of the story. If the stories seem to resemble "ordinary life," then very few things happen with a beginning, middle and end. You often can understand things in retrospect, or something will happen that will precipitate a change that will be rooted in a lot of things, or it will anticipate a lot of things. But I don't think that most of us lead orderly lives, and it wouldn't be very possible for me to write a story that went along with some status quo that I don't even see in operation.

JP: As your characters try to order their lives, they look to the past so often that it almost seems like returning to the "scene of the crime."

AB: It's true. I think I've very rarely written anything that doesn't invoke the past at some point. At what point that occurs, though, varies a bit. The story that I read tonight, "Home to Marie," certainly could have been told in reverse order. It could have had a different so-called "punch line." It's really just an emotional decision, in a way, if all your material is there, to try to figure out how you want to present it. I'm not saying that *anything* is okay. I don't think you can set a reader up for one set of expectations, and then just reverse course in the story. But I do think that the same information can be given a lot of different ways.

I've juggled a lot. I very rarely make endings beginnings, but I quite often lop off beginnings, because I write many pages before I feel my way into the material. And those things often do have more to do with the character's past, how they habitually talk, the physical descriptions. Finally, if you've got it right in your head and you are clear on who they are and you can animate them, you don't need an introduction. I mean, what's more interesting: two hours into the party, or when you're walking through the front door?

JP: A passage from your story "In the White Night" reads, "There were two images when you looked in the finder and you had to make the adjustment

yourself so that one superimposed itself upon the other and the figure suddenly leaped into clarity"—which, it seems, could almost serve as directions
or a warning label on the side of your fiction for how readers should get
through a Beattie story.

AB: Hopefully, that's how the details will work. As visual images, I think you
need to have things intensify, and for me as a writer, the way to make something seem more real is to go at it several times, rather than declaring that it
is some one thing. There are a lot of people who are extremely good at that.
Carver, he'll give you some banal landmark—a lamp on a table—and by the
time he comes back to the table for the third time, you know the lamp is
there and it's glowing, whether or not he says that it is. That's just a working
method, in a lot of ways. It also has to do with a certain personal view of
things, and I'm not very interested in looking at the surfaces of things except
as starting points. I'm willing to go with the visual detail that strikes me, but
it has to be appropriate to the material. It's fairly random if something is
going to capture my attention, and when it does, I think you have to hound
the reader a little bit about what that means.

JP: As in "The Longest Day of the Year," where at the end a golf ball rolls off
the table and rolls next to a dust ball? Here you have an obvious symbol of
action, motion, all that rubber at the core. . . .

AB: And the leisure life. And here are people who can't afford the place that
they're staying in and have to move, and their marriage is also breaking up as
well. But those are the details that keep happening that you *would* notice in
that situation if you were those people, more than other things. Rather than
taking the long view, they're more apt to notice there *is* a dust ball in the corner, rather than to trying to imagine themselves in some particular way a year
or so down the line.

JP: What I was thinking of was not so much motifs—although they're certainly present in your fiction—but about the way your characters tend to
reexamine their childhoods, or estranged couples will meet at houses that
hold pleasant memories. They engage in a nostalgic return of some sort in
order to find meaning or healing. You also use a lot of mirror images and
doubling. Has life become so complicated that, like a poem, it has to be
"read" more than once for your characters to really understand what they're
going through?

AB: Well again, it's a personal view, and a lot of the time I'm going to look for things to reinforce that. It seems, from my experience, to have been proven true that a lot of the time people don't see a thing succinctly in the moment, but whether or not they even want to see that thing, other things accrue— and those things are often things from the past that allow the person to more fully see what's happening in the moment. In other words, I'm not talking about people who are out on a quest, or people who are simply sitting and trying to articulate a problem to themselves. I'm talking more about those off-center, unexpected moments when people do find that they are thinking about the present, and that it's been influenced by the past.

JP: Sometimes your characters do work at this kind of thought process or conditioning. Your stories often feature game-playing as a diversion but also as a controlling metaphor. The "don't think about" game in "In the White Night," for example, is quite different from the game-playing in "Honey," where the main character actually works on a kind of mental conditioning. She looks at all the people that make up her circle and thinks to herself, *think about the positives, think about the ways in which they're wonderful,* and that works only briefly, because shortly after that the bees swarm in and destroy that internalized Kodak moment, and an unattractive side shows through. To me, it's as if your characters are deliberately trying to make some sort of return trip, or deliberately trying some mental conditioning.

AB: Like I said, I'm very interested in the ways that people come to terms with things, and I'm very interested in the accommodations that they make. I think a lot of the time I tend to show it more through gesture. I tend to show it less through elements of plot or describing something directly. I think it's an exception that you found a character in "Honey" who is militantly think- ing of herself, *I must now think of the world a particular way.* Usually the characters don't articulate that. But I'm not the best person to introspect about these stories, because I have a vested interest in not doing so. If it were someone else's story, I probably would be more willing to pronounce upon it than I am my own stories. I essentially agree with what you're saying. You can apply those things very habitually to what I write. I guess, beyond the fact that I would take that as a given—which, some people might dispute, cer- tainly—beyond the fact that I take it as a given, only the specifics matter, and that's where the stories become really distinct from one another. It's not just that the theme is now seen in one terrain with one set of characters and so forth. The whole idea of double lives, or triple lives, I hope that there's an emotional resonance that makes them seem as if they can be transplanted to more than one space.

JP: You experiment more in the latest collection with strikingly different narrative voices. I'm thinking of "Installation #6" or "Television." How do the new voices arise? They're quite unlike the "New Yorkerish" voice which has typified your characters' speech.

AB: I didn't really realize that until I collected all those stories together, and then I did think that *What Was Mine* was a good title for the book, although it was not originally titled that. A friend of mine gave me that title. Initially it was just called *Windy Day at the Reservoir and Other Stories.* But the whole idea of *What Was Mine,* there are a lot of different people, and they *are* distinct voices. The thing is filled with monologues. Who knows why a thing like that that becomes interesting to a writer at one point, versus another? When I sat down to write "The Working Girl," for instance, I wrote the first paragraph which began, "This is a story about Jeanette, who is a working girl." And sitting there, I thought, "Oh, Ann, you *can't* execute another story in which you make the presumption that you're the omniscient narrator. I mean, *really,*" So I undercut it by interjecting a real question. In effect, the question was "Really?" and it ended up being a kind of deconstruction of a short story, and I suppose a kind of admission of what the process is, too. But I was funning with myself there; it's not that I wasn't in earnest about what I wrote, but for whatever reason I didn't mind letting people see the skeletal system. Why not?

JP: In some of the newer stories, you deal with people who actually use contractions, who begin sentences with conjunctions. And in *Picturing Will,* the style is even more complex, more fluid, less stylized than the short stories with their subject-verb-object patterns.

AB: That was deliberate, and partly it was because I realized I was going to be taking years out of my life. You want to set yourself some tasks if you're going to do such a thing. However silly they might sound, I just decided that I was going to write compound-complex sentences for a change. Who knows why? I just thought I'd see if I could do it, but I had to find a reason for it. It wasn't even my notion when I started writing that book that the italicized portions—the journal entries—would be attributed to any particular character.

And when I did decide to do that, when it looked like it was overly conceived, in a way, that it was calling attention to its own form by having the author's voice come in, at first I thought about giving them to Jody. But then I realized no, no, no, no, no, you can develop a whole other plot—even if the reader realizes it only in retrospect—by giving the journal entries to a much more unlikely person. But the difficulty there, of course, was the obvious one of straddling the line between writing it so explicitly that the reader would catch on very early that it was Mel, and therefore ruining the surprise of it—ruining the reverberation of it when you find out at the end—or not doing enough. They're a bit flowery for my taste. That's not what I meant by wanting to write compound-complex sentences. I was trying to write a journal that, once I had attributed it to that character, would have been written in the voice of someone who was a poseur. They had to sound stiff enough to be believable once you found out who they were, but not so stiff that they just put the reader off for 90 percent of the book. It was a hard problem.

JP: You've referred, in the past, to things like point/counterpoint, and counter melodies. Steinbeck used to call them "interlocutory chapters," and it seems as if you have relied on these devices, these breaks, in order to give the narrative some sort of texture, some sort of relief, or "counterpoint," as you say. I don't want to lead you here, but you seem to be growing more and more fascinated with the whole process of authorial intrusion.

AB: I'm more ill-at-ease with the notion that anyone might think that I was defining something in the story, and I realize that you can't anticipate these things and you can't, in effect, write an apology. But I think for my own sake, to be able to look at the story and to point to the fact that there *are* ambiguities, complexities, contradictions, etc., is a pleasing notion to me. Because I'm just the sort of person that, if you tell me one story, I won't pay much attention to the story that I'm hearing, or I'll put it in the context of something that I choose to put it in the context of.

I'm not really very interested in information. Information is random, so it would be very hard for me to write something that was on some level informative—you know, four hundred pages of a novel—and to put out something that might be mistaken for being "definitive," that would not be at all pleasing to me. If I could do such a thing, I guess I would stand on the street corner and shout it at the sky, or passers-by, or whatever. I don't think that's what the writing is about at all. It just puts me at my ease, personally, to indicate those counternarrative things, if for no one else but myself. It is to create texture. You're totally right about that. I could have gone with many other systems, and the ones I've come up with, certainly they were chosen for particular reasons, given the work. But they have to be there.

JP: Space is sometimes an issue. There's a woman in "In the White Night" who experiences the death of a daughter, and her husband, shortly after the death, follows her everywhere—almost as if to intercept whatever grief she may launch into. And the minute he goes to sleep, it creates that space for her to grieve, or, as the last line suggests, to make that necessary small adjustment. Do you find that as a writer you need similar space in order to relate to the characters?
AB: That's a very good observation. I never thought about it, but probably on some level, yeah.

JP: How do you relate to your characters? It seems to me that you're fascinated by the distance between author and persona.
AB: I think I just plain try to put enough information there so they're believable. I mean, I try to examine them closely—that's how I relate to them. But it certainly wouldn't be of any interest to me to be directly analytical, because I don't even think people would believe it—not the readers that I was interested in having as readers, anyway. You know, that just doesn't seem to me to be the purpose of fiction.

But believe it or not, I'm certainly trying to do a lot of things by delivering the detail or information between the lines. I hope you will realize that I might have given you the same set of facts, but in a different order. I'm trying to elicit particular emotional reactions with the stories, and I'm quite aware that the way I structure something and the way I omit things, as well as the way I include things, can create or fail to create a real world in the story.

JP: In the past you've talked about private lives and secret yearnings. Are these yearnings, in part, responsible for creating the impossible distance that separates your characters?
AB: I'm hard-pressed to think of a writer who doesn't have characters with secret longings. I mean, Raymond Carver is about nothing but longing in a lot of ways. I could think of any number of people: Tobias Wolff, Richard Ford. . . . Those unstated things that happen off the page are so often what

contemporary fiction is about. They're not empty spaces—they're referential spaces. So I don't think I'm distinguished that way from other writers.

JP: Your characters don't travel as much as they used to.
AB: That's because I travel too much.

JP: But they're still as alone as ever, still not connecting with each other, for the most part. What keeps them distant from others? Personal space? Or are yearnings the culprit?
AB: I don't know that it's just secret yearnings. I don't necessarily assume that my characters have any more social skills than me or anybody I meet. It's a problem to communicate—it's as simple as that. It's extremely difficult. I don't think that, in a lot of ways, this is a culture that really asks people to communicate. It's a culture that asks people to listen. That's why people are so hostile.

JP: In some of your early stories, the connections between characters were so tenuous that they would do anything to relate to one another. In the case of "A Vintage Thunderbird," it was the car that served as the main connection, and in another story, it was the Weimaraners. Now though, it seems as if objects are less the bond between characters than an associative method of leading them somewhere else.
AB: I think that's true. Even *Chilly Scenes of Winter* was a novel about an obsession. Charles would find external things that would remind him of Laura all the time. He took all these things to be signposts and guides. He was projecting like mad, it's as simple as that.

The whole idea of anti-materialism was much in the air when I was going to college. So if we're talking about stories that I wrote in the early or mid-seventies, I was often surrounded by a lot of people who professed not to want material possessions, or who were happy not to own furniture. It was certainly to your credit to have only what could fit in the trunk of your car, including your cat.

I saw a lot of acting-out on the part of a lot of disenfranchised people who were militant about not being ensconced in the world, who were not going to live the status-quo, who were going to have a free-wheeling existence. What they tended to do, on however sad or humorous a level, was often to fixate on their pen, or something like that. They didn't have any furniture, no fixed address, no telephone number, no way to get in touch with them, but they absolutely would have had an anxiety attack if they had lost their favorite pen! I never failed to see that, on some level—whether or not they admitted it—there was something that they held onto, and very often in an extremely exaggerated way.

So to some extent I think it was much more typical of the things that were around me at the time when I started writing. It seemed a more common, almost social preoccupation, whereas that has vanished pretty much. I don't mean that I don't still know people who live out of their cars and their trunks. I do, as a matter of fact. But not so many, and it doesn't stay interesting to keep discussing, either.

JP: Fixations point to something meaningful, don't they? For an author, as well as a character?

AB: When I was doing *The Burning House*, the copy-editor at Random House wrote me a letter saying, "You and I know these are distinct stories, but if you keep naming the characters Andrew or Andy, the clever reader is going to go through trying to zig-zag and make a pattern between these stories, so don't you want to rethink it and call Andy 'Paul' sometimes?" And that was entirely true.

She also pointed out things like—we're talking about maybe fifteen or sixteen stories—six or seven times somebody has a headache, which seems perfectly believable in terms of what people suffer in the real world, and I was always sending them off to take an Excedrin. That is, in fact, what I take. I don't take Bufferin, I don't think of it as the generic *aspirin*. I think of it as Excedrin. She said, "They're going to think you're getting a kick-back from the company. You've got to change this. Nobody would believe that every character everywhere is taking Excedrin." Point granted. I was so fixated myself that I didn't *know* I was fixated.

Essentially, I know what you're saying, and you're not talking about those small betrayals of myself—you're talking about elements of plot, that I mean people to be fixated on external things that bespeak private desires. That's true. Nevertheless, you can't be too sophisticated about it. I'd trip myself up all the time.

JP: In "The Longest Day of the Year," when the Welcome Wagon lady comes, just the sheer irony of her arriving when the marriage is in dissolution is awfully funny. But as she begins to prattle nervously, she starts talking about kids in the neighborhood. That gets her to thinking about rabbits and turtles that also used to be in the neighborhood, which gets her to thinking about the squirrel acrobatics. That leads her to recalling a traveling carnival, which leads her to recalling the animals her husband used to win for her at the carnival and at that point the narrator concludes: "I was coming to understand that she was suffering too." What tipped her off that this woman was suffering? Was it nostalgia, the process of association, a projection?

AB: To tell you the truth, I put that line in and took that line out half a dozen times. I'm still not convinced it should be there. In fact, I'm convinced that in the long run I probably made the wrong decision. I should have taken the line out. But I didn't want the woman who was being visited by the Welcome Wagon lady to seem like anyone's fool, either. I didn't want to condescend to her in any way. She just happened to be a victim in one way, and she happened to encounter someone who more overtly thought of herself as a victim. It was playing off of those two vulnerable positions and having them understand each other for what they were, but still not really being able to do anything for one another, or even to get past that without a lot of awkwardness. I certainly wanted the story to be as awkward as those real life encounters can be when somebody just starts spinning out of control and you realize that they're saying more than they want to say, than they know they're saying. That was really a consideration again of trying to figure out how to make the woman in that story not seem to be dense. That's why I gave her such an overt line.

Of course, as a writer, what I was trying to do was bring in everything from the natural world—the rabbits that used to run around before the place was so sophisticated—to the natural world in sort of an unnatural caste, the way the world looks when there's a carnival. Carnivals really are extraordinarily strange. This carnival happened to be strange not in the conventional way, but strange in terms of how the Welcome Wagon lady had to talk with the carnival man. It's almost as though, if you listen, everyone will tell their story. And it'll be slightly off the point if you believe there's just one point—that is, it'll be slightly off *your* point. It won't be slightly off their point. Does that make sense?

I realize as much as the next person that there are things that people expect to hear. Certainly, I'm that way. I'm used to people making a lot of small talk with me. Everybody is. You sort of expect that. To make the story seem real, you do have to have that level of small talk, in some way, so that you can make people comfortable enough to when you reverse the tables, they have a frame of reference. If you just launch these characters in some wild way, it would seem to me an affront, as much an affront literarily as it would be conversationally.

JP: I thought that perhaps some of your characters were just using language as a mask.

AB: Oh, that happens too. I certainly admit that. Even the story that you were talking about, "In the White Night," which begins: Don't think about a cow, don't think about a river, don't think about a car, don't think about snow. Absolutely. That's a mask for not having any real communication during the evening, and as the story goes on you find out why these people would have everything invested in *not* wishing to communicate. What painful conclusion would they arrive at if they did? Probably no conclusion, just more pain, you know? A lot of my stories are about masks, a lot of them are about the smoke screens, the facades, and so forth. Nevertheless, considering the characters, they have to vary. It did seem to me that the Welcome Wagon lady might kind of veer out of control because of who she was, in that setting. To tell you the truth, I encountered such a Welcome Wagon lady.

JP: I figured you might have.

AB: I did. I very rarely write things that are true. And it was only true to the extent that there was a lunatic Welcome Wagon lady who did come to visit near the end of my first marriage—not my third marriage, as I made it in the story. She uttered a great line that I could never use; when she unrolled the map— this is her dialogue, and I never remember dialogue verbatim, but I've remem- bered this for twelve years—she said, "I believe they have neglected to imprint the map." It would either look far out, or it would look like the writer was just writing outrageous or bad dialogue, to have someone say that. She was no idiot. She must have known she was speaking bad dialogue, but it was a mask. She was anxious, and it was a blank piece of paper. She was completely unnerved. So a lot of the stories I write, I think in some way, it's true I want to lead into things. I let people be unnerved, but it's not all going to be revealed. You have to do things externally to give a context within which the dialogue can be read.

JP: I thought it was also great use of a symbol to have her sit in the chair that her husband had neglected to properly glue—as she herself is coming unglued.

AB: You may call it a symbol, I call it my life! As Flannery O'Connor said about her character's wooden leg in "Good Country People," first and foremost, it is a wooden leg. You may want to say that it's loaded, that it's a symbol, but first and foremost, those were the lousy chairs I lived with for years. By the way, it didn't crack, and she didn't go down. But years later, I realized my anxiety was so great that I had not considered that the chair *wouldn't* break. So I wrote the story and let it happen. A retake.

JP: You do a lot of retakes with your characters.
AB: I do, yeah. I do a lot of retakes.

JP: Your stories seem so driven, at the core, by underlying emotion. I get the feeling that at the heart of a lot of your stories is a Welcome Lady who, given the right door, may just spill everything. You know?
AB: Again, that's certainly my sense of the world. I don't know if it's the case that I had a particular personality and therefore I became a writer, or if it's because now that I'm a writer, people come up and say things to me because they think they intuit a particular sensibility. I mean, it's very hard at some point to ever sort that stuff out. Whether or not I had become a writer, I think just conversationally I would still be sitting here saying to you, "It's amazing what people will say overtly." Forget about *covertly*. And it takes really very little to get them to say things that might make others uncomfortable. But we live in such a state of fear that, without realizing it, we're always putting out signals that we don't want to hear things.

If you think about the day you spend in New York City, or something like that, the cab driver has a rehearsed routine that he's going to tell you. Can you think of the last time anyone has been interested in your opinion on public transportation? And yet, everybody travels by public transportation. I just flew in today from San Francisco. No one on the plane made eye contact. Not only did they not want verbal communication, they didn't even want to acknowledge that you were sitting in the same space they were sitting in. This is something of a strange situation, really, if you sit back and just take an overview of the thing. But to tell you the truth, I do think that everybody's a volcano. And I often find out that they are. Today I was reading in the *Paris Review* an excerpt from some book that's coming out about Raymond Carver. They talked to a lot of his friends, and somebody in the course of that said that Ray always said, when the phone rang, "The phone's ringing.

The world will change." That's all it takes. I feel that same way. Otherwise, I would not have an unlisted phone number and screen calls. I do believe that the phone rings and the world changes. So naturally it would interest me to write about that happening.

JP: Your characters often draw attention to the fact that accidents often shape their lives.
AB: Or *seeming* accidents.

JP: And in one case, it's a literal accident. I can't remember the name of it, but there's one where the main character realizes that the accident was a turning point.
AB: Oh, you're right! In "What Was Mine," she has the car wreck.

JP: What about Irony and Pity, the name of your corporation? Is that a nutshell expression of how you feel toward your characters, or about the world?
AB: It's a nutshell of what I feel about being told to incorporate. Years ago I had a scandalously inept accountant who told me to do this. It's been nothing but grief ever since, but I did do that for business reasons. I had to pick a title for my so-called corporation, and you know the line, right? A friend of Jake Barnes in *The Sun Also Rises* sings, "When you're feeling. . . . Oh, give them Irony and Give them Pity"—which, when I read it, I just burst out laughing. I was probably sixteen when I read the book. Actually, my ex-husband came up with the best name. It was "Wasted Inc." That's pretty good—but the one that I came up with was Irony and Pity, because I thought it was so funny, and it stuck with me all these years.

JP: Speaking of "Wasted Inc.," I was going to get a group of over-the-hill basketball players in the university intramurals, and we were going to call ourselves "Abilities Ltd." We also had a diet contest on campus, and the English department chose, for our team name, "As I Weigh Dying."
AB: That's very good. I have no ability with puns. It's strange. And often they have to be explained to me. Those don't, but often they do.

JP: And *do* you have irony and pity flowing through your work?
AB: I hope so. I don't know that the irony is so strong. It's often remarked upon to me, but I'm not sure. There are lots of readers out there, and

I almost think that the irony isn't surprising to them. I almost think that readers take my tone as a matter of course, whereas a lot of critics are very alarmed by it, and I'm not quite sure why. It doesn't seem to me to be that shocking a thing. I think people get it very quickly when I read aloud, or even just people who have read my work privately, who talk to me. They understand the level at which it's ironic. It doesn't seem to stop them dead. It often seems to stop the critics dead.

JP: When you say "stop them dead," what do you mean?
AB: To make them analyze the work only in terms of where and when it becomes ironic, to overlook any other impetus of a piece, to speak only about where it's ironic and to form opinions and assumptions—even if they've only become personal opinions and assumptions about me based on them.

Look, here's an example: *Twin Peaks* on television. Were you shocked and amazed by *Twin Peaks*? You couldn't be; you've read literature. That was only shocking in the context of its going out to a television audience. And that audience shouldn't have been condescended to, to that point. Television, as far as I'm concerned, has always essentially condescended to the public. I think there are any number of writers who are communicating clearly to their readers—not condescending—and being understood. But it's only when people come in to do a so-called critical study of this book that they stop dead at point A, as though its remarkable. It's not remarkable. You can find irony in Flaubert.

JP: I wanted to wait until a relaxed moment to hit you with the "M-word," so to speak, since you seem to have bristled when minimalism was mentioned in previous interviews. Yet, you admit to having felt Hemingway's influence, and if Carver has been called the godfather of minimalism, Hemingway is certainly a precursor. A passage from your story, "Snow," even reads like a minimalist dictum, or a rewording of Hemingway's "Iceberg Theory" of omission.
AB: Yeah, that one's been turned around as a baseball bat a lot of times: "Any life will seem dramatic if you omit mention of most of it."

JP: That's come back to haunt you?
AB: Sure. I mean, you can always point to the sentence in a book that some critics are going to use to turn against you. And then you just think, am I really going to take it out?

JP: Why do you take it as a baseball bat, though?

AB: Because it is always invoked in a negative way, it's always been used as a dismissal. That line has never been used positively. It's only used negatively. It's only been used as a substantiation of someone's own foggy notion of what so-called minimalism is. I don't mind the comparisons. I don't mind a serious discussion about Raymond Carver, Ernest Hemingway, and me, heaven knows. I think I'm in great company. It's just that I rarely get serious discussions. And as you realize, many interviewers simply mean to be provocative: the "Oh, you're so cute if you're mad" approach.

I think most people who know me well think that I do have a pretty wild sense of humor. But I'm really serious about this writing, and maybe I was falsely protected, in that being in the academy for so many years, and graduate school, and teaching, and so forth, I don't know that people tossed things off the way a lot of interviewers do when they talk to me. I'm not sure that it isn't just a fatuous element to the process. So I don't necessarily take people at their word if they say that what they most want to talk about is minimalism. A lot of people need a drop quote. If you're talking to a journalist and they're working under deadline pressure, what do you think they're going to use as a drop quote, what do you think they're going to put in bold type? A conservative statement? An explanatory, normative statement . . . or the one outrageous thing that you said? It's almost inevitable.

JP: I don't think there's anything wrong with minimalism, except that it's been taken too far. When Carver got into his revision of "The Bath," that story about the baker, he expanded it into a larger version he'd call "A Small, Good Thing," as if to say, We've taken it a little too far.

AB: I've got to tell you the truth, though. Current information has it that what you're seeing as the second version, the longer version, was the original version. And Gordon Lish edited it, so that what you saw was Gordon's version of minimalism. It was never Raymond Carver's. Very unfortunate. And until proven otherwise, I believe that.

JP: I had a friend in graduate school who submitted a story to the *Quarterly*. It was a wonderful story, and Gordon Lish turned it into a minimalist story. He took out all the contractions and chopped it up so that it was no longer fluid, and said he'd publish it if my friend would go along with the changes. He did, of course, because he wanted to appear in a prestigious literary journal.

AB: Dreadful. There are as many bad editors as there are bad janitors. Every building isn't beautifully clean. I have a good editor, Joanie Evans, and she line-edited *Picturing Will*—she and Julie Grau, who works with her—and before that for five books I had the same editor, Rob Cowley, and he line-edited every book. He'd put down twenty chapters in my living room floor and crawl on them to see if I'd repeated an adjective from chapter one to chapter four, or if so could I combine the one from chapter four and throw out the other. Very inventive, hard-working people. Personally speaking, I realize my experience is narrow and has been exemplary. Roger Angell, at the *New Yorker*? Brilliant! An excellent eye. Ninety-some percent of the time I agree with the change Roger wants me to make. It's a terrific skill, but I've heard too many horror stories about editors who feel they have some mani-fest destiny that has very little to do with the material put in front of them not to be suspicious. So yeah, beware of the editor, until proven otherwise.

JP: Your short stories in the new collection, I don't know when they were written, but the difference in style between this collection and *Picturing Will* is just incredible. One would come under the heading of that so-called mini-malist school, and not just because it's leaving things out—because stylisti-cally you're relying on simple sentence structures, the absence of contractions, the absence of adjectives, and yet in *Picturing Will* I found myself thinking, is this the same Ann Beattie I've been reading?
AB: Well, it depends upon the situation. The treatment hopefully is particularized.

JP: When many young writers engage in what they consider minimalism, they usually combine it with their idea of Chekhovian slice-of-life, and they end up with a piece of nothing.
AB: Look, if I had to generalize, I'd say that what I dislike about a lot of so-called minimalist writing is that it has no clear trajectory. I can't look at anything if it seems that there is no coherence that I can even ferret out. My sensibility has nothing in common with that, as far as I know. I'm interested in how things are put together to form a whole. I'm really not very interested in the kind of egocentricity that I see in a lot of so-called minimalist writing. I'm not going to sit here and trash people, but I kind of wish that when Tom Wolfe wrote that piece a couple of years ago that was originally published in *Harper's*, and he was speaking, I thought, generally and rather vaguely about

the "K-Mart school of realism" and so forth. What writers does he *like* who invoke the K-Mart, and which writers does he *not*? There's a world of difference. Come on, you can't say categorically because you put the K-Mart in something, you're a faux naive or an empty-headed person. There are plenty of empty-headed writers around, but which are *not*? I would have been happier to have had names named, even if I was one of them, than to have not quite understood what his perspective was on all of this.

JP: According to theory, the final stage of any genre is self-parody. And I'm wondering if minimalism has reached the point where it has become parodic, except in the hands of people who really know what they're doing.
AB: I think even "parody" puts too nice a word on it. I don't think its parodic, I just think a lot of it is bad. When something is complex, there are ways to read between the lines. You might not agree with my interpretation, but if we sat with a Carver story, I could at least tell you where I think something is being said that isn't verbalized, and how I think he's led into that, and so on. I believe I could do that. But I don't believe any such thing without just projecting wildly or imagining some story that wasn't there with somebody who was a lesser talent than Carver. It's not the first mode to be misunderstood. You have to remember that when modernism came in, people were kicking and screaming. Now we speak about "postmodernism" as though modernism is taken for granted, and now there's this often self-referential, humorous, even parodic thing called "postmodernism." Did modernism become legitimized because there's now so-called *post* modernism? I don't think so, unless you're ignoring history.

JP: "Postmodernism" and "minimalism" are only buzz-words?
AB: Yeah, which is why I'm very ill-at-ease in having questions asked about that. If I am to take something seriously, what am I being asked?

JP: Alright. The simple sentence style, the preponderance of articles, the absence of contractions—the "I am" instead of "I'm"—what do you feel it accomplishes in a story?
AB: It has a kind of staccato effect, and it has a kind of deliberate artificiality about it that lets you know that, since you are going to *I hope* give the benefit of the doubt that the writer is not a fool, that that artifice is being invoked for a purpose.

JP: So it's almost an acknowledgement of the writer/story relationship?
AB: Yes, it is, in a way. It's a kind of tacit admission on the part of the so-called authority figure—the writer—that this is a put-up. It's literature, after all.

JP: Would you go so far as to compare this style to the impressionists—of drawing attention to the process of creation, of diminishing the illusion?
AB: I would almost compare it to the superrealists, myself. I would be more inclined to think about [Richard] Estes, or somebody. Yes, it's the natural world, but it's so *hyper*. Is there ever a moment in which you really stop to think about the world that way? I don't think so. Yes, it invites you because it looks like a photograph—I could easily think of a lot of photographers who try to do the same thing—but there are no moments in which time is frozen that are quite that perfect and complex that stay perceived for long. You may indeed pass by a store window when you least expect it and see that the light is even in a way that allows you to see reflected things, blah, blah, blah. Then you go right on. In other words, it doesn't correspond to what you really physically linger in in the real world. It does correspond to what you wish to consider aesthetically and linger in. It's a refinement and an exaggeration masquerading as being normative. And that's true a lot of the prose style you were discussing.

Carver, for instance, if you think about his sentences, they are short, declarative sentences that vary greatly in emotional intensity, or that give you sudden, sharp, shocking new information that would be difficult to verbalize. The first story in the selected stories [*Where I'm Calling From*], "Nobody Said Anything." It's about the kid that stays home from school and he has a fight with his brother. He is always the good guy, his brother is always the bad guy. The brother is made to go to school. The mother leaves, and he suddenly decides that he's going to go fishing, and he's going to do just what he wants to do. He's a pretty calculating little kid. And then it becomes rather shocking. You feel like you're also playing hookey from something. There you are, and it is as though you're watching this kid as a ghost, or something. The kid doesn't know that you, the reader, is there. It's as though you're looking through a keyhole. You know the way Carver does that, suggesting that you are looking at something extremely private? So you find out that the kid is quite calculating, the kid starts to go off fishing, stops a couple of times to masturbate, finally decides he's going to to see what he can do, meets another kid who tells him that the two of them can team up to catch a big fish.

Three-quarters of the way through that story, where you might *think* the shock was *aha*, the character of the child is being revealed, that's very inter- esting and very dramatic. And *oh*, now we're even watching the kid mastur- bate, that's even more sensational in a way. And then, wait a minute . . . there's a runway with airplanes on it. It's the last thing you ever would have expected in that story. You have, really, three-quarters of the way through that story, nothing but neutral sentences—whether they refer to shocking things or normative things. And then you find the airplane, which is more shocking than shocking, because you remember that there is a larger world and you think about the intrusion of technology and all this framing stuff that is going on in society. It pulls a million more punches than "Big Two-Hearted River," and it means to be essentially a retake of the same story. You can't help but think about Nick Adams going armed into the woods when you read that story of Carver's. I'm sure he's alluding to it.

But if you look at it, there are sentences of eight words maximum: "I walked to the water. The water was still. I heard an airplane." Wait, an air- plane? I mean, that's not counternarrative, but it is an immediate admission that there is a larger world, that you're not just looking through a keyhole. You might want to look through the keyhole, but somebody is watching you in their peripheral vision. That's the airplane. It's so beautifully constructed. It's a sentence that varies only in emotional intensity from the construct of all the preceding sentences. And when he comes back to it a second time, it's not just that the character heard a plane, but that the runway apparently is very close to where they are fishing. Well, what does that say about this sad fish that they catch? We all know that the rivers are polluted. We all know that everything—industrial parks, landing strips, whatever—are just contributing to this ecological problem. I don't think that it's a pro-ecology story, for God's sake. I'm not that simple-minded. But I think that the constant larger framework, referred to with no more emphasis on its delivery than the other things, can hit hard—can hardly fail to hit hard, if you're a good reader. It becomes another problem if people don't know how to read.

JP: So what you're trying to do, then, in your own fiction when you're using structures like that, is to achieve the equivalent of superrealism, where you have a heightened sensibility to the world at a particular moment in time?
AB: Yeah.

JP: How much forethought goes into crafting a story with that much suggestiveness or implication? Does much of the "planting" occur in rewrites?
AB: No. At this stage of my career, more than 50 percent of what I attempt to write ends up in the trash. If the stories don't start to take on a larger life, I just can't follow through. I have to be surprised in the story in the same way I'm surprised constantly in daily life—that something is said by non-sequitur or that somebody who is a minor character turns out to be a major character. Along with saying that, I have to realize that there are also a lot of things gestating that I don't realize are gestating until I sit down to write—that I'm making comparisons between things in my mind that are not factually related, and so forth. I might have an overheard conversation in a fictional setting, or that fictional setting might be tinged by something real—what my best friend's kitchen really looks like. But I tend to write about things that are so-called "real" only to the extent that they begin to transform. And if they never transform, then I feel like I'm a reporter. I feel like I'm just there to write about the interior of this room, or something like that, and that is so deadening in a fictional context that I can't continue.

JP: You say "if they don't transform," but don't you nudge them just a little?
AB: I nudge for several pages—four, five, six pages, if I'm writing a story—and then, if in spite of all my nudging, it just looks like something I could equally describe in an essay or pick up a camera and photograph, then there's nothing to be revealed with the advantages of language that we have when you're doing a story, when you do more things to build up in a particular way, where you can use imagery to be evocative.

JP: Is it a first line that will grab you, a character, a sketch, a situation?
AB: Never a situation, because that would too closely resemble plot, and I never do know that. You're right what you said earlier. It is an emotion that starts me, and then the visual image comes. The visual image may eventually be discarded. I can write several pages to orient myself to the world that I'm talking about, and then there could be a line of dialogue, and I could realize then or later that the line of dialogue is the true beginning of the story. I mean, the first forty-nine and a half pages of *Chilly Scenes of Winter* were thrown out, so that the novel now begins with a line of dialogue—in French no less—because it took forty-nine and a half pages to wade into the material, explaining how Charles and Sam came to know each other, what the

house looked liked that they lived in, blah, blah, blah. Very nice, once I know it—then I can fly.

JP: Did that happen with *Picturing Will* too?

AB: Oh, everything in the book happened with *Picturing Will,* as it were. It was very hard for me to catch on to what I was doing. I had to write a lot to see what shouldn't be written. Even when I did figure out what my notions were, and which characters were major and minor, and, to a large extent, how the book would be organized and so forth, even then it was a real problem to figure out how it could be done as directly as possible while still keeping the readers' interest.

In other words, it seemed like a book that could turn very discursive, and that would be a terrible disadvantage. It's an entire book about storytelling. Everybody tells a story. They actually sit down physically and *say* things in that book.

This is probably the first time in a novel that I so clearly let myself be the manipulator. To have dropped twenty years out of the text, you could only think it was the author's decision to do so. That was quite calculated. What could I do, though, to make that seem not like a cheap shock, or not shocking beyond the obvious shock of suddenly realizing here we are in the twenty-first century in section three, was really the question, really the hard thing to do. A lot of things to me, in the rough draft, had seemed clearer that either remained not clear or problematic to the extent that. . . . I think a lot of people were right.

A lot of friends gave me feedback on that manuscript. They knew what I had meant to write. They were very good in being able to say where I had not been clear. Case in point: I thought I had created a pretty cold Jody. Not only that, but that there was that dimension to her character rather early on. It was so much *not* there, or it was so subtly there. The opinions on Atget are not my personal opinions of Atget. I created a character who would have, as far as I'm concerned, a rather odd and insufficient response to Atget, because I meant to indicate something about her character. Point granted in retrospect. I don't think everybody's going to say, "Aha," and spring up out of his or her chair. I think I really had to go back and do what people told me and I finally went back and wrote that scene where her friend hits the deer, and you see Jody jumping out of the car and saying, in effect, I'm going to now photograph the scene for my art, and "Thank God for the invention of the auto-winder." I put that sentence in point-blank; I knew perfectly well that, at least there, I was announcing something about her character. Therefore, at the end, when you find that she is more than a little removed and more than a little egocentric, if you look back you may not think of her as simply a person under duress and trying to do a hard job as a single mother. Hopefully, in retrospect, the book will become clear. The last image gets superimposed on the first image, if you will.

JP: There's a lot of superimposition in your work.
AB: Constantly. And this one even gets to refer directly to photography, so it became lots of games within games with that book.

JP: We talked a bit about this already, but superimposition is so close to revisiting the past, of trying to make more sense of it a second time and having it come into focus.
AB: Maybe it's wish fulfillment. I mean, in point of fact I don't do that. I don't go back to see houses where I've lived.

JP: And yet your characters are, dare I say, obsessed by it?
AB: Again, I think to some extent these things are obviously personal, but in another way they really do reflect what seems to be demonstrated, to me. It's something that I think a lot of people do, but it's not autobiography.

JP: Something else in *Picturing Will* that struck me is that you included some graphic sexual scenes. That's also new territory for you, isn't it?
AB: I was absolutely shocked when the motel door closed and I realized what was going to happen. I didn't realize until that door closed what I had intuited but not verbalized to that point. We all know these people like Haveabud, who seem to be completely out of control in an almost charming way. Very egocentric and narcissistic, they are very interesting to watch from afar. Close the door on those people and, they're not any less crazy than people involved in the status quo, and often more so. So that was interesting, but that was not fun to write. I have written things on many occasions that haven't been fun to write.

JP: You were pulled along then.
AB: Yeah, feeling claustrophobic, feeling trapped—that I had led myself into my own trap that I had not articulated to myself.

JP: Does that happen in a short story as much as it does in a novel?

AB: It tends to happen on a more personal level in the short story. I don't want to write these things to personally reflect my private life. That's not the point of them at all. It tends to happen more with writing a line that is indicative of something to me. I wrote a story years ago called "Playback," and it had a garden hose, and I personally had not seen a white garden hose until very recently. I was visiting a friend's house on Long Island where there was this wonderful green lawn and millions of things to observe. I was so stunned, because I had always seen green garden hoses all my life, and I just remember the image of that glowing white hose there in the green grass.

Several years later, when I was writing about that back yard in a completely fictional context, having nothing to do with that man or with me, I remembered only then—I had forgotten it all these years—that image of the white garden hose, and as I was typing the rough draft of the story, I had the character think that it was the East Hampton equivalent of the snake in the grass. And I suddenly realized, at that point in the rough draft, that I had been writing, in effect, something that deliberately referred to the Garden of Eden and to the whole fall of man. Just to have come to that realization and to have written it so quickly, then, I guess it's almost like automatic speech or a Rorschach test, where you spontaneously say what it is that you're thinking. I couldn't help but think that was very indicative.

JP: Your world—at least the characters that you write about—has been somewhat restricted—and I hope that you don't take that in the wrong way, but. . . .

AB: I try to make my personal life as restricted as possible!

JP: What do you do to keep your writing fresh?

AB: Try to empathize with new people. To some extent, the monologues in this book, you've got everybody from a Welcome Wagon lady to guy who does installations for his brother's artwork, and so forth. Put yourself in the mind of somebody that you're not.

JP: So you don't exactly do field work like Mike Royko of the *Chicago Tribune,* who frequently goes to Billy Goat Tavern to sit and talk with the common folk?

AB: I don't ever do direct research. I mean, I don't do things thinking that I'll file the experience away and use it. I have to admit that so many things have come back to me in writing—not conspicuous things, but the overheard conversation or the ordinary detail that becomes the telling detail in the fictional context does occur to me, so I have to say that my tentacles are out, whether I mean them to be or not. I'm always knowing things I don't *know* I know until I sit down to write them. I don't even find any necessity to express them directly. I myself am amazed at how those things both reoccur and are changed by being put in a fictional context.

JP: How do you remain open to surprise and discovery as you're writing?
AB: That's a hard one. How do you? To some extent, I have to struggle more now, than when I began writing, to keep other concerns out of my mind. I never sat there thinking of pitching this to such and such magazine, or what will critic X think about this. I still don't, but so much of my life is encroached upon now in ways pertaining to writing, that it becomes harder and harder to just plain drop out for a week. Even I must admit—maybe it's my age, too—now I'm more tempted to listen to the phone, even if I put it on automatic pilot until five o'clock than I am to let the phone go for three days. Either I have not learned to manage my time very well, or I now realize it cannot be managed well. It's not any longer very interesting to shut out the world.

JP: Do you have a routine that permits you to do that?
AB: No, I have defenses, to some extent. Phone answering machines. But I do agree with Carver. If I go and take the mail from the mailman's hand—I'm not saying this facetiously, either; I've done that instead of having it dropped through the slot—and I've been absolutely amazed at what gets revealed before the mailman leaves the front door.

It's like hopping stones across a river or something, you know? It seems logical until you get out there and you realize that the river is wider than you realized, and you've only got three stones. And I think people tell their stories that way a lot. If the mailman stops to say something to me, he may mean it to be quick and anecdotal, but something either triggers something in his mind, or I look taken aback, and he goes on. And as he elaborates, like the Welcome Wagon lady he finds that he's in deeper, and it can all happen so quickly.

I think people are always vulnerable. You try to pretend that you're not and to keep that out of your conscious mind, but in point-of-fact you are. And as a writer, you really do have to—at least for the physical act of writing—sequester yourself as much as possible. It's enough that these things have been percolating in the subconscious, and hopefully will come to you when you're writing.

JP: So human connection isn't important to you?
AB: I try to forget it when I'm writing. It wouldn't be possible to write if I remembered it. Also, I must say that, with a few notable exceptions, including three damn years on *Picturing Will*, I mostly write short stories that either don't work out—and in the course of a *day* they don't work out—or else they do. I have three to five pages of rough draft very quickly. They either get abandoned right away, or they do work out. And in most cases, some very primitive sort of a rough draft exists in a matter of hours, whether it be three hours or six hours. We're talking about a fifteen-page story, not "Windy Day at the Reservoir." I can drop out for that long.

JP: How many rewrites does each story undergo now?
AB: Well, "The Longest Day of the Year" probably had six words changed. It was written in three hours. "What Was Mine," the title story of the new collection, had six or seven rewrites before it went off to the magazine.

JP: "In the White Night"?
AB: Right off the typewriter, and that's a rare exception, too, That hardly ever happens, anymore, and when it does, it's something very brief, like "Installation #6" in the new collection. I was sitting on a plane, as a matter of fact. I had very little paper, so the analogies I came up with—like the way people glare at you when your reading light goes on in the airplane, or the way the horizon line looked outside—were because I was on an airplane. I was flying from New York to Houston. I was killing time. I just had a couple of pieces of paper, so I wrote.

JP: Would it be possible to have you do a walk-through on a story?
AB: Well, the genesis of "In the White Night" . . . which, I was told after the fact, is apparently a term for a hangover. I had no idea. You have to understand, this is the same person who wrote "The Burning House" having no idea that it was the Buddhist name for the body (laughter). Didn't know it. Got to "The Burning House" by way of "ladybug, ladybug, fly away home, your house is on fire. . . ." But I can't tell you what made me sit down to write, "Don't think about a cow."

JP: That was the first line that came?

AB: Yes. I wrote a story years ago called "Dwarf House," a story in the first collection, and the first line is " 'Are you happy?' blank said, 'Because if you're happy, I'll leave you alone.' " It seems a good beginning, in retrospect, but where did that come from? Then I wrote, " 'Are you happy?' McDonald said," because I had eaten at McDonald's that night. And now there is an article that exists talking about "Ann Beattie: The Imagery of Old McDonald's Farm" and blah, blah, blah. Just amazing! Sometimes a line will pop into my mind, "Don't think about. . . ." Remember that game?

JP: To start with a line like that, a line of negation and denial or repression, pretty much summarizes what the whole story is all about.

AB: Sure, but only in retrospect did I know that.

JP: That line didn't force you to go in that direction?

AB: No. They often start with an image. Had it begun with "Matt was standing in the doorway," I think even the doorway, it doesn't say anything to the reader, particularly, but emotionally, I would see that doorway more clearly than I was describing it.

Anyway, it really did begin with "Don't think about a cow." So here was somebody saying some perplexing thing, and I had no frame of reference for it. Then you've got the next paragraph. Suddenly, I have to root him visually. I have to put him in the temporal world in some way, so I start them naming things. But I remember when I moved them out from under the protection of the Brinkleys' porch—"the cold froze the smiles on their faces"—I suddenly realized that what seemed to be the case, was not really the case at all. That's a tacit admission to the false level on which they're discussing things, if you know what I mean. The choice of the words, "the cold froze the smiles on their faces," that did something for me. Then I knew it was about cold. I knew about doorways. I knew about all sorts of stuff.

And then, "don't think about an apple," I was actually thinking of [René] Magritte's painting. I had written "don't think about a cow" just randomly, as far as I know, but then when I wrote "don't think about an apple," suddenly I was seeing that painting and wondering, why am I seeing that painting in this context? What's that doing there? Why am I putting that there? So I let it stand in the rough draft, and later we get to it. Later the light, which is red, yellow, and green—the green becomes the apple again. So there you are with the layering. Again, I'm just talking about the physical creation of the story. I'm not talking about how to deconstruct the thing, or anything like that.

JP: Your characters do exactly what you do. They free associate, going from one object to the next, one element to another, in a modified stream of consciousness.

AB: What may start as "free association," that has to stay there. But it has to intensify, then, within the free association. It has to build. I mean, there are a few thrown-in lines, but not generally speaking. At some point, I got to the turn in the story before the first space break, and here I'd written all this stuff that set the scene up, what's going on, and then I had to create my story. So then I knew my characters. I knew what they were doing now, why were they doing it, and who these people were who thought in terms of images.

I did spend time in the hospital when I was a kid. It is nothing that I ever have reason to think about, but once I had started writing this story, which had nothing to do with the way it really was in my life, I could remember my father so distinctly sitting on that hospital bed. He's a very tall man, and even as a little girl, I knew that he looked extremely foolish. And he was out of his element with the plush animals and me horribly ill in this hospital bed and my mother backed up against the door. And I just thought—well, what I never thought at the time, what I only know now, really, being an adult—is that there were unspeakable consequences to what was going on. It became, certainly, worse in the story than it did in my personal life, but "there were two images when you looked through the finder," and there certainly were, "and you had to make the adjustment yourself so that one superimposed itself on the other, and the figure suddenly leaped into clarity." So it becomes more her story, in a way, only at that point.

In retrospect, I can see that I could have anticipated. But had the man in the story not gone to sleep, it could have become his story. I could have dramatized. I could have gone from the battlefield and to the animals in the hospital bed. It could have become his story, but, in a way, because she's deferred to him all along, and everybody's out of control—the drunks are out of control, that's why they're hollering this nonsense game; the snow is out of control, because who can control snow? Her memory is out of control, because suddenly something that she knows in one context becomes almost surreal in another. When she stopped at the stoplight, the real world they occupied was out of control—so what are you going to do about illness?

The battlefield is not a random analogy. You can compare a bunch of animals thrown on the floor to many things. The stakes are high, if it's a battlefield. Those things became emotionally loaded enough to cue me as to where I was going. And in the end, I had a friend who was extremely tall, and who always slept this exact way. It had nothing to do with the world of the story, but when I started imagining what it would be like to have the father's life, I suddenly thought of my friend who was disproportionately tall, draping over everything because nothing was large enough to hold him. When the woman goes back to the fetal position at the end of the story, you know that she is regressing, then you make the analogy between her and the daughter, the young child, the younger person who died.

To some extent it started with the external world, it got very claustrophobic, it got, I hope, revelatory, and then where do you take a story from there? Back to "Go," right? Back to the outside world. But by then, hopefully, the wooden leg is loaded; the snow is more weighted than it was. It's not a neutral snow anymore. And I have to admit that I was thinking of the ending of James Joyce's "The Dead," when Gabriel Conroy goes to the window and sees the snow that's not the same snow at all. He's thinking of it as blanketing and uniting everything; I was thinking about that, about Dublin, when Conroy looked at the window at the snowman, and I thought that's interesting. Let's see what the snow means in this story.

So in effect, I just said what the snow meant. And also, snow's in a lot of my stories. That was easy to write: "the sadness set in, always unexpectedly, but so real that it was met with the instant acceptance that one gave to a snowfall." Well, that sort of brings back the normal everyday world. Who's going to get freaked out by seeing snow on the ground? But if you really think about the consequences of that, it means that the world is different, stranger, a little bit out of control. And so, hopefully, has the story been. I wanted it to be a controlled story about people who were out of control. And it only be reinforced by having the natural world be out of control.

JP: I once taught a course on "Middle-Aged Crazy: Updike, Carver and Beattie." Students, light years from their own mid-life crises, read the books as if they were fantasy. But they were fascinated by Updike's ten-year re-examinations of Rabbit Angstrom. Have you ever thought about how your characters, though you don't revisit them, have changed over the course of the years that you have written?

AB: Without realizing it, when I started writing, although I was not writing autobiography, I was writing about things that I was curious about, and I was writing about people who weren't exactly like me, but that I certainly thought on some level I understood. I was interested in an almost speculative thinking about those people. I think I've backed off that. I think now you can be speculative all you want, and that won't begin to approach the complexity of what you're dealing with. I just plain didn't know that then. I thought there was some virtue, some personal satisfaction to be taken in that kind of speculation—in going out on a limb, in imagining spacemen coming to earth to take pornographic pictures, or something like that.

When I was writing *Falling in Place*, Skylab was falling and nothing could have been a more perfect metaphor if I had invented it, and I didn't even have to invent it. But now I'm quite skeptical about those things. I don't want to go for the easy thing, even if it is the perfect thing. I'd rather go for something more off-kilter, hoping that it might reveal something in a slightly more complex way. I don't mean to totally dismiss the earlier stories, saying that they were expedient, but I now see that I was kind of bedazzled myself.

JP: The same is true of your readers, presumably.

AB: I do feel a little bit more like I realize my position as the author. I realize when I'm creating a keyhole and having people look through it. The scene in *Picturing Will* in the motel with Haveabud was, in effect, that. Where do readers stand physically in terms of these people that I'm thinking about? I don't ever think about the readers in rough draft. But as I'm trying to make the story seem very actual, then I *am* thinking about the audience. I am thinking about what should be there and where should it be and when should I go private, when should I not? I think I'm less prone to go private than I was earlier. When I was writing a story like "Downhill," I was presuming to go into the mind of an extremely disturbed woman, I would make those leaps. Fine, that's that. But now what I think I'm interested in is texture or the variance of things—counternarrative. I can't help but realize it as a calculated effect. And knowing that I'm onto myself, I don't want to overuse that device either. I'm on guard.

Generally speaking, I think that the focus is narrower now. I don't mean narrower in terms of honing in on something, but that there is a particular kind of thrust to the story that doesn't have to encompass some of the things the earlier stories had to encompass. There's a difference. Part of it is that I simply understand method better than I used to.

Ann Beattie: An Interview

Robert W. Hill and Jane Hill / 1996

From *Five Points* 1.3 (Spring/Summer 1997), 26–39. Reprinted by permission.

This interview was conducted in York, Maine, on September 13, 1996, in the home Beattie shares with her husband, the painter Lincoln Perry. Her first book, *Distortions*, a collection of stories, and *Chilly Scenes of Winter*, a novel, were published simultaneously in 1976. Since then she has published five additional novels, including *My Life, Starring Dara Falcon* (Knopf, May 1997), on which she was making final corrections at the time of the interview. She has also published four additional collections of stories and several nonfiction books on artists and photographers.

Beattie was once identified as the most imitated story writer in America and has often been called the spokesperson for her generation (she was born in Washington, D.C., in 1947). However, her work reveals a texture and complexity that such easy labels belie and a keen sense of humor and irony that her responses here verify.

RWH: I've recently reread *Another You* (1995) and literally today finished *Chilly Scenes of Winter* (1976) so that I could see the first novel and the latest published one. You spoke earlier about how much you feel you have learned about making novels in the years between those books. Could you elaborate on what you feel you've learned?

Beattie: There certainly are a lot of changes, as far as I'm concerned, and there are things in the last few books that have sort of become second nature that were not things I would have resorted to in the books before that. I think one thing is that I have stopped thinking . . . well, not wanting to be didactic . . . I've stopped thinking that unless I make things somewhat more apparent than they were in, let's say, *Chilly Scenes of Winter*, that people are necessarily going to read the books that I hope that I've written. So I think they're more directed in terms of how they're structured than the earlier books. But this wouldn't have been a concern at all. All I'm saying, basically, is not that

140

I think I could trap people or anything like that, but that it certainly is perplexing to me, and I'm always wondering if there are some concessions I can make, so that what I want to say will be more apparent; can I do that at very little expense? And the answer usually is yes.

But what it usually requires is showing something of the structure, the underlying structure of the book. I almost think of the more recent novels as being somewhat multilayered and three-dimensional, whereas the others seem to me (*Chilly Scenes*) to be only linear.

When I began, I had no feelings really. I didn't know who my audience was. I still wouldn't outguess it, in terms of saying I know who my audience is. But the idea of relying heavily on dialogue seems not only not very interesting to me, partly because it's quite easy to write, and it's quite easy to do things that proceed by using a lot of dialogue. But, for me, it's intruding myself into the text to have exposition. I didn't have that in the early books, and now I wouldn't really like not to intrude myself in the text. I mean it takes years to write these things. They're a lot of trouble. I'm not trying to have, à la Philip Roth, a character named Philip Roth standing there in my work, but I'm more willing to show my hand.

RWH: Again, because I looked at *Chilly Scenes* so recently, I noticed the technique of your having a character, say Charles, speak in dialogue and immediately correct himself silently.
AB: Oh, really?

RWH: He would say something and then immediately think that he didn't really mean that, but it was the only thing he could think of to say then, or whatever, and then he would go on. It's very smoothly done, and I was aware of how you're sort of moving in and out, layers of thinking versus layers of overt conversation. That takes another form in a work like *Falling in Place* (1980) or in *Another You*, where moving in and out means you go to the interchapters in *Falling in Place*, or with *Another You* you've got this expectation that somehow we are going to interweave the past stories from the letters with the ongoing emotional and eventful development of the other plot, the main plot.
AB: Sure. Exactly. You have to trust the writer, obviously, to do that, but when I was going through early drafts of *Another You*, I didn't have letters at the end of every chapter. I had them there intermittently. And the point was well-taken by my editor that you can play games, in fact, but you have to let people see

very overtly that it's a game. You know, there has to be some method, however subversive that method is in terms of how you're evoking them. And that was easy enough to do. The problem then was making the letters *not* a direct kind of alternative narrative to what was going on. And, you know, it's sort of one of those cases like don't think about a pink cow, or something.

It's very hard to write something you're sure *isn't* related very directly to what's gone before, and you think, oh god, you have the same sensibility, you're apt to come up with the same images, the same rhythms, and so forth. So those were hard to write and have them, as I say, not be direct and obvious commentaries on the chronology of the present.

Jane Hill: It struck me as I was reading the end of *Chilly Scenes of Winter*, and Charles is rather suddenly pouring out all of his past memories of Laura, all the details of the things that he did know about her. That was a kind of landslide, too, of a different sort, whereas *Another You* has this momentum into the main plot, the more current plot, concluding with that sort of wonderful last section, with Martine's story. There's something very similar, in a way, if not formally, structurally, that giving up a lot of information about Laura at the end of *Chilly Scenes*, and then so much clarification is given in the last section of *Another You*. Both have a sort of acceleration of pace, an acceleration of kinds of information that we get, that we are perfectly prepared for, I think, in either book.

AB: Well, it's interesting. One of the obvious things when you're writing a novel as opposed to a short story, if you're not going to deal with chronological time, you have to make it apparent that it's not just an error on your part that you're not dealing with chronological time.

But what is chronological time? In other words, if I truly repress things, and suddenly have some reason in some point in my life to either speak of those things or introspect about those things, or whatever, that seems to me as valuable a thing, or as real a thing, certainly, as so-called chronological time.

JH: . . . and as current a thing.
AB: Yeah.

JH: And *there*, it's there. It's really, truly there.
AB: Yeah, it really is there. But, to my way of thinking, it wasn't that I was playing a game with the reader in *Another You* and that I might have put that

information anywhere. I thought, no, it would really only be when Martine got to this age . . . at that point in real chronological time these things would be very likely to appear whether she wanted them to or not, in a way. So it just seemed to have some basis in chronological time, but to negate the whole concept of chronological time, or to make you question, "Well, if it's chronological time, so what?"

RWH: In a very clumsy way . . . I feel sort of sacrilegious bringing this in . . . but the way that *Bridges of Madison County* deals with letters of whoever, and the brother and sister discover all the mother's. . . .
AB: I can't say I've read it.

RWH: No . . . basically, the children receive the letters or diaries or something that the mother had written, where she explained her relationship quite easily. And they say, oh, well, this is what went on; it's sort of nice that Mom had a life of her own for a week or something. That clumsy use is . . . very instructive for the skillful incorporation of letters and the gradual discovery of the deepening of complexity that you get in *Another You*. The other is clearly a gimmick of some kind.
AB: But, of course, with mine, it's not that the right people ever notice things; it's the wrong people. It's an effect that the reader notices. But still nobody (in the novel) ever knows.

RWH: It's a wonderful touch, having those letters put under a rock under the ocean.
AB: And the way Marshall is told about that, he does a double-take: "Excuse me? what? what? what?" Yeah, that was fun to write.

RWH: I guess I can't imagine how you *imagined* that. I really am always astonished at the explosiveness and the fertility of your imagination. Things just pop up all of a sudden, and, *WOW*, I hadn't thought of that particular image, and there's no way I could have predicted that that would happen. . . . It just seemed so unutterably right—one of the astonishing things about your work, as well as the sort of accuracy of the realistic language, and all the things that you've been talked about for. I think, when you were in Japan, you said you were talked about—"Minimalism! Minimalism!"
AB: Yes!

JH: I wonder, there are five published novels, and *Love Always* (1985) happens to fall right in the middle and also coincides pretty closely, I think, with Larry McCaffery's observation about your reluctance to write about anything except the immediate present. But the question of what's the immediate present is the same thing as the chronology question.

Anyway, it's interesting and probably coincidental, I realize, that it's in *Picturing Will* (1989) and *Another You* that you move deeper into the past in bigger sections of those novels.
AB: Yeah.

JH: In *Another You*, huge parts are set before your birth so that, in a way, you're going deeper into the past even than your own experience would allow. So, as I was rereading *Love Always*, it seemed that it is a transition novel in some ways, that it moves from the sort of immediate present, as in *Falling in Place* and *Chilly Scenes*, to . . . it's certainly more in keeping with them in that it's a linear narrative, basically, of that summer, when Nicole comes to Vermont. But then it also goes back into Lucy and Jane's childhood. Some of that's in *Falling in Place*, and *Chilly Scenes*, too, of course, because Charles thinks back to his childhood memories and so on. It's not that these people are totally living in the linear present. But then the past becomes a fully developed structural part of *Picturing Will* and *Another You* in ways that you can almost see.

I guess partly it's the narrative voice getting more and more confident with moving in and out of time and being able to clue the reader: "These are not just mistakes I'm making, but part of an ongoing sense of what *is* the present and that the present takes on more and more dimension as you move through the career."
AB: Well, I'm also dealing more with people of a different spectrum of age, really, than I was, than I usually . . . well, obviously Jane and Lucy's mother is older than they, and so forth, but I mean it's right there in the same time period, really, whereas it's another world that I'm telling about in *Another You*, really a vanished world, in a way.

That's what you always have the trouble with, the problem with how to integrate these things without being arbitrary about them or hokey, like "he remembered that" or some direct flashback or something just so pitifully transparent like that.

But it's interesting, when I was doing the first draft of *Love Always*, the ending of the book was Jane and Lucy's mother talking. It's the same sort of device that I finally came back to and certainly used much better in *Another You*. But, at the time, I was persuaded that . . . well, I mean, the polite interpretation would be that it was too radical, and that it was kind of grandstanding. But I was really talked out of it on the basis that somebody whose opinion I respected said to me, "OK, you've had the whole book have a kind of staccato, a sort of implied hysteria about it, and then you get to the end, and what if the reader just thinks you're saying, 'Oh, but by the way, I'm Ann Beattie and I can write really lyrical prose: want to see it?' " Well, obviously, no, I don't want that. I mean, that's really counterproductive. And maybe that was the case, I don't know. I reshuffled it. I don't even have that draft of the novel anymore, but I had one friend who argued particularly strongly for it. And she was very happy to see *Another You* take the form it did.

But I think maybe I do agree with my friend who cautioned me. I think that wasn't the time or the place to do it, but it was an idea that stayed in the back of my mind. Of course, it's always so interesting who gets the last word. *That's* the novel. I mean, who gets the last word in life? Probably the nurse's aide or something like that. But who gets the last word in a novel is very important.

JH: Even in *Chilly Scenes*, which has the most tightly limited point of view of any of the novels, it's Laura's story that gets the last word. Charles doesn't even get the last word in that novel.
AB: Yeah. He keeps telling someone else.

JH: So technically it's a person the reader doesn't even know, in whatever way readers know characters. But then in all the other novels, there are any number of people who could have had the last word.
AB: Uh-huh.

JH: That becomes a huge decision about what the effect of the novel will ultimately be on the reader. The last word, the last image, or whatever.
AB: Yeah.

RWH: How much do you, as you are rethinking how to do the novel, and getting ready to do another novel, how much of your energy is given to conscious conception of a structure for the novel as opposed to a structure that emerges from the story?

AB: Oh. it emerges from the story, but I suppose there are certain constants about me, a distinct sensibility, in a way, in that I do look at, sometimes, things that are very oblique being very determining forces and subtext being more important than text . . . you know, in things like that, just because, I suppose it is as simple as that it is my view of the world. Inevitably and, I think, with less reluctance now because I'm older, and as I feel slightly more adept at what I'm doing, those things are going to be *right there*, to be examined rather than to seem hunches and stay buried in my mind. They come out in other ways.

So I don't usually have structure in my mind when I start a novel. For example, these letters were not even initially part of *Another You*. I thought that what I was going to do was have some mid-section that really would transpire in a different time frame. But, again, that was *so* artificial. I mean, before I got one page of it written, I knew that was dead wrong.

RWH: George Garrett's *Elizabeth and James*, I think, does a little bit of. . . .
AB: Yes. George is great at that.

RWH: . . . what you decided not to do, actually, which was just to set a section in another time. And then move. . . .
AB: Yes. If you can pull it off, you can pull it off, and George certainly does pull it off.

RWH: Yes. I hadn't thought about it until you were describing it that way.
AB: But that always is a question for me because I am always writing in the present, and what do you do that hasn't been done a thousand times before that might seem very convincing, within this particular work, to evoke the past?

RWH: I understand how distant incidental pieces of writing can become, but I've recently reread much of the text, not all but much of the text, in the Katz book (1987) and also your introductory essay in *Flesh and Blood* (1992), which is particularly fresh in my mind because one of the things that you said rang a bell. You talked about how as a writer you appreciate those photographs. As a writer, you wanted to be able to convey a sense of the form, the understructure, sort of the skeleton, the superstructure, without demystifying the clothing, that is, of the outer area. That's a wonderful statement.

Somehow it reminds me of what you were just saying about keeping a certain sensibility and yet still somehow having conveyed to the reader . . . It's like a symphonic composer. You have to convey that these little turns and surprises are, in fact, on purpose, so you repeat them . . . at least once to say: yes, I did that particular dissonant progression on purpose. It wasn't a mistake in the orchestra or whatever. And it could be the same sort of thing with writing. It struck me that your sense of the implicit narrative that lies under art, and photography, is very congenial with your aesthetic theory about writing.

AB: Oh, I don't think these things to be definitive. I might be more apt to think of that about something that I read than about some thing that I'd written. At all times it's in the back of my mind, too, not to disparage what I'm doing, in some ways, that this is just what it is: this is a story, not over-complicated, not always successful. It's a book—just a book. It's not anything anybody can carry around and rethink their life from, directly. I mean, if they want to, that's very nice. I highly doubt that such thoughts are all in the text a lot of the time.

But the tacit admission that it is artifice seems to me to be more and more necessary to put there. And I like that about photography, too. That is why I'm so attracted to it a lot of the time, because it seems to be a quickly captured moment, and yet, if you could find out the stories behind the pictures that you would take to be that, inevitably they're not. Inevitably they're posed. The exposure's been taken repeatedly; the person's gone to the site, repeatedly, and so forth. Why not say that that's involved in the process and it's still a great photograph. Does it matter that *Moon over Hernandez New Mexico* wasn't snapped with an Instamatic? Nobody thinks about that, really.

But that whole thing about process, you know, that's so overwhelming to the artist. I sort of wonder why that isn't more a topic of discussion, in effect, within the work itself.

RWH: Well, partly because, I guess, that certain kinds of artists—I think of ballet dancers—who work particularly hard to show that something is effortless, that it's important to them to appear not to be breathing hard or not to be straining, that if you show strain then somehow that immediately undercuts the effect. I think there is a tradition in art that it must appear artless in some way. And it *is* fraudulent.

AB: I think often the discussion is what you're saying, but I think of little girls always being told by their mothers when they're getting too ga-ga about the ballet, "Well, you should see their feet! You don't know how long they have to practice. You don't know how many are anorexic. You don't know." And now we even have all this documentary evidence that all these things are true. It tempers it, you know, it does; it's meant to temper it. It's somebody saying, in effect, something pretty nasty: You can't have your illusions, you know? But I'm pretty tempted to say to people you can't have your illusion either.

RWH: Actually, I agree with that position very much, but I'm also very much aware of readers, students, particularly college students, and others, the general reading population, who want in effect to sort of give themselves up to whatever the illusion is of the world of a book. They give up to that world and *escape* into it—that's a common word that's used—or they just want entertainment, that sort of expression, and then, what that implies is that we want *not* to be aware, with this sort of skeptical eye, of the feet of the ballerina. We want to go and have the lights fool us into thinking that people are actually floating and flying.
AB: But, with that, it's filed away.

RWH: I agree, really, I do. But then I am reminded of—is it Charles (in *Chilly Scenes*)?—who says something like "I just know too much," something like that? Wishing he could push back, but he just knows too much. I noticed that Jane had underlined that sentence in her text.

This constant flood of memory for people who have that kind of memory, and that sort of constant inescapability of human experience for some people, is something that other people really, first of all, can't experience and really can't figure out why you would need to. What's the value of being skeptical and thoughtful and somehow straining after a book that they think of as entertaining?
JH: Which suggests something about you can't *have* your illusion. Having re-read some of your novels in the last couple of weeks, I wonder if you would talk a little about *The Great Gatsby. Chilly Scenes* and *Love Always* strain very openly to connect to *The Great Gatsby.* . . . It happens very late in *Chilly Scenes* when, I guess, Sam says to Charles, "What is this, some Gatsby thing you think, where there's a green light at her house?" or whatever.

And then on the second page of *Love Always* somebody says about Ruthie, she's kind of a woman like that woman in *Gatsby*, or whatever, and then the Gatsby thing gets worked out in more detail later in the novel. And my reading of *The Great Gatsby* is that it's a book that says exactly that—you can't *have*, or *possess* is maybe a better word, you can't possess the illusion. That's the point of *The Great Gatsby*.

Are you conscious of *Gatsby* as a part of that structure under those novels?
AB: Yeah, absolutely. In a way, there's the American myth, and then there's Gatsby's revision of the American myth, but I think that's become more dominant, in a lot of ways, in the culture, than the initial naive myth itself.

I'm not a hundred percent sure, though. I mean, I think a lot of people might just read *The Great Gatsby* and think it's too bad it turned out that way in the end. They would think it's something other than what it is. And I think they read the same book you and I read and think, well, that's a tragedy.

JH: The ending of *Love Always* . . . I mean, the choice about where to end the story. To have him in bed with the recorder, watching the video . . . if I were writing a critical essay about that decision, I might say, that's the late twentieth-century version of "and so we beat on, boats against the current," the ending of *The Great Gatsby*, you know. We're striving for that sense of wonder Fitzgerald says the earliest explorers must have felt. So we sleep with some-body else, which becomes this constant going back, striving, for an illusion. But at the same time we construct the situation so we're not allowed the illu-sion. And it did not occur to me the first time I read *Love Always*, how much it is about *Gatsby*, and how much the title is from Gatsby's deluded notion about Daisy.
AB: You can't recapture the past. Why, of course, you can't. . . .

JH: Well, but Gatsby says, Why not? Of course, you can.
AB: Exactly. there you have something being telegraphed to the reader. I mean, if you're reading that totally, if you're reading that correctly, you understand what Nick Carraway is doing there. This isn't just Gatsby talking to himself in his kitchen, or something like that. I mean, if you see why it's framed as it's framed. You know, you read that with one intonation, and if you're reading blind to those things, then Gatsby tells the truth. And that's the fatal flaw: Gatsby tells us that Gatsby tells the truth.

JH: Of course, once I started thinking about this, for Jane (in *Love Always*) to be killed on a motorcycle in a traffic accident, at almost the same structural point in the novel that Myrtle is killed in *Gatsby*, and then for Lucy to be left to sort of clean up the mess in much the way that Nick Carraway is left to do that . . . the parallels make *Love Always* a commentary on the American dream and the American novel sort of simultaneously.

AB: That's why I can't help but invoke it. I mean, its almost as though, yes, I understand there's a predecessor for what I'm doing, I'll just put my cards on the table here. I don't see how you can get away from that book.

JH: When I was reading and I was talking to Bob about this, I was saying that the flap copy of the paperback of *Chilly Scenes* talks about Hemingway and influence. And in the McCaffery interview he talks about Hemingway, and you say, yes, of course, I'm aware that there are influences on my style here. And Irony and Pity (the corporation under which Beattie's work is copyrighted) is a Hemingway reference.

But your subject matter seems much more Fitzgerald-connected than Hemingway-connected, and that just hadn't occurred to me at a really conscious level until I started re-reading *Love Always*.

RWH: And Hemingway has a much more cramped approach to getting information out in some way that I find unsatisfying, in contrast to Fitzgerald, where you do have a sense that there's this genuine, almost generous spirit of the giving of the book, giving out to you in some way. Instead of this sort of parsimony somehow about it, that it's not just the clean, stark style, but there's something that always struck me as sort of mean-spirited and withholding somehow, unlike, at the wildest extreme, you have Faulkner and Wolfe—that sort of giving, giving, giving. But with Hemingway something else is happening. Your work seems much more like Fitzgerald's on this point.

AB: Fitzgerald is really giving those series of images, the way things are juxtaposed. That's not anything particularly meaningful to Hemingway. He'll repeat something or something will augment in terms of its importance or whatever. But Fitzgerald is much more interested in pastiche, in a way. And I probably got that from him. So am I, but again it's a question of temperament: and it does seem to mean that that's the way things come out. I think that there are certain Hemingway stories that, if you were to see them as a photograph, they'd be almost parodic, they'd be so wildly apparent.

I mean, you see "Big Two-Hearted River" and you see the natural landscape, and then you see the guy's brought whatever he's brought, a bottle of champagne and his imported sardines or something like that. Yes, it's a cheap irony . . . you get it right away. I don't think there are any cheap ironies. When I think of the rainbow of shirts in *Gatsby*, and so forth, those things continue to come at you. That doesn't seem like a cheap-shot photograph. That seems something you could look at forever and you can't figure out, you know, because the boundaries are other than in the photograph.

RWH: It's even a wild scene in the Redford movie. The shirt scene is one of those things that your critical awareness goes out the window when it comes at you. You don't even have to think about that. You're just sort of overwhelmed.
AB: He's very good at that.

RWH: How do you see your short stories in relation to the novels? You suggested that you see a difference in the stories of *Distortions* (1976) and those of *Burning House* (1982). I wonder if you see a similar progression, something that's running parallel, collaboratively, with your story-making as with your novels.
AB: You mean the stories vis-à-vis the novels? Gee. I don't know. It's not as though I sit around thinking about these things. But I wouldn't think so. I really wouldn't think so. I wouldn't at all. In other words, because I'm not very upset about the notion of chronological time to begin with when I'm writing a story, I always feel automatically that with one big thing, one big potential liability, I'm in effect off the hook to begin with. That alone—and I'm not saying everyone is equally traumatized by that—but that's a big one for me to get around, knowing that I have to grapple with that. And I can't think of anything else that's that categorically that much of an issue.

RWH: When you have very, very short stories and very long stories, do the long stories seek a different audience, a different market?
AB: No, because I just figure nobody'll publish them. I must admit I may be proven wrong, but it still seems to me that they could come out in book form. It's just that nobody will have read them before they read the book. For all intents and purposes, I mean, I can think of exceptions. *Ploughshares* just printed a very long story. *Salmagundi* is printing a long story, but the national magazines won't touch the length that I'm writing now. And I'm still writing them, I mean, because I can't do other than what I'm doing. I'm a little perplexed myself, but it's not because I think, oh no, my markets dried up.

I mean, I've written a lot of twenty-page stories that I've been very attached to but that have been consistently rejected everywhere. So it's not as though I feel if only I had written this at half the length it would be a shoe-in somewhere. Probably not, you know.

RWH: Well, let me sort of redirect the question that I asked a minute ago. Do you think that you're writing longer stories as you are developing your expertise as a novelist? I mean, you've said yourself you're developing a sense of the novel, and is this in a way also leading you to deal with more complex, longer stories?
AB: I wouldn't be the one to answer that. I wouldn't be able to introspect about that. I don't really know if that's the case at all. If anything, I think it's sort of a change in me, and that it's getting projected onto the material. I don't mean that sentence by sentence I think I'm more long-winded.

I hope that it isn't as simple as that, you know. But I guess that I do think more and more that mysteries . . . it takes a while to convince somebody that a mystery is really a mystery, whereas before I would have taken that as a foregone conclusion, and. . . . Who knows why?

JH: I think, just thinking of the story in *Ploughshares*, that it goes back to what you were saying about being more willing at some level at this stage in your career to show your hand. But part of showing your hand comes with the fact that, in terms of content, there's less that's definitive to show. I mean, in that story, it takes a really long time. . . .
AB: Yes, I do believe that. I do believe that, in fact.

JH: There are lots of things that could have been pursued as a shorter story, more in keeping with what you wrote twenty years ago, maybe. . . .
AB: Yeah, yeah.

JH: . . . but there's some connection of all these things that is even more mysterious than the sort of crystalline exploration of one of them, and there's no way you could anticipate in the first, say, ten pages of that story, the image that would end it. The two characters that the story focuses on at the end have literally not had any connection throughout. As you're showing your hand more and more, it's partly because there's some sense that what there is to show definitively is less and less clear.

RWH: Or less and less interesting to you. And if it's less interesting to you, then it's just not worth being shown.

JH: I would say there are three, maybe four, potential stories that you could have developed sort of left-handedly as a story that you would have written fifteen years ago, maybe. But that's probably not as interesting as the intersection of all of those modes.

AB: Absolutely true.

JH: I just read that story last night, and I have to go back and think about it, but that also suggests why the story has to be longer, to a certain extent. Because part of what's going on is the narrative present working toward some comprehension that I can show as much of what I think about this as is in this story, but really I can't show anything definitively or clearly.

AB: And yet put many things there so that people know you don't think one of them is definitive. If you put one there, they're very apt to think it's something definitive.

JH: It would be read the way an earlier story might be read.

AB: There were times . . . one thing leaps to mind when you say that . . . I remember when I was writing the story "Shifting," which was written in the late seventies . . . quite a long time ago . . . but then, I did have a very . . . I'm at a loss for a better word . . . lyrical, it seemed to me, ending, and I was just intuiting because I never knew specifically what the ending would be. In the long paragraph that comes at the end of "Shifting," she's thinking again about this piece of sculpture, and you know, if she were an artist she could slide her hands down and do whatever, whatever—I knew it was so good, and it would serve so perfectly, but I just couldn't do it. I just couldn't. And I wrote the whole thing. And look at it without the last line, it's fine. It's absolutely fine. You know, it's *too* shapely. It's deceitful, too shapely.

And I remember sitting there and thinking, boy, if I don't get an ending within two minutes, the whole story's gone. And I really had the feeling I wasn't going to get it in two minutes. And initially the first line of the story didn't help me because . . . now it's something like the girl's name was Natalie and the man's name was whatever. That got added when I went from the ending back to the beginning.

But see, then I would have bracketed. . . . I bracketed it then. I wouldn't bracket that now. You're right, I'd just gone off into left field in a way, to prove my point. And that's very well said, but suddenly I realized what I had to say was, "This was in 1979, Philadelphia." Yeah.

Information's in, it's all over, but what's the information? You know what I mean, raising so many questions in that. But it's very . . . and sometimes . . . too, the story "The Working Girl." I guess I just got tired of being adept. You just have to be terribly critical of yourself . . . I'm probably not critical enough. But that was really a kind of primer on how a conventional story might be written, saying that this, I hoped, it was not. Almost a Q&A sort of situation. So that chomping at the bit from moment to moment and feeling uneasy about what I was doing even in the story form, to say nothing of novels.

But you're quite right that the way to say that things are very, very complex is to, in effect, do a multi-paneled painting, not to do one painting with all these things in it, and you hope you include enough to carry all the connotations you want. Usually you can't. How can you? There still is only one perspective.

JH: And the implications of the next conclusion there go back to "I know too much." Even though it's a multi-paneled painting, someone's mind still has to be holding it all in the structure, however loose or arbitrary that structure seems, and so at some level that's where the artifice comes in. While all of this is complex and multi-faceted, there's also an intelligence—and presumably, if the story works, at least two: the writer's and the reader's—that are able to hold it all there and see it as artificially revealing something that really can't be revealed.

AB: Which probably doesn't negate it, but, nevertheless, at the same time, you do hold it in part of your mind that this is also artificial.

And the same thing totally too with those sections in *Falling in Place* that really sound like notes for most of them. Some of them are meant to be slightly more shocking, and more worked over, than others. But basically they're intrusions that might have been there all along if you knew this person's perspective or if you knew the complexity of that situation that you don't yet know, or whatever, on and on. And really it's a way of starting for me, I'm sure I have told you that. I was writing so fast, the rough draft, that I was making notes to myself and I suddenly thought, the notes have an immediacy and a relevance that I wouldn't possibly know and why should I try to integrate them into the text? They're my notes.

And it's much more artificial, say, if Donald Barthelme's writing *Snow White*, and suddenly there's a quiz: What do you think of the characters so far? I think that's very amusing. I mean it's a device that's overused, and generally I'm not taken with metafiction at all. But I must admit that the first time I read that book I thought that was incredibly radical and *just* the way to make that point. I really thought that was smart.

JH: My graduate students who studied *Falling in Place* this spring found the italicized sections of the novel to be the key to their relationship with the narrative presence of the book. They found them gestures of intimacy and help and attached—and this is what's interesting to me about the artifice thing because their link to the main storyline, not to mention the italics, calls attention to the artifice of the book as a printed thing and so on.
AB: Yeah, exactly.

JH: Yet they found them almost like—I'm paraphrasing their language, of course—whispered asides *just* to them, which they found much more intimate in the way they want a book to he intimate with them than the longer, to my mind, much more rationally meaningful—you know, if you really just want to know who these people are and what they're doing, the Roman-type sections probably give you more to hang on to. I think at times that they saw the italicized sections as very much part of the narrator's relationship with the reader: you and I understand deeply what we've just read or are about to read in ways these characters couldn't possibly know and understand.
AB: Snapshots versus portraits.

RWH: To some extent you have an opposite effect in the letters of *Another You*, where there's a sense of objectified distance somehow, that the letters are there and they come in and introduce more mystery. And it's even in another kind of language and clearly in another kind of time. You're carrying along here not the sense that I'm going to go deeper into this immediate situation, but that I'm backed away now and I'm clearly going to draw two lines and I hope they'll come together and I hope I will understand at some point.

So that pushing us away is a very effective thing there. It's more, maybe a little more, like Steinbeck's effect, when he has those interchapters, where he's suddenly shifting to a natural scene: let's objectify this human condition and

put it out there. You're saying, in part, let's objectify, let's show the human foreshadowing of what we're doing here in this past time and past language.
AB: Yeah.

JH: It has struck me as I've been thinking about your work that there's the whole "spokesperson of one's generation" thing. And there's a deep and profound irony in the fact that when the generation that one is the spokesperson for seizes control of the academy that the first thing they do is proclaim the kind of fiction you write is not what we really should be studying or talking about.

It's a real jam to be in if one's work is one's work, and to have been, I guess, embraced, only then to be told you're too much like us, you have nothing significant to say.

I'm being hyperbolic to a certain extent, but does that ever cross your mind? Does that ever just seem incredibly weird to you?
AB: Ah. . . .

RWH: Politics and deconstruction and all that. The people of this generation are those who've taken theory more seriously than fiction in some cases.
JH: And your upper-middle-class baby-boomer kids who now think the only literature worth reading is about anything except upper-middle-class baby-boomer people. It's like, that's my literature; therefore, it must not be discussed, or something. That seems pretty weird to me.
AB: Part of my answer is that, maybe as opposed to what I'm doing with form, which isn't—I'm not deconstructing when I'm writing. I'm augmenting when I'm writing, actually, or doing variations, or doing whatever, improvisations and things like that. It doesn't seem, well, for example, why would this criticism be directed at me but not at Don DeLillo? First of all, no one is tempted to deconstruct Don DeLillo. You know why?

JH: It's too hard?
AB: They take it to be overtly political. That would be my quick answer as to why he doesn't come into this. Not that I think our writing is anything alike. But I think what a strange thing that people haven't fallen into the trap of trying to do that. But, no, they wouldn't because they can see its social connection. They mistake, I think, its social connection, but I think I understand what it is that they're perceiving.

JH: I was saying to Bob when we were talking about this, you know, the whole cultural materialist approach to literature, and we have to talk about race, class, and gender. And I've talked to people about your work who say your work has nothing to do with any of that. And I'll agree that it has little to do with race. But it has everything to do with class and gender in an infinite number of ways. Maybe it's that it has to do with the class that critics are most likely to belong to, and so the class they're least willing to discuss. At least that's my theory there.

AB: Interesting. That's interesting.

JH: And whatever questions it raises about gender—the exact people that would be leading the discussion of race, class, and gender want to think they have all that straight, they're beyond that discussion, when your fiction illustrates that no, those people aren't any more beyond that discussion. . . .

AB: Uh-huh.

JH: . . . than. . . .

RWH: . . . well, in their lives. . . .

JH: . . . the teeming masses, or whatever.

RWH: If you know any of these critics, if you know these academics, then you know their lives are not nearly so orderly and righteous.

JH: One other thing I'm continually amazed at, and *Another You* is the perfect example of this, to have lived on the periphery of the academy, how dead on the portrait of the academy is, and the president of the university, when the donor comes and they have the sherry in the board room. . . .

AB: Well, I think the academy understood it was being indicted in that book. I don't think they felt they were being found out. They just thought, we've already been indicted better by Alison Lurie in *The War Between the Tates*. And then they went through every so-called academic novel, whereas my friend Michael Silverblatt said, "People repeatedly mistake setting for theme in your work."

JH: Yes.

AB: They do. They do. Obviously, if I'd wanted to have something rooted on the college campus or transpiring there, I wouldn't have written *that* book. But I didn't realize how much of a red flag it was, and frankly—I admit it—it led it to be so misperceived that if I had it to do over again, I would have set it in an advertising agency.

JH: Or any other environment.

AB: Any other environment. It was interchangeable. I mean, you can find other situations in which it's very likely that a very young person will be the protégé of a much older person. I mean, it just leaped to mind, of course, because the hierarchy is right there in the academy. So, in effect, it's not only a world I know, but it was kind of expedient. And I thought, well, that's obviously not what I'm looking at, and I need to find some profession for somebody who's very inward and who has the sort of life of the mind that's a sort of blunted life of the mind, need just to set up these polarities in terms of age and so on and so forth. Obviously, it would jump into anybody's mind.

JH: Then it would be an obvious misreading to say that this is an academic novel trying to expose the hypocrisies and foibles of the academy, because that's just setting?

AB: Yeah.

JH: Not what the novel is about?

AB: Oh yeah. You don't hear Professor Lawford in there giving his lectures, or anything like that. It's all just, you know, he's chomping at the bit—talk about chomping at the bit—he's out of there every time he can be out of there. I actually added that chapter. I was advised, very strongly, that there was not enough reality to Marshall in terms of what he really did in the world, other than floating truth. So in a way I'd been my own worst enemy. I wanted a floater, and I had a floater.

But, again, you have to make people—the reader—you have to make them close enough to your character that they're really going to think of this as a real character. So I had to do *something* that pertained, and I certainly was not going to do the stock classroom scene or the fighting with colleagues scene or the whatever scene. . . .

RWH: The tenure fight.

AB: Yeah, the tenure fight. At least it wasn't that. It was one of those sort of odd backroom things that do go on all the time, but that people outside the academy don't necessarily know go on all the time. But it wasn't even in there when it was turned in to the publisher.

RWH: To what extent do you feel that you're consciously part of this development and undoing and development again of the novel as American, as an American enterprise? Do you see yourself, I mean not just *The Great Gatsby* or in connection with Fitzgerald, but as part of the ongoing business of making novels—that's not just the right word—well, the artistic effort, the artistic enterprise, of making the novel of America in the last twenty years? And do you see yourself bouncing off of other kinds of novels? You mentioned DeLillo. . . .

AB: I see myself admiring other novels, and it's hard to tell. . . . I tend to find these other novels reinforcing rather than something that I'm a part of. In other words, I don't really see any common denominator between Tim O'Brien's *In the Lake of the Woods* and Don DeLillo's *Mao II.* I mean, I could force the issue and, you know, they're not totally unrelated or whatever. But I suppose that I certainly don't think that in being at odds with the form of the novel that I'm wrestling with something that other people I admire aren't wrestling with. In terms of our level of success, I don't know, I mean, I'm sure I've said to you before, I'm not my own favorite writer. I mean, I'm most excited if there's a new book out by Tim O'Brien, not if there's a new book out by me. It's the truth.

I just don't think in those terms. I wouldn't know. Even people who are appreciative don't tend to speak to me in terms of placing me or to tell me what they think, vis-à-vis other people they are reading. They might mention, and they do mention, other writers. I mean, I can tell pretty quickly when somebody comes up and means to compliment me and they tell me what else they're reading, and I clearly am the best of that lot, I'm not so complimented. You know what I mean?

But if people come up, and they've got this cast of stars that they're reading, as far as I'm concerned, then I'm very happy to be in that company. But they're not measuring me in terms of those people. And I guess I think of the people that I really admire, who have such distinctive world vision—like Stephen Millhauser would be another one—I think of them as working such particular territory, and then my question is, is the form of that book, is the whole delivery of that book appropriate to what they're trying to do, given the *somewhat* sameness of their concerns?

And the same thing with me, I suppose. But I don't tend to compare them to each other; I tend to compare them in terms of their own work, with the rest of their work.

JH: In the McCaffery interview, you talk about being in graduate school—I thought this was great, and this may be the difference in someone who winds up being a critic and someone who winds up being a writer—that you would read all these books, these novels, and they were wonderful, and then you would have to go and ask. . . .

AB: What time period they were in?

JH: . . . were these written at the same time and, that sort of compartmentalizing and saying, OK, the eighteenth-century novel is this, for these reasons. . . .

AB: Yes. Yes.

JH: . . . and . . . that's why you didn't finish graduate school because, why do *this*?

AB: Yeah.

JH: And it seems what you're saying here is that you read each book on its own terms.

RWH: Well, within a writer's context.

JH: The first question is, is the form of this book the obvious and best connection for the material with this writer's perspective and so on? So that's looking at novels as discrete creations rather than this linear story of the novel as it evolves. But I thought that was so funny.

AB: I haven't changed.

RWH: Jane and I were talking about writers that you specifically mention in your own novels. Fitzgerald is one, but Jane Austen is mentioned often, and Henry James is mentioned often. . . .

JH: . . . Mr. Yeats.

RWH: Mr. Yeats, who has a very limited novelistic career. We also had begun to talk about strong similarities with William Dean Howells. Do you know Howells' work? Have you read Howells?

AB: No.

RWH: Because there really are some very interesting similarities that make your work. . . .

AB: Wasn't he always upset about money?

RWH: That's Melville who was always so upset about money. I don't know about Howells, whether he was or not, but he had a long career with realism, and his attitude about realism and his writing about the middle class, sort of the defining subject matter for the realist novel. It wasn't a grudging toleration of those people that he wrote about. There was a genuine affection for them, and recognition of their difficulties, their foibles, their limitations, their whatever. And you really have that, too. You have a genuine generosity, compassion, or, maybe I'm tilting the word a little too far, a sense of not just tolerating to put up with, but a genuine entering into middle-class, upper-middle-class territory that a lot of writers can only be—T. C. Boyle and others—can only be cynical and bitter about. And it seems to me you don't do that with your skepticism.

JH: Just come out and say what you think about T. C. Boyle.

RWH: Is this wrong? So I guess I'm thinking Jane Austen does that, too, in a certain way, but she deals with a more narrowly defined set of people, a narrower class than you do.

AB: Yes.

RWH: James . . . Jane basically corrected me on this . . . she said, James really does aspire to the upper-upper more, but he seems to be condescending to the middle. But you really deal well with those people in a way that is reminiscent of Howells. You do have a more brilliant lyric gift.

AB: Yes. Howells. . . .

RWH: The lyrical gift is not part of Howells.

AB: I hadn't heard that it was. Maybe that's what kept me away.

JH: I also think that in *Love Always*, the conversation between Piggy Proctor and the doctor, when he has to go and identify Jane's body, where he learns that there was this poet that the name *Passionate Intensity* [a soap opera in Beattie's novel] is from is a wonderful conversation. He keeps trying to work the conversation back around to that poet guy and that line from the poem. That could also be read . . . the subtext of that could be read as a conversation with your readers to that point, and that many of your readers might be Piggy Proctor . . . who might have consumed these texts assuming that there's just this surface but there are references and sort of an awareness of a tradition of literature. . . .

AB: Right.

JH: . . . on which these texts are built. . . .
AB: Right.

JH: . . . that just kind of misses them.
AB: Yeah.

JH: And not even that they would resent having it pointed out because Piggy seems like perfectly thrilled at this idea, but he also seems ticked off that they're paying this writer who just stole all his ideas. The subtext there is partly about, again, the relationship between creator or writer and audience, and Piggy Proctor seems perhaps. . . .
AB: Well, I wasn't aware of it. . . .

JH: . . . a type of reader that every writer must encounter.
RWH: No reader out there is going to have the full literary context of what you have. Nobody. Because you've read, in combination, things that nobody else has ever read.
AB: Right.

RWH: So, I guess part of the good-humored tolerance I was getting to earlier is that even in points of the reader's ignorance, you seem to be okay about that, it doesn't seem to be so . . . you're not shaking your finger at everybody for just *not knowing* all of those things, in the same way that you fairly glibly make references to popular culture and so forth throughout that there's no way that a lot of people are going to have reference to the particular items you name.
JH: But because *Passionate Intensity* is a soap opera, it's obviously intended in the novel to be working on two levels because there are the people who "read" it and are deeply moved . . . But then there's the writer . . . and if the doctor watched *Passionate Intensity*, but he doesn't. . . . they can understand that there's a joke going on here. And part of the problem is that the doctor and the writer don't connect. The doctor has to talk to Piggy Proctor, and he says "WHAT?" And the writer has to talk to Piggy Proctor and he's going "WHAT?" So the joke gets lost unless the reader gets it. There's something there about how people react to your work in general, I think. They think because the mystery of the surface is preserved, there's nothing but the surface.
AB: Uh-huh.

JH: There's a foundation and a skeleton and a texture upon which. . . .
AB: So that is the danger. That's certainly the danger. If you do it very well, that's the danger.

JH: That, and the assumption that also seems to be there, even for readers who would know, who would read that scene from a more informed perspective, but that again who think there's nothing political going on here, that there's no statement being made about the culture. That lack of recognition, that misunderstanding, I have to term it, is just a mystery to me.
AB: Yeah.

JH: I don't understand why those two things don't connect.
AB: Well, similarly, the mere presence of a Piggy Proctor, named Piggy Proctor, is *clearly* an alteration of tone. I mean that is something that jumped out of a Tom Boyle novel. I mean, come on.

RWH: Or John Irving.
JH: Or in *Love Always*, there's the scene very early, where you write the whole summary of the year's episodes of the soap opera: the series has ended and this is the situation that Nicole is in. And the prose there is so different from anything else in the book. You've got this writing in a certain mode. And then, of course, Cindy's letters are another mode entirely, and the juxtaposition of that with the other things that happen in the novel would suggest that certain comments are being made here. . . .
AB: Yeah. Yeah.

JH: . . . and not just that these are *real* things. In other words, the linear time thing is deceptive because the linear time suggests that all of these things are simultaneous and equal to a certain extent, but the real idea is that there are all these gradations and fluctuations.
AB: Well, John Updike didn't miss it. Updike reviewed the book and talked about why it was extremely serious and picked up the tone of everything, as he would. So, I don't know, again, it becomes a question of what can you do? I mean, what are you going to do? Lose John Updike in order to convince some other people. . . .

JH: . . . Piggy Proctor. . . .
AB: Exactly.

RWH: When you—and I know you've done interviews, and you've certainly had newspaper reporters and questions at book clubs and you've taught classes and all of those things—are there questions or patterns of questions that you keep running into that suggest that people really don't understand what's going on in some of your work, that you wish you could sort of pound the table and say, "No, no, no. You need to get this"?

AB: The ones that puzzle me, that do keep coming at me, don't really have to do with the work *per se.* No, because people don't tend to ask those questions in an audience.

RWH: They want to know when you write during the day?

AB: Yes, in fact. If I were teaching someone, they might come up and say I read your story thus and such, and you know the ending? Maybe somebody in an audience that doesn't particularly like the ending might say I don't understand how to read the ending, or something like that. That sort of thing happens. But I'm not giving so many readings and running into that so habitually that that really takes me aback all that much.

No. I think basically that implied in a lot of the questions—and I wouldn't assume at all that it's necessarily restricted to me; I'm *sure* it isn't restricted to me—what people want is for you to tell them that you are like them. You are very much like them. You have not *seemed* to be like them, but you're up on that stage, and they're projecting wildly onto you. They love or hate your clothes. They think you're a millionaire or that you're in desperate straits. You know, there's no in-between, no gray area. You are not a gray person. You are a black or white person up there on that stage, and they are very nervous that you are up on that stage. You didn't put yourself there *really*, you know. Somebody brought you in. Somebody flew you in. You didn't just fly in to be there and get to be there. It makes them very nervous. And often they like you very much and/or your work, or they come around to like your work very much. I mean . . . to digress briefly, I can't tell you the number of times I went to Raymond Carver readings and saw people coming out hugely changed, saying, I GET IT! You know . . . same thing with Donald Barthelme. Once they heard him, once they saw him and heard him and realized that he was dead-panning, and it was okay to laugh, HAH! the relief was palpable!

But the thing I'm always telling my writing students, which relates to this, is that people will always want you to spend a lot of time assuaging their personal anxiety. You don't have time to do that. You're worried enough about, are you going to sell this? You don't need to have somebody say, do you know

the statistics? You probably won't sell this, what will you do? You just
don't need to have these things verbalized. Well, that is a slightly obvious
example, but, in effect, people are always saying—categorically—you almost
don't exist. Well, this is true, anybody who's freelance in the United States,
anybody who does the career for many, many years, anybody who doesn't
have a teaching position, or some other position they're doing, or married
to someone who has money, or with someone who has money, blah, blah,
blah. It is highly unusual. So what they're saying to you is, you're highly
unusual: account for yourself. Well, you've only got so much energy. Why
should you?

   This is easier to say to young people because I'm really rooting for them.
I don't think I can change the perceptions of somebody my age. I mean,
I don't take other writers aside and say, you know, you're pissing in the wind
bothering to answer these people. You know, it's not going to get them anywhere, and it doesn't do anything for you if you're rude to them. But I do
think that there is a point when you can still say this to younger writers. You
really can tell them that they don't need to assuage other people's anxieties.
And, furthermore, it's next to impossible to do because the people will then
become nervous with the next person who's on the stage. They take it from
the top all over again.

JH: It's not permanent about the interaction between an audience and a person reading his or her work, that an individual person must. . . .
AB: . . . account. . . .

JH: . . . undertake this process of accountability to the audience.
AB: Yes. Yes.

RWH: I wonder to what extent that is affected by people's relationship to television. That is, they can't get Phil Donahue or somebody to come into their
house literally although. . . .
AB: But you think they'd . . . look at the reaction to somebody like Oprah
Winfrey. There you go. Statistics tell us that when Oprah looks slim and
lovely, people are made very nervous. She loses an audience. When Oprah
puts on weight again, the audience is right back with Oprah. You know?

RWH: It is amazing. It's similar to what you're saying. . . .
AB: Uh-huh.

RWH: . . . they want you somehow to be them.

AB: You could be a version of them. That's all right. You could say, I'm you, but I spend more time indulging my creative impulses than you do. And then you can even say things about your life like, well, I don't have a job. I don't have children. I did indeed plan it that way. But, in point of fact, you see, I have twelve hours a day that you don't. Whoo! But then, on to the next case. Wait a minute! What's your story? You know what I mean? As long as there's anybody left to look at them, they're going to have the same amount of anxiety.

JH: When you read in Atlanta—and you may not remember this—but you were reading from *Picturing Will*, and a woman in the audience stood up and said, "I thank you very much for coming and reading to us, but, really, why did you have to put this child-molestation in the book?" And I think what was behind that question was that she wanted you to stop.

AB: I made one faux pas, one faux pas, and in the future, I should do it differently—that's the implication. Right.

JH: And she wanted you to assure her that this was just fiction and for the purposes of plot or something. . . .

RWH: And that you mightn't do it in the future. . . .

JH: Right. That you would never write about such ugly subject matter again. But it was obvious from your answer that you were saying, well, this really happens in the world and that you're just observing the world around you. And I'm sure that answer was very unsettling to her because it did not indicate to her, first of all, that you agreed with her views about the world. . . .

AB: Oh, uh-huh.

JH: . . . but there was no way that you and she were going to meet on common ground about this issue. . . .

AB: Uh-huh.

JH: . . . and that her needs had very little to do with art or your reading or you.

AB: Oh, she would be just as upset if she were reading an essay and someone dropped a very dirty word into the essay and the rest of it were eloquent.

JH: Yes, it had everything to do with her and her wanting her version of the world confirmed. It is sort of an odd thing to ask of an author.

AB: Oh, but even people who've been out publicly, I think that they, too, are of two minds. I think they do want to be personally validated. They want to connect with it, and they want to say, yes, I already knew that. But, of course, you're no good if you're writing things that people already know. And so they'll come as close as they can, well, that's sort of like what happened to my neighbor. It didn't happen to me . . . it's sort of like what happened to my neighbor. But then, now, you as a person, you in effect did that. To have written it is synonymous to them with having done that. And then they want you to answer very quickly, why did you do that? And they want to say of the neighbor, why are you the sort of person that you are, but of course you can't say it to the neighbor. You have to say, would you take my paper in?

So they think that it's a more public mode, in a way, and that you're sort of a stand-in for all these other people, too, that they want to be validated by but that actually, because they're real people, only confuse them. But you, since you have created you—they think the work is you—since you've created you, just, then, tell me exactly what goes into the recipe and why you decided on those ingredients, as though there's some objective way to *exactly* make an apple pie.

JH: But it's also, I think, one of the things that makes people uncomfortable about your work. It starts in the novels—certainly with *Chilly Scenes*, where you make the protagonist male—and then in every novel after that there are these multiple perspectives and it's really hard even to say who the protagonist of the novel is. That even if you show your hand more and more, they're less and less able to say who you are. . . .

AB: Uh-huh. Uh-huh.

JH: . . . and part of their purpose in reading fiction, I think, is to think that they know the author personally, and so, because your fiction doesn't invite . . . they can't make a one-to-one correspondence: oh, Charles is Ann Beattie.

AB: Uh-huh.

JH: That expectation is constantly undercut by your fiction.

AB: I think you're right. I do think you're right.

JH: So that when you appear before them, it's even more important, more imperative to find out what the recipe is, who you are, because they can't really even speculate what the ingredients are to a certain extent. Whereas, if John Updike stands up and reads the story about the man who's roughly John Updike's age and his feelings about his religious faith are waning, or whatever, they assume that Oh, poor John, the church hasn't gone well for him. Whether that's true or false is not material; they think they understand . . .

AB: They're categorically reassured.

JH: Right. And if you subvert that expectation or your work subverts that expectation . . .

AB: Well, I tell you, you must be right because the novel that I just finished, that I turned in to the publisher, was actually—it was actually said to me by someone that, well, thank God, now, I, a woman, was writing a story about a woman. And, in fact, I'm writing a story about a woman who has an involvement, not a romantic involvement, but a great involvement with another woman. This all pans out! As though this was calculated, too.

JH: At long last she is revealing the recipe for who Ann Beattie is!

AB: Uh-huh. Now this person, I assure you, is not personally that dumb because he is in marketing.

Apparently it was a big problem of *Another You* that a woman was writing about a man. There are quite a lot of women in the book, you know. I do understand that Marshall is a guy. But it seems almost an occasion to talk about the intense effect of women on everyone's life. Other women, men, everything. That's what it seemed, if anything, I thought that was the orientation of the book. But the bottom line was that I was a woman writing about a man.

JH: I did that paper on the Uccello story, and I wrote the guy and sent him the abstract, and he called me and said, oh, we must have this. I hardly think of her as a woman at all.

AB: I know, you wrote me.

JH: I mean, the panel was about women writers . . . and he went berserk because it suddenly dawned on him that you were a woman writer. Oh—we could have Ann Beattie! I mean, what do you say to these people? It's not like you have an androgynous name. You're not like Flannery O'Connor and your name would. . . .

AB: Yeah, I know well, I know. . . .

RWH: There are so many misunderstandings that float around . . . maybe that's part of the mystery or whatever. But I'm always amazed when people don't understand that you are funny . . . you know, that there's something super-serious about. . . .

AB: They usually do when they come to a reading.

RWH: Exactly. That reminds me of what you said about Carver. Hear Carver read, hear Barthelme read, and hear Ann Beattie read, and you say, oh, this is really funny. But I've been in class, and I've had to say, Does everybody understand? Lighten up a little bit. This is a funny line here. And for some reason they want to come to it with this too-serious quality. I don't know. Maybe it's that surface we talked about.

JH: But this also goes back to the whole politics and gender thing because the presumption is that a woman writer writing in the late twentieth century, if she will be discussed and marketable, taken seriously as a woman writer, must be writing a book that can be labeled from page one as a woman's book . . . and will pursue woman's subject matter, woman's themes, whatever those are. And, again, your career, your novels have pretty much defied that expectation, on the surface at least. . . .

AB: And so, to some extent, I've lost out commercially. I have.

JH: Well, at some level one writes the books one has to write. And what can one do?

AB: Sure.

RWH: And the proper audience finds it. It does. It has.

Author Ann Beattie Lives in the Sunshine, but Writes in, and from, the Dark

Margaria Fichtner / 1998

From the *Miami Herald*, 17 May 1998. Reprinted by permission.

KEY WEST—"You think I'm cheerful?" Ann Beattie asks, jerking her head forward, clearly exasperated.

For half an hour, Beattie, unquestionably one of U.S. literature's most adept explorers and interpreters of the unraveling edges of life, has talked with patience and candor about her work, her readers, her new collection of stories and her attachment to this old resort town where she and her husband, the painter Lincoln Perry, now spend more than half the year.

Beattie is, in fact, a great talker. Her lilting tic of elevating statements into questions—"So it's kind of interesting?" "That didn't come as a surprise to me?"—is inexplicably soothing. And like the sputter of a moped on the street out front or the unnerving scream of the caged bird in a neighbor's garden, her tumbling words and staccato laughter weave smoothly into the ambient undertones of this spring morning.

Almost before you know it, you have a string of stories: about Beattie's turn-of-the-century farmhouse in Maine; about the course on the unreliable narrator she taught as a graduate student ("I used *The Good Soldier* and Andre Gide, and I put in Rose Kennedy's *Times to Remember . . .*"), even about the BULLS—rubber stamp with which she decorated students' papers. "It got so tiresome writing marginal comments that were polite about things that at bottom you just shouldn't have to be polite about. I was spoken to harshly by my teaching supervisor more than once. I probably should have had a stamp that said STOP. I suppose that would have been better."

What else would have been better: Your last question, if it had been less clumsily framed—What cheers you up?, say, instead of the odious What makes you cheerful?

"Actually, I would have to say I'm a pretty dark person," Beattie insists. "My husband often describes himself as a short-term optimist and a long-term pessimist. In other words, he thinks that the Earth is a goner; Planet Earth is gone, but he's never really worried about the next day. I'm the exact opposite. I think, 'Oh, tomorrow. Oh, God.' I have a good sense of humor. I'm a sociable person, and I'm much better when I'm with other people than when I'm left alone. But I certainly am a moody and, I would say, not very happy person.

"I'm not kidding. I am writing about the things that trouble and puzzle me more than the things I think, 'Oh, I understand this,' . . . I don't think I've got it figured out at all. I think I know what to do that I think is a clear avoidance of pain, and I think I understand what things do please me, writing among them. But it's with some effort. Those stories don't come out of great optimism."

Even readers only marginally acquainted with the inarticulated longings; the fraught, grabbed dialogue; the ambiguous endings and troubled, passive characters that to varying degrees typify Beattie's stories and six novels will find much to move and perturb them in her latest effort, *Park City: New and Selected Stories.*

Beattie fans will welcome the collection not only as a showcase for the timeless qualities inherent in its best-known early dramas—"Dwarf House," "The Lawn Party," "A Vintage Thunderbird" among them—but also as disconcerting evidence that although Beattie's characters have survived to almost the end of this post-everything decade, not much has changed for the better.

And although many of the people who inhabit the collection's more recent stories have drifted, as the fifty-year-old Beattie herself has, into a more or less conventional, secure middle age of nice cars, remote controls and other reassuring props of the status quo, they continue to drift in lonely orbits, conversing in scary non sequiturs, self-absorbed but clueless. They are specimens of detachment, indirection and unease:

An English-literature professor makes the student he is dating read his 1,200-page novel before he admits to her that he is married. Another man has MOM tattooed on his arm because he is mad at his wife and, besides, her name—Angelina—is too long to fit inside the scrollwork. Someone else buys a pair of lavender panties for his wife even though they have been separated since her old boyfriend moved "right into the house" to recuperate from brain surgery.

A woman tries to fine-tune her screenplay about Thomas Jefferson's servant/lover Sally Hemmings, which originally began "with the mounted heads of animal trophies brought back by Lewis and Clark that were hung on the walls at Monticello talking to each other about the odd goings on at night." And, in the "The Siamese Twins Go Snorkeling," set in Key West, a rudderless bartender/housesitter named Harry DeKroll, whose aspirations center on his daily hit of cafe con leche and the novel he will never finish, transforms a sponge into sculpture and plays pranks with a trick phone that makes him sound like a girl.

Where does Beattie find such people? Why? The well-dressed woman she once spotted sitting on the curb, sobbing, at Key West's airport ("What do you assume? You assume she might have hurt herself, right?") may never make it into print, but then again—

"I think what's captivating to me is something that's all around, that on some level I either empathize with or can't come to terms with," she says. "Something that provokes a fairly strong reaction and yet isn't my life."

Born in Washington, D.C., Beattie was a "painfully shy, very quiet, very introverted" only child in an adult-oriented setting. Her father was an administrator with the government, "and because my parents liked me a lot, they never would have considered hiring a baby sitter. If they went visiting for the evening, I went along, so I'm sure that helped me to be the fly on the wall. I'm sure that from my child's perspective I stored away a lot that I wouldn't necessarily if I'd been home with the baby sitter watching the tube."

Beattie started to write as a graduate student living in Eastford, Connecticut, "a working-class town most people still have never heard of. It had an ax-handle factory and a woodworking shop. I was . . . living in a house with a bunch of other people, and what I wrote about was what I saw every day. It's not to say this is 'Ann goes to the ax-handle factory' or something facile like that, but on some level . . . if you do go to the ax-handle factory there are more common denominators around than you sometimes think. It's incredibly easy to find genuine common ground.

"And that's what these stories are. They're the same thing I would do in conversation if thrown together with somebody who potentially interested me, who had a life that seemed extremely different than mine, but that on some level some part of me would connect with.

"I have no trouble with connecting with disenfranchised characters. If you take a story like "The Siamese Twins Go Snorkeling," no, in fact it is not my worst fear that one day I will wake up and be completely out of my mind and only able to go out and get a cafe con leche. I don't think I'm that precarious, but . . . I believe the precariousness is real, and there are some aspects of it that I understand very well.

"I'm flying by the seat of my pants, too. I don't have any guarantees. I've also chosen Key West, and I do, to some extent, see myself as a marginal person. Examining people who are more marginal than I am to see how they've put things together is very illuminating."

How she puts things together can be, too. "I don't really know what I'm writing a lot of times when I go into something," she says. ". . . I think that when I first start dealing with images I have an intuition about how far they'll radiate. . . . It's like doing the set for a play." And then like directing it. Folded into *Park City* is a piece called "Waiting," which started out as a story about a woman whose husband has taken off across country and whose dog has died. "But I had to bring the dog back to life. I realized that what she was going through was so horrible I didn't need to have the burial of the dog at story's end."

And when Beattie was writing her novel *Falling in Place*, "my hands went off the keyboard" when young John Joel shot his sister, Mary. "I didn't know he was going to shoot her until a page or two before . . . so when it happened, I knew it was absolutely dismaying but completely correct. But then I thought, 'Now where? She's dead!' and it really took me longer than the average bear, probably an hour of deep thought, to realize, 'No, you can be shot and just be wounded. I can resurrect her.'"

Park City, due in stores in early June, reprises twenty-eight selections from previous collections and adds eight new ones. The title story and two others—the murky, hilarious "Cosmos" and "Windy Day at the Reservoir," in which the death of a retarded man becomes a metaphor for everyone else's disillusionment—are really novellas, evidence of the once-minimalist Beattie's drift into more complex forms.

"I thought of the early stories often as being a kind of snapshot," Beattie says. "But for whatever reason—maybe I'm just getting long-winded in my old age—there's more exposition now. I don't know why it's more interesting to me to say more things rather than less and have them be, as I hoped they were in the early days, absolutely loaded with meaning. Now, I don't think you have to load things quite so extremely. You don't have to crop the picture quite so severely."

Beattie is sitting on the sunny second-floor deck of the house she and Perry co-own with a friend. She first came to Key West in 1982 on vacation, and the town routinely crops up as a destination or reference point in her work. Her last novel, *My Life, Starring Dara Falcon* which was so severely trashed Beattie "felt I'd been kicked in the teeth, and my head's still ringing," begins "I was stretched out on a lounge by the pool at a hotel in Key West when I found out the news. . . ."

More news: Beattie is at work on her seventh novel. When it is finished, she will hand it to Perry, "and then I sit right down across from him and look at him like"—staring—"this. If he goes like this"—scratches her nose—"I think he's bored. . . . He's helpful, because he'll say, 'I know what you should do,' and the idea is so bad that I'll think, God, I can't do that and it puts me in such a panic that I immediately come up with some alternative."

But now, Beattie is sitting across from you. She writes in a cozy former guest room at the other end of the house, past the white stuffed gorilla clad in her old tattered nightgown and the doormat that says You Are Here. Always Beattie has told us Pay Attention to the Small Things, to the routine, indirect and pixilated details, to the pink-dyed hard-boiled eggs that are someone's idea of a breakfast treat, to the snowflakes that fall "like wadded-up tissues headed for the trash," to the small pink baby shoe glued to a taxi's dashboard, to the two dozen awful black-blue tulips someone else has sneaked out of the house at night to plant in the geranium bed. They are life's tumble and drift. They build character and characters.

"You have to get these characters to be intimate to the reader," Beattie says. "I don't expect you to like them. I can't actually say that I like them. In fact, the older I get the less inclined I would be to have Mr. DeKroll over for a cup of cafe con leche at my house, I'll tell you. But at the end of the story I would hope that the reader would think that this isn't just some kind of aberration.

As the whole story transpires, I want them to realize that this is something to think about. They don't have to come to the conclusion, 'and I like it,' because I don't come to that conclusion. I come to the conclusion 'it disturbs me,' and that's why I wrote the story to begin with."

Ann Beattie at Home

Dawn Trouard / 2004

The interview was conducted over two extended sessions on October 1–2 in the Maine summer home of Ann Beattie and her husband, artist Lincoln Perry. Beattie was expecting the page proofs for her eighth short story collection, *Follies* (Scribner). She has published seven novels in addition to her work on painters and photographers. Beattie is the Edgar Allan Poe Professor of Literature and Creative Writing at the University of Virginia.

The house itself is full of light, eclectic décor, and assorted constellations of books, sculpture, photos, paintings, and toys. Life was very much in-progress and Beattie's pleasure in her marriage and the work she does is palpable. The couple was preparing for their annual winter relocation to Florida and the house was in various stages of departure. The interview was punctuated by Perry's occasional appearance in a doorway to corroborate a story, embellish an account, or provide sustenance.

DT: Of your three homes, the last place I expected to meet with you was the one in Maine. What's it like living amongst Mainers?

AB: Like being a ghost. I mean, sometimes I say to my husband when I look at *Preservation* magazine and see those little ads in the back for what look like wonderful Georgian mansions in Tennessee and they're fifty-five thousand dollars, I think that's what we should do. That's what we should do! And he says, "What do you like about that?" and I say, "Nobody would know where we were, and we wouldn't even have to have a telephone." He says, "Well, you could take your telephone out, and that *is* the life you live in Maine." It's quite true. I think if you don't have a history with the place and you don't have any easy way to connect, like having kids in school, or a need to be part of certain groups, you can have a great deal of anonymity.

DT: Can you have too much anonymity?

AB: [smiling slyly] I really have pretty much failed in making friends.

175

DT: Is there a book store in this town?

AB: No. But a lot of books appear FedEx, delivered right into my hands because publishers send me books. And I order from Amazon and I go into Cambridge once a year. I shop in Harvard Square for books, then I have dinner with Don Lee and he drives me back to the bus. He can't believe that I won't drive in Boston.

DT: Even with your map and phone directions, I had to stop four times to get help from locals just to find this road. I missed it three times. It seems they haven't made it all that easy to even get to you.

AB: No, but it's not about making it easy. In Maine, it's really, really not about making it easy.

DT: Does that carry over to householding? I notice that you have lots of projects around the place—the garage, some work by your porch? Are these your projects or are they couple projects?

AB: They're not all my projects. Sometimes I have a project that isn't Lincoln's, but he's a Gemini, so often he has a project that isn't mine. I was on record as saying that as far as I was concerned the garage could fall into the ground and we could park in the driveway, rather than pay to do all the repairs. It was endless. So finally Lincoln wrote a check to pay for the garage repair. I still have a very bad relationship with the garage. We're still waiting for the patio guy. We've had several appointments. He's supposed to come. But he never actually does.

DT: And is writing a check the same as getting someone to come do the work here?

AB: Very rarely, unless it's over a certain sum, can you get anyone to come do any work under any circumstances. And, if so, not during the time period they said. We waited three years to have the outside of our house painted.

DT: Was there a waiting list? How selective are the house painters in Maine?

AB: I don't think they liked the colors.

DT: And, do they give preferences to Mainers?

AB: I can only assume [laughing]. I can only assume.

DT: So of the areas not under construction, do you have a favorite space in this home?

AB: The living room is nice, and I love the color of the walls, but it will always be the living room, you know? I can't get over the fact that it's the living room and therefore I almost always avoid it. Except in cold months when it's very nice to be warm in the living room. I like the kitchen in some ways because you can see in many different directions, and also because it's the mail sorting room and there's room on the walls for paintings I really like, instead of spice racks, or whatever we're supposed to have in there. I also don't feel that there are any particular things required of me in the kitchen, though every now and then my husband looks very hopeful that I might cook. There's a kitchen island but there's not a table or chairs or anything like that, and I wouldn't want them. I like to lean on the island like it's a big flat lectern, though there are a few stools for people to sit on if they want. I like to feel like I'm improvising. We've even lugged the TV onto the porch, hooked up lots of extension cords, and simulated our own drive-in movie theater. The changing light through the summer viewed from the porch is one of our favorite things.

DT: [Laughing] Would it help your wait list ranking if you make Maine news? "Couple torched among pigs with faulty electrical hook-ups."

AB: [Laughing] We're very attached to the pig lights on the porch. They're the last things I put away when we close the house, and when they're put up again, it indicates that summer has arrived.

[At this point the door bell rings and the longed for semi-mythical patio man arrives.]

DT: With three residences, do you have different supplies and favorite things in each house? Do you have duplicate libraries?

AB: Well, believe it or not, one triplicate is a grammar book [laughing]. I occasionally need to check something before I send a piece in, so I do have a copy of Harcourt Brace . . .

DT: Standard bible?

AB: Yes, the very standard bible. I have that everywhere. I think I probably have a book of mythology everywhere. I probably have *Grimm's Fairy Tales* everywhere too. I know I have Flannery O'Connor's *Mystery and Manners* at all three places, I know I have a collection of essays with Joan Didion's "Why I Write" in it. I think it's called *The Writer on Her Work*. It has very good essays in it. I can never tell when I'll be called upon to write something and there are certain little touchstone essays that are just so wonderful that even though I remember them pretty well, I think "Oh great, Didion would be the perfect source to look at for that." *The Great Gatsby* is in all three houses. But works of fiction tend to be one place or another in order to thwart me, because they're never where I need them. Of course with Lincoln the essential reference work would be the Atlas.

DT: I noticed that in addition to the strings of pig lights around your porch that you have dragon flies in the first floor bath. Is there a theme?

AB: No, I love toys and I do think they are visually exciting, and they serve the purpose of undercutting any notions I have of seriousness. So does our friends' dog, Sandy, who comes to stay for a month or so every summer. I would feel inhibited, having nothing but nice antiques. I sort of equate formality with things that are expected of me. Artists don't usually want to deal with such things; they really don't like expectations. I'm an odd mixture in that I do like things to be in their place, and I like to have comfortable chairs, but I like rugs to be as wildly patterned as possible and houseplants to be from nowhere in the region. It's my temperament: I try to undercut seriousness as much as possible. And also, I love odd little things, whether it's a series of photographs of someone I don't know, or some lamp that has a story attached to it (my lamps have quite good stories attached to them), or something absurd, like the frog pitcher that reminds me of the way Pavarotti stands when he's going for the high notes that our friends Bob and Jane gave us. There's almost nothing anywhere we live that doesn't have a story. I've always had a cluttered desk, and everything, everything, is meaningful. In fact, if I'm going someplace new, like the time Lincoln and I spent a couple of months in Rome, I take along a panoramic picture of my Maine desk because I know it'll reassure me that I can make a big mess again on a new desk and everything will be okay.

The photograph has to do for a while, because how could I immediately find fifty amusing things in Rome to make an instant landslide? As a joke, once, I went out and bought lots of vegetables and draped my Missoni scarf over a corner of Lincoln's drafting table and had an instant still life set up for him to paint when he came back.

DT: Does the clutter calm you or does it play a role in your writing?

AB: When I'm writing, I find that when I can't see the details of what I'm writing about distinctly any more, it helps if I can actually move my eyes to something real, something I can appropriate. If it's right in front of me, it'll do for the moment. The writing may be revised—the artichoke might disappear—but in the moment, it will keep me going. At some point, if things are distinct but become too disembodied, it's helpful just to be able to look at the simplest thing—a little vase or a framed photograph or something like that; they're "grab things" and they're the little life rafts that keep the story afloat. More often than not, they stay in the final version.

DT: Do you advise your students to keep clutter or just tell them about "grab things?"

AB: I do try to indicate to them the point at which I start to feel either that things are too vague, or that I've become too myopic as a reader. That's usually the result of the writer keeping the external world too much at bay. In other words, there need to be little moments of chaos: those erratic little intrusions you always experience when you least want to in real life. What I try to do is get them to avoid writing things that are hermetically sealed; to find places where they might open up a story with a bit of randomness or an overheard song or a flower pot that falls for no reason. The story can't really go out of control, but there has to be the possibility that it might. It's a sort of wink given by the writer to the reader that the writer knows perfectly well he or she is working within narrow parameters, but that there is a larger world. I question extreme order all the time in the fiction writers' stories. They make fun of me, of course. They'll put in one sentence, almost like they're throwing me a bone, almost as mockery: "At this point comma a bird flew by the window." I'm made much fun of for saying, "No bird ever flies past the window? The character has looked toward the window three times. What has the character seen?" These are small things and they sound funny in paraphrase, but of course I'm also expressing my philosophy of the story. If the unexpected starts to intrude in the lives of the characters, too, the uncontainability of life tends to make the story more convincing.

DT: Did you get such practical advice from your teachers?

AB: I did get very astute marginal notes from J. D. O'Hara, who taught at the University of Connecticut, though he wasn't my teacher. I was scared to take a class with him. I'd be even more scared this many years later. Frank Turaj, who taught me in undergraduate school, persuaded me very subtly to learn to read, and J. D. O'Hara was invaluable in letting me know what I might aspire to as a writer. His notes were absolutely wonderful because I could look at them privately, I could look at them in my own time, I could understand without embarrassment, especially after I began to catch on to what his way of reading was and what he was looking for. I admired it, and he really taught me a lot.

DT: How did he get a hold of your stories? I'm picturing him skulking about saying, "Give me that story. . . ."
AB: Almost true. He stopped me in the hallway one day and said that he understood I was a short story writer. I was a graduate student—B minus all the way—but another student had told him my real love was writing stories. He said he'd be curious to see what I wrote. So I gave him a story and he crossed out lines, asked questions, put the story back in my mailbox, and then I gave him another story and he did the same thing, and finally we had a real editor/writer relationship going. It was incredibly kind of him. I try to remember that, not so much when I'm teaching (though probably my students wish I would remember), but those times I might be able to do a young writer a favor.

DT: I know you were doing doctoral work in literature when you broke through as a writer. Do you believe going to a Writing Program benefits aspiring writers?
AB: Look at the numbers of MFA programs these days. You're talking to somebody who avoids the expectations she feels people have of her in her own living room. There are so many of these programs now, and there's no going back. Of course there are good things about them and there are bad things about them. If I'd known I wanted to spend my life writing, I wonder if it would've occurred to me to go to a Creative Writing Program. I'll never know, because it wasn't at all clear to me (and that's no reflection on my students it is clear to), that I was going to find writing stories so endlessly interesting. I wasn't thinking about specializing in that way; I was thinking about what period of literature I might specialize in. I was also avoiding work. I'm really glad I had all that reading time. Maybe it would have been better if I'd been part of a writing program, but I was lucky enough to do okay being lost.

Now, an immoderate number of people are rushing into MFA programs. It's obvious that it's an industry that is sustaining and perpetuating itself. A few years ago when I met Patricia Hampl in Prague she made an extremely good point. She said something like, "Because the regular curriculum is so theory-driven, students who want to study literature have started going into Creative Writing because you're still reading the book at hand; you're still talking about formal concerns about how that book was put together." I hadn't gone back to teaching at that point and I was surprised by the information.

DT: My biggest frustration with your reviewers has been how often they miss your comedy or balk—or almost disapprove—at the overwhelming ironies you capture. Forget appreciation for how your sentences pop or the stunning emphasis of the finales. What do you do with student writers to help them get irony, humor, emphasis?

AB: Even though they're writers, I work with them almost continually as readers. There are good things and bad things about going to readings, but writers who are good readers of their work do help students understand not only what they're hearing, but by extension, how that keen hearing can lead to good writing. I can remember some audiences, years ago, who were rather hostile to Donald Barthelme's stories. Once they heard his delivery, though, once they got the tone, they felt relief, and they were rolling in the aisles. And believe it or not, even after constant exposure, not everyone understands Raymond Carver's tone. At first, many people had a tin ear for Carver; they had no idea that within these very serious stories there were hilarious, deliberately irreverent moments. And there were. They got it when Carver read, too. So, in some ways you want them to hear their own voices, but you also hope they'll hear echoes of other voices worth admiring. It's fine if they want to sit in their room and read their own stories out loud, but they also have to develop that ability to hear when they've done it right and when they've done it wrong. In general, beginning writers are rather afraid of humor, because it's potentially so unmanageable and also sometimes so unrecognizable, even to them.

I think very often when students read a confusing line they do notice that it's different than other lines, off-kilter, but humor isn't the first thing they think of. They fear the writer has made a faux pas. A student will say, "Wait a minute, this is really weird, why does the character say something so dumb?" It's okay to ask the question, but asking also takes you farther away from the spontaneous, instinctive response the writer means to elicit. Don't overlook the obvious. The writer wrote a deliberately silly sentence so you'd laugh. The writer did it because writing good dialogue gets boring. Or because he knew his girlfriend would like it that she got the joke. It's as simple as that.

DT: So, maybe part of the solution is Jon Stewart needs to start a reading club to teach reading. Forget Oprah.

AB: Oh, that would be great! Jon Stewart has an automatic advantage in that it's visual and he can give you a sidelong look, or he can put his head in his hands, or he can roll his eyes and express emotion without relying on words. He shows a clip of something inherently absurd, he lets just the right amount of time transpire, then he communicates with expression, rather than with words. But that's not analogous to how people read, unless you train them to read that way: "Wait a minute, pause after that paragraph, be Jon Stewart after you've read that paragraph and then you might be on the track of what the writer is trying to do."

DT: So, maybe the handbooks that accompany literature anthologies should provide stage directions instead of fact-based questions about the story. Or *The Daily Show* could produce handbooks for literature.

AB: Yes. I'm sure Jon Stewart's questions to go with a story would only enlarge the story. So often the questions developed for stories are terribly reductive and absolutely unanswerable—even by the author. I actually think it would be a great idea to have philosophers and your mechanic writing the questions.

Sometimes you can get quite far into a discussion about a story before you realize they haven't understood something on a very basic level. Or if something's a satire and based on something else. I'm guilty of it, myself. I just tend to teach things that I do get. One of the funniest teaching stories I have happened when I taught a story by Frederick Barthelme that I really like called "Box Step." I was not communicating with the students very well, I could tell. The problem finally occurred to me. I looked at these young kids and said, "You know what the box step is, right?" They shook their heads no, so I sprang up from my chair and said, "Here's the box step." I finished, and they continued to stare at me—at least, those who weren't looking at the floor. I said, "It's the first step they teach you so you could move around the

floor even if you didn't know the tango." I did a very mechanical box step
again, bringing my feet together in a sort of militaristic way, and I said,
"That's the box step." There was complete silence. Of course they were humil-
iated for me, that I had done this odd dance twice. Finally somebody raised
his hand and asked, "Professor, where would someone do this?"

I guess if nothing else, if I go in there and inadvertently show them I'm just
a person in her own little world, it makes for a livelier connection to the work.

DT: I fell into despair years back when I noticed they'd felt the need to gloss
maître'd in "Babylon Revisited." I was lamenting this at a conference and in
perfect English a French scholar said, "It really *is* over for you people, isn't it?"

Any secrets on teaching complexity and nuance?

AB: One thing that I had my graduate students do that I thought was helpful
had to do with noticing the careful level at which an excellent story is crafted.
I went through an Alice Munro story myself, and I footnoted and cross-
referenced it and pointed out every allusion I got. This was Munro at her
best, so of course everything was loaded and about to explode. I wrote longhand, because I was lying on my sofa and so many hours were required. My
minimum notes came to about fifty-five pages. Then I had the students read
what I'd written, read my footnotes, then later I had them footnote their own
work. Not to show the class, but to show me. I wanted them to also account
for why every single word was in their story. Their stories got to be a lot more
carefully written. The danger, of course, is that when everything's in close-up,
a story can come to seem very schematic, too perfect, in a way. But as an exercise, I thought it would be interesting. Then I brought in some footnotes I'd
made of a story I hadn't yet distributed that I thought was pretty obscure,
and said "Here are my footnotes. Read them, and when you're through, tell
me what you think the story is." They considered all the cultural references,
all the allusions, everything I managed to mention, and had a fine time spinning their wheels about what they thought the story was. And also, don't
think I didn't learn something about that Alice Munro story, even though I'd
read it several times before and thought I understood everything about it. I'd
realize that a footnote on page twenty was inadequate, because by page
thirty it was a much more complicated matter. So I would have to go back to
re-footnote page twenty. This was my idea of great fun. It has been suggested
that I take up computer solitaire.

DT: I've heard you read your own stories (and they can be bought through Audible.com and Amazon.com). Do you think there will come a time when no one much wants to actually read words on the page, preferring to have the author and others just read to them through ipods? What will be lost?

AB: I think people will always want to open books because it's like the excitement of opening a package. And what you find inside, with a book, is present after present. Also, people like an excuse to hunch their shoulders and slip low in chairs and be elsewhere. Always elsewhere.

DT: A friend of mine suggested that I not ask you the traditional question, what is your biggest regret or to name the thing you'd do differently, but instead, ask you the question, what's the thing you think you did right?

AB: I think my perseverance was one of the biggest factors. I was young, and I didn't realize that I was persevering; I was just doing something I was compelled to do, and fascinated by. I guess writing a lot and also hanging in there was the thing I did right. Other things were out of my control. They're largely out of everyone's control, like whether the *New Yorker* will accept a story or not. They might or might not have ever accepted my work. I kept at it. I figured out a lot of stuff when I was making the transition from reader to writer—not to say that I didn't have very, very good feedback from friends, which helped enormously. But I don't think there's any substitute for teaching yourself something.

DT: What projects are in the works now?

AB: I'm writing an introduction to a book of my husband's paintings: *Lincoln Perry's Charlottesville*. It should be out by Christmas.

[At this point Lincoln Perry returns from the backyard and asks Ann to join him and the patio man.]

DT: Is there anything you had hoped I'd ask before we end? I got a great price on my patio in Orlando. I know you've been waiting for this encounter for some time so I don't want to hold you up.

AB: Come with me and tell him about your bargain price and prompt service. Take a picture of him, too, so we'll recognize him if he ever comes back.

Index